The ATLAS Of
CATS
OF THE WORLD
DOMESTICATED AND WILD

By
DENNIS KELSEY-WOOD

Photography: Animals Unlimited; Dr. Herbert R. Axelrod; Tom Caravaglia; Lew Clark Studios; Donna Coss; Jal Duncan; Lewis Fineman; Isabelle Francais; Florence M. Harrison; Michael J. Hodits; Dorothy Holby; J'Sens; Kel-Don Associates; Dr. Robert C. Koestler; Larry Levy; Si Merrill; Miceli Studios Ltd; Pete Miller; Phil Morini; Robert Pearcy; Fritz Prenzel; Progs; Purina Pet Care Center; Ron Reagan; Vincent Serbin; Joan Serles; D.H. Shagam; Skotzke and Lucas; Kevin T. Sullivan; Sally Anne Thompson; Dr. Arthur Topilow; Louise Van der Meid; Joan Wastlhuber; Len White.

Wild cat drawings: John R. Quinn.

Owners: The author wishes to thank the owners of the cats portrayed in this book and to apologize to anyone who was inadvertently omitted or improperly identified.

Joselyne Aalbu; Allaborde Cattery; Annouchka Anderson; Mr. and Mrs. Joseph Anderson; K. Dale Baer; Elaine Bartosavage; Sharyn and Richard Bass; Ruth Bauer; Mr. and Mrs. Gil Belanger (Shamba Lotu Meiko of Grenouille, Japanese Bobtail, p.306 bottom) Mrs. I. Bentinck; Herbert and Brooke Berger; J. Berger; Pat Bergman; M. Borofsky; Dr. and Mrs. John W. Boyd; Lisa Bressler; Irene B. Brounstein; K. Brown; Debbi Burke; Rae Ann Christ; Maria Corpolongo; Betty A. Cowles; Nancy T. Dodds; Mr. and Mrs. F.M. Dreifuss (Beachmor Jessica, Scottish Fold, p.323); Hobbs and Ethyl Dubois: Kate and Karl Faler; Mr. and Mrs. Lewis Fineman; Frosticat Cattery; Donna Fuller; Tobe Goldman (Ch. Khufu's Streaker of Bast of Temeh, Egyptian Mau, p.297); Lieseiotte A. Grimes (Gr. Ch. Ti-Mau's Szabo Aki of Die Lili, Balinese, p.232); Chester and Ann Gris; Gary and Karen Haddeman; Geri Hamilton; L. Alice Hanbey; Vickie L. Hansen; Claire Harden; Barbara and Erika Haukenberry; Bernard H. Hayduk; Linda Hazard; Priscilla Herrick; Pat Herrmann; Mike and Beth Hicks; JoAnn Hinkle; Ruth Hodges; Barbara Hodits (Mi-Ho's Haiku, Japanese Bobtail, p.305 bottom; Mi-Ho's Mikeneko, Japanese Bobtail, p.305 top); Elaine Hughen; Jaanus Cattery; Carolyn Jennings (Camotop's Chandra of Niacus, Balinese, p.231); Linda B. Jones; Christine W. Keightley; Rosemary Kendrick; Irene and Bella Kertay; Fay Kinsey; Ruth Kitsmiller; Dr. Robert C. Koestler; Mr. and Mrs. Chip Kruyszczuk (Gr. Ch. Mr. Lee of Far East, Japanese Bobtail, p.306 top); N. Laino; Jose Langevin; Marianne Lawrence; Allan and Louise Leber; Larry Levy; Rose Levy; Hans and Karen Lindblom; Elita Cooper MacNeil; Juli McAlister; V. McFarland; Dana McKinnon; Elaine Marsh; Don Martin; Pam Martin; Dean Mastrangelo; Betty L. Meins; Jean Mill; Mary Minium; Maria Mladjen; Anthony Morace (Gr. and Dbl. Ch. Mor-Ace's Delilah, Egyptian Mau, p.145; Dbl. Ch. Mor-Ace's Hephzibah, Egyptian Mau, p.298); Phil Morini; Ruth and Bob Morris; Rebecca Nan; Daphne Negus; Michael E. Nelson; Ruth and Paula Nessenkar; Jean Osborne; Shelley Page; Lenore Michelle Paulus; Sharon S. Paulus; Marie Phetteplace; Purring Lane Cattery; Mrs. P.N. Ramsdale; Gayle Rasmussen; Doris and Chinn Reese; Anne Reichle; Debbie Rexelle; Glen Robinson; Mary Robinson; Carol Rothfeld; Catherine Rowan; Grace M. Ruga; Dayle Russell; Robert Salerno; Norma and Bob Salsman; Joan Searles; Margaret Seybert; Joy Smith (Shawnee Bataloosa of Kejo, Bombay, p.279); Lyman and Elena Stewart; Tord and Suzanne Svenson; Dennis Thomas; Ruby J. Thompson; Mr. and Mrs. George Q. Thompson; Susan P. Tilton; Wanda Tomaski; Mr. and Mrs. Thomas Torio (Ch. Gelin of Torio, Turkish Angora, p.351); Karen A. Votava (Bryric Patchwork, Scottish Fold, p.303; Bryric Trick or Treat, Scottish Fold, p.326; Mr. Morgan Le Faye of Bryric, Scottish Fold, p.325); Victoria Waldron; Patricia Nell Warren; Joan and Alfred Wastlhuber; Len White; June Young.

Distributed in the UNITED STATES by T.F.H. Publications, Inc., One T.F.H. Plaza, Neptune City, NJ 07753; in CANADA to the Pet Trade by H & L Pet Supplies Inc., 27 Kingston Crescent, Kitchener, Ontario N2B 2T6; Rolf C. Hagen Ltd., 3225 Sartelon Street, Montreal 382 Quebec; in CANADA to the Book Trade by Macmillan of Canada (A Division of Canada Publishing Corporation), 164 Commander Boulevard, Agincourt, Ontario M1S 3C7; in ENGLAND by T.F.H. Publications Limited, Cliveden House/Priors Way/Bray, Maidenhead, Berkshire SL6 2HP, England; in AUSTRALIA AND THE SOUTH PACIFIC by T.F.H. (Australia) Pty. Ltd., Box 149, Brookvale 2100 N.S.W., Australia; in NEW ZEALAND by Ross Haines & Son, Ltd., 82 D Elizabeth Knox Place, Panmure, Auckland, New Zealand; in the PHILIPPINES by Bio-Research, 5 Lippay Street, San Lorenzo Village, Makati Rizal; in SOUTH AFRICA by Multipet Pty. Ltd., Box 235 New Germany, South Africa 3620. Published by T.F.H. Publications, Inc. Manufactured in the United States of America by T.F.H. Publications, Inc.

Contents

Kittens and cats have become the friends of countless numbers of children and grown-ups alike. More and more people continue to find room in their multi-pet households for a feline companion.

PREFACE

When I was invited to write this book on cats I was both delighted and yet somewhat apprehensive as to the way in which this should be done. Over the years many excellent general books have been produced, so how was this one to be different, for, of necessity, it clearly had to cover much of the same ground as all others. I have therefore tried to give greater consideration to certain subjects that I felt had not been overworked in comparable titles. At the same time, the text still includes detailed discussion of all topics one would expect to find in such a book.

The position of wild felids has been given special attention because few books intended for domestic cat owners devote much text to them, yet these are the very people who I have found to be most interested in such information. This is thus, to my knowledge, the first "pet" cat book that cites every living species of wild cat and gives a thumbnail description of them. Many observations on wild species have direct application to domestic cats, so the natural history of cats is briefly discussed together with the question of conservation—surely the most pressing problem facing most wild felids.

The mind of the cat is a topic that, in recent years, has at last attracted the attention of zoologists, and here the cat's character is explained by considering the way a cat has evolved and the effect that domestication has had, and continues to have, on the psychology of felids.

In all general cat books I have read, the genetics of the breeds and of their colors and coat patterns is given very sparse coverage, yet the subject is of immense importance to those who breed and exhibit pedigreed varieties—and may well be of more than passing interest to any cat owner. For this reason the subject has been given more detailed discussion, but hopefully in a basic manner that will be found usefully instructive.

A shorthaired cat finishing up a bowl of milk. Cats come in a wide variety of colors and patterns—there is something for everyone.

Another departure from the norm is that I have not attempted to provide a catalog of feline diseases—most of which the average cat owner would have little hope of diagnosing and even less chance of treating; these matters are best left to veterinarians. The most likely ailments and major diseases are cited, but, additionally, the text looks more carefully at the role of bacteria, virus and fungi as being an essential prerequisite of good health; an understanding of these microorganisms will greatly help in avoiding, rather than treating, disease.

The chapter on exhibition was the most difficult for this author simply because I have never exhibited a cat in my life. This was not, however, without advantage, for it meant I found myself asking much the same sort of questions that a beginner would ask. I have thus not presupposed knowledge and have tried to work systematically through the often highly complex systems that govern the exhibition of cats. Further, I have endeavored to make the text as applicable to a British reader as to an American, as the two nations differ considerably in their approach to the subject.

When it came to the breed descriptions, I attempted to keep these to the minimum, but sufficient to give a reasonably sound picture of the breed being discussed. The wealth of color pictures, which is a hallmark of TFH, ensure that the reader is left with no doubt as to what the breed looks like. Where a breed is associated with a genetic abnormality, this has been pointed out so the novice is aware of the possible negatives of such breeds; these are often glossed over in books or not mentioned at all in some. The establishment of abnormals is an unfortunate consequence of the popularity of numerous animal species—it is a reality that cannot simply be ignored.

A final inclusion within the text that is not normally found in general works is consideration for those, admittedly few, people who decide to leave home and country with their cats. I have indicated the very minimal requirements, in terms of documentation, that will be needed for the more likely destinations.

As the whole of my working life has been involved with animals, much the greater part specifically in the preparation of books on pets, the one thing I have learned above all else is that no matter how much one studies a subject, there is always even more which remains unstudied. One can only admire those who specialize, for it is from such people, via their own works, that we are all able to advance our knowledge.

I express my thanks also to the following people, and the organizations they represent, who provided me with valuable information without which this book would certainly have been the poorer: Susie Page (American Cat Association); Lynn Karlesses (Cat Fanciers' Association); Leslie Bowers (The International Cat Association); Bridget Kolonich (American Cat Fanciers' Association); Barbara A. Haley (Cat Fanciers' Federation); Mrs. J. Barham (Governing Council of the Cat Fancy); Judith Lindley (Calico Cat Registry International); Susan H. Plante (Canadian Cat Association); Daphne Negus (Cat World International); Mrs. Denise H. Reed (Pedigree Petfoods Education Service); and X.A. Doyle (Department of Primary Industries, Australia).

To Roy Robinson (geneticist) I give my special thanks for giving freely of his time in order to answer my numerous questions on the genetics of cats and other animal species.

Any person attempting to write on a subject that is itself composed of many subjects must accept the fact that he is liable to make errors—

A pair of kittens whose attention has been caught by something on the lawn.

certainly I am no exception to this comment; it would be a rare book indeed that did not generate objective criticism from those more knowledgeable than the author on the different topics discussed. If errors there are, then these are mine alone, and I would not attempt to defend them but would explain them to my critics on the honest grounds that Dr. Samuel Johnson did when asked why he called the pasterns of a horse the knees—his reply was, "Ignorance, madam, pure ignorance."

It would be unthinkable to conclude this preface without making very special reference to four people who have played an incalculable part in my life. First, my mother and father, both of whom encouraged my interest in animals from my earliest years; Dr. Herbert R. Axelrod, surely the most remarkable man in pet book history, who has been far more to me than simply my publisher; and, lastly, but by no means leastly, my wife Eve, who has accepted without complaint the many sacrifices that have been required in order that I could pursue my own interest in all animals and in books devoted to them.

A lovely white kitten taking an outdoor stroll.

DEDICATION

To William, Muffet, Oliver, Domino, Marmalade, Tinkerbell, Minka, Tabbetha and Rustin—every one a character that has given us so much pleasure by sharing their home with us.

Whether you choose to raise a cat from its playful kittenhood to maturity or to purchase an already full-grown cat, it is a good idea to find out about the needs of your new feline before you bring him home.

INTRODUCTION

On a global basis it would be quite impossible to say which is the most numerous pet in the world; this is because in many countries dogs, cats, rabbits, and other domestic animals are not always regarded as pets in the sophisticated way that they are in the more wealthy Western countries. Only in a relatively few countries are there national clubs or societies which actively monitor and promote the various pet breeds, which are often tolerated for practical reasons more than for being household pets by specific use as such. However, each year the number of true pets increases and the cat is unquestionably amongst the top few such animals. In analyzing the reasons for the cat's popularity, one underlying advantage it has over just about any other animal one could hope to own is its sheer convenience.

We can, of course, make cat owning a very costly and complicated affair, and where pedigreed cats are concerned this is inevitable up to a point, but in its most basic form, applicable to many millions of owners, a cat's needs are those of sound nutrition, grooming in certain breeds, and a sheltered place to sleep—much beyond that a cat will happily take care of itself. Given a goodly degree of handling whilst it is a kitten, most cats will reward the owner by allowing them to stroke it, lift it up, cuddle it, and generally spoil it. If they feel inclined to, they will answer and come to the call of their name, but in each of these aspects it should be clearly understood that these are concessions on the cat's behalf and not rights you can demand or expect simply because you own the cat—this latter point being a legal situation rather than one the feline would agree with!

This independent and sometimes seemingly aloof character of cats is not suited to all people, whose desires from a pet are such that other,

Top to bottom: Gray and white kitten; a white kitten stretching its legs; brown and white kitten.

more tractable, natures found in dogs are better suited to given needs. A cat cannot be trained in the same way as can a dog, yet this does not imply that a cat will not respond to given situations; it can be taught many things—where it should not go, what is not desirable (such as attacking a pet bird or climbing up the curtains), but it will not respond to specific commands in the same way as a canine. The cat sees no advantage to itself in such matters and its evolution is not based on any need to have reliance on the complex social structure that is an integral part of a dog's life. However, it is as wrong for cat owners to say that dogs are subservient as it is for dog owners to accuse cats of being disloyal and somewhat unintelligent creatures. Such terms may have meaning amongst humans, but they are as grossly misleading when applied to cats or dogs, as is the use of the words brave or cowardly in the animal context. One of the major problems—often perpetuated in many books—in caring for animals is the temptation to apply human morality to our pets, to compare given traits exhibited by different species, and then to use these to either support a given species or vilify it.

A cat is not a dog or a rabbit or a horse; it is a cat, and it must be judged and cared for with this and only this in mind. It is the objective of this work to bring to the open-minded reader its benefits and its pitfalls; how it thinks and why it looks and reacts as it does; how it feeds and how it breeds; its potential ailments; and, finally, the many forms in which it is available. It is hoped that the reader will find it essentially a practical work which considers the cat as a single pet, as a subject for breeding, and as an exhibition animal.

To many millions of people the cat is the ultimate pet—to others it is far from this. These are subjective matters only determined on an individual basis, and cats are no less individuals themselves, so that many comments made about cats in general may not be applicable to given individuals. Domestication does have the effect

Contrary to popular opinion, a cat and a dog can become good friends, especially if they are raised together from a young age.

A young ginger tabby kitten and spaniel companion.

Above: Tabby and white cat with a very surprised fox. **Below:** Cats have always been known for their jumping ability.

of suppressing certain traits found in wild animals; were this not so domestication could not take place. In cats, however, the extent of domestication is relatively low in many breeds, whilst being more obvious in others. There is thus plenty of scope for potential owners to seek the sort of feline they desire. Beyond the advan-

tage of being convenient pets in their general welfare, cats do have another benefit when viewed in their non-pedigreed state: they are far more predictable, sizewise, than are dogs. The difference between a large and small cat is insignificant when compared with that found in dogs, so when selecting a cat, be it pedigreed or wholly mongrel in origin, the owner is not likely to find that the pet grows to a size not bargained for. In features, too, felines show very little change from the basic wild pattern. No other very popular domestic pet can make such a claim other than certain very small rodents such as mice, hamsters or gerbils, or a few bird species.

Given consideration for its general welfare, there is no doubting the fact that a cat makes a super pet, and within the breed section of this book will be found more than sufficient choice for all tastes. Some are extremely popular, some are quite rare, some may prove more difficult to keep than others, and some show a higher movement away from accepted feline traits than do others. Throughout the book is featured a truly magnificent collection of colored photographs that will give the reader a very clear idea of what each breed looks like, so it is hoped that in this volume both the beginner and the confirmed and experienced cat owner will have at their fingertips a single and useful reference work that can be used for many years.

A pair of Siamese kittens and a white kitten.

NATURAL HISTORY

Cats have always interested humans for a number of reasons. Some are large enough to kill us and have done so since we first started to evolve as advanced primates, others plunder farm livestock, whilst yet others have coats so beautiful that females for thousands of years have often thought they would look better on them than on the cat! Cats have been used for many years as hunters to aid sportsman—and they are still the number one mouse and rat catchers on farms, in homes and on commercial premises. They have figured in folklore and legends and have been associated with witchcraft, and they have been worshiped as gods.

Given these facts, you would think we know a great deal about them, yet quite the opposite is true; only in relatively recent years have we begun to understand their habits, lifestyle and needs. Indeed, it is true to say that other than the domestic cat, and a few selected zoological garden examples, the vast majority of cats are still somewhat of a mystery to us. Cats are very secretive creatures, so much so that it was only in the late 1960s the last species was discovered on the southernmost island of Japan, Iriomote Jima. Most people are aware of the more obvious felids—such as lions, tigers, and leopards—but how many readers realize that there are over 30 wild cats and around 200 subspecies of these!

Left: A young kitten intent on stalking. The behavior of domestic cats has much in common with that of their wild relatives. **Opposite:** The tongue of the cat is covered with papillae which serve to remove meat from bone.

Although the cat has been associating with humans for centuries, just recently have we begun to study feline behavior in depth.

Virtually all wild cat species are in decline compared to the position of only a century ago, and many are actually on the brink of extinction, a number of subspecies having become extinct already, and within most of our lifetimes. Whilst we spend countless billions of pounds or dollars in looking after our domestic pet felines and even greater amounts to give ourselves the capacity to blow up our planet, we spend, by comparison, virtually nothing on studying and preserving the wild species from which our pets evolved.

The whole question of animal conservation is, of course, both a topical and complex problem. However, the basis of what is being conserved assumes a knowledge of the various animal groups, and the hard facts are that, where felids are concerned, most cat owners are just not aware of the numerous wild species. It therefore seems appropriate in a work such as this that the cat as a wild animal should be given some exposure. Apart from its value in helping us to understand our pets, it is hoped that readers will find the facts most interesting, maybe even to the degree that they prompt further study in more specialized books. Just being aware of the numerous wild cats is, in fact, the first step toward helping them to survive for future generations to see.

THE CAT FAMILY

Cats make up a remarkably uniform group of animals that differ in size rather than in physical appearance, so they are easily recognized as being cats. They are housed, in respect to scientific classification, within the family known as Felidae. This is one of eight families that make up the large order known as Carnivora—the flesh-eaters.

The carnivores range in size from the tiny weasels of a few inches in length to the enormous Kodiak brown bear—the world's largest terrestrial predatory animal. Other carnivores include the well-known dogs, foxes and wolves as well as raccoons, hyenas, badgers, otters; lesser known examples are the aardwolf, the fossa and the olingo.

Although carnivores are flesh-eaters, a number of species have modified their habits over millions of years so that today they may eat much vegetable matter—in some cases exclusively, as in the case of the pandas. Others will take both plant and animal foods and are termed omnivorous, but the cats have chosen to remain prime predators, though all will occasionally take fruits, and many, including the mighty tiger, are known to eat grass, probably as a medicinal tonic rather than as a food.

The fact that domestic cats are not far removed from their cousins in the wild makes them fascinating creatures to observe.

The specialized tongue of the cat is one of the feline's most distinguishing features.

Rarely does an animal have a single diagnostic feature, so only by considering numerous features can one actually attempt to define a cat. Although detail differences in anatomical parts figure in determining whether a given animal is or is not a cat, for our purposes the following are the more obvious of a felid's features.

1) The muzzle is of moderate length, never approaching the proportions seen in other carnivorous families.

2) The jaw bone is relatively short.

3) The number of teeth is typically 30, though slight variations may be found in certain species. The canines are usually well developed, the incisors less so.

4) The digits are 5-4; this means there are five toes on the front feet and four on the rear. One of the front toes does not touch the ground but is found further up the foot on the inner side. It is clawed the same as all others.

5) The claws are housed in sheaths, so are not visible—or only partly so in some species—unless the cat is scratching or about to attack or to defend itself. The cheetah is the singular exception to this rule and is unable to retract its claws other than during the first few weeks of its life.

6) Felids are digitigrade in their stance; this means they walk on their toes—as opposed to bears which walk on the soles of their feet (plantigrade) or horses which walk on their nails (unguligrade).

7) The tongue contains sharp, backward facing papillae with which to groom and also to remove meat from the bone when feeding.

8) Coat patterns may be spotted, blotched, striped or solid colored. The felids exhibit a wider range of colors and markings than any other carnivorous family.

9) The tail is usually, though not always, long; it is covered with fur—but never bushy to the extent seen in other families (i.e. dogs, foxes, wolves, skunks).

10) The forelimbs are usually shorter than those of the rear.

FELINE CLASSIFICATION

The way in which scientists arrange things, be they minerals, periods of time, plants or animals, always seems complicated to those not familiar with the terminology. Certainly this author found the principles of taxonomy a rather boring subject when it was taught at school. However, it became quite impossible to have any meaningful conversations about wild animals without a basic understanding of taxonomy, so the subject was studied again and, surprisingly, was found to be anything but boring, for it enables one to read technical texts, articles, and other material without the necessity to be forever reaching for a dictionary.

Zoological classification enables one to refer to whole groups of animals without having to state specifically which individual species are being discussed—this is implied by the terms used. The present system was originally devised by the Swedish naturalist Carolus Linnaeus, and modern taxonomy is deemed to have commenced with the publication of his tenth edition of *Systema Naturae* in 1758. Though much modified since then, it has proved a sound basis to work with in spite of the fact that it is not ideal. It is known as the binomial system of nomenclature. The system is based on the Latin language; this overcomes the obvious problem that is immediately created if one were to attempt to use French, English, or any other modern language. It happens that in the days of Linnaeus, all scholars used Latin, so its choice was almost automatic.

The ranks: Under the system stated, one starts at the apex, rather like a triangle, with the common feature of life itself. This is then divided into two broad divisions based on certain features. Each of these divisions is in turn divided based on further features, and the process is repeated many times until one arrives at the individual breeding groups, known as species, which thus make up the base of the triangle. The divisions are known as ranks, and whilst there are many of these, certain of them are regarded as being more important than others and are termed obligate ranks, to be used whenever the full classification of a group is cited.

The further down the ranks one goes, the more are the features shared by the members of a given rank. Cats thus have more in common with dogs and bears than they do with mice, but they share more features with mice than they do with birds, and so on. Although obligate classification stops at the species rank, there are further divisions below this. If we take the lion as an example, there are in fact nine subspecies of lion—all differing slightly from each other (two that have become extinct in this century) and all forming separate breeding populations in different geographic regions.

The species: Actually defining a species is far more difficult than it might at first appear; however, for our purposes it is a group of individual animals that are similar in appearance and which, in the natural state, will freely interbreed and produce fertile offspring which are similar in appearance to their parents. Such a definition means that a cross between a lion and a leopard is thus not a species but a hybrid, even if it is fertile; generally it is similar in appearance to its parents. Such a union would never happen in the natural state, where the lion would kill the leopard if it was able to get hold of it!

In the case of the domestic cat (or any domesticated animal), it is given the status as a species simply because its origins are not known for sure. The small felids present the taxonomist with many problems because domestic cats will actually freely breed in the wild state with a number of cat species, indicating not only the probable mixed ancestry of our pets, but also just how closely related many wild species are to each other.

Species name: The specific name of an animal must always be a binomial, which is made by adding a trivial word to the genus of that animal; only when this is done is an animal identified. It is customary to write the species name in a style different than that of the main body of text. This is why you will see species names printed in italics; this also applies to the rank of genus if it is used by itself, but to no rank above this. All rank names must begin with an initial capital letter, but trivial names always commence with a lowercase letter.

Subspecies: A subspecies is indicated by adding a second trivial name to the genus, thus forming a trinomial—again it commences with a lowercase letter. When there are numerous sub-

A young Ocicat. The popularity of exotic-looking domestic breeds (e.g. Ocicat, Egyptian Mau, etc.) seems to reflect the increasing concern for wild cats and their environment.

CLASSIFICATION OF THE HOUSECAT

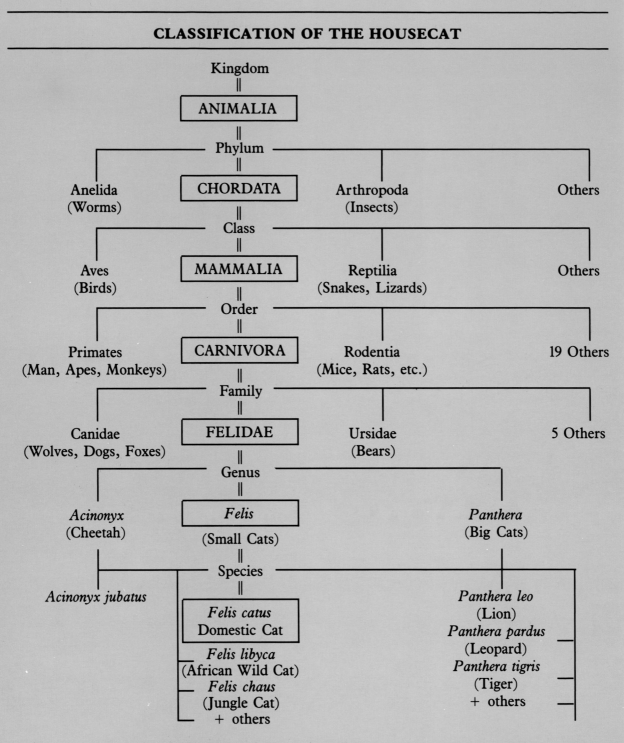

In the above table, the classifications of the more well-known animal groups are given purely to show the believed degree of their relationships with cats.

An adult cheetah, *Acinonyx jubatus*, with its young kit. Cheetahs have features in common with both big and small cats.

species, the very first one to have been named is indicated by having its trivial name repeated. Such an animal may not be typical of the species but is an example of the type that the species is based upon; it is thus a sort of archetype. Such a subspecies is known as the nominate race. The lion thus has the scientific name of *Panthera leo*, but if we wish to be more specific about which lion is being discussed, we could then cite *Panthera leo leo* (the nominate race, now sadly extinct) as compared to *Panthera leo persica*, the Indian lion (yes, there are still lions in India to this day).

but changes in order to accommodate the latest information on a given species or other rank. As a result, research may indicate that a species is not as closely related to another species as was thought for many years. It is then transferred to a more suitable group. Secondly, the system of nomenclature is governed by international rules. Any competent authority is free to produce his or her own classification on a group of animals based on personal views of the importance of given features. It is then a question of how many other people of authority accept this or that version of a classification, and thus how often it is seen and used.

CHANGES IN NOMENCLATURE

Initially, those not familiar with scientific classification are often confused by the fact that an animal is listed as being of a given name in one book but a different one in another. For many years the lion was known as *Felis leo* but is now *Panthera leo*. Such movements from one genus to another are quite common in zoological circles, and this is for two basic reasons. First, taxonomy is never static, as some people believe,

The white Persian may seem light years away from the wild felines but at times it will exhibit similar behaviors.

A mother cat grooming her offspring. Even the maternal instincts of domestic cats are akin to those of the wild cats.

As it happens, cats have been the subject of much heated discussion amongst zoologists, so felid classification is constantly being revised. Presently the use of a numbering system is adding to the arguments, but these matters should not deter the student, who will quickly find that things are not nearly as difficult as might at first be thought, once the basic principles are fully understood.

THE ROLE OF CATS

All predatory animals fulfill a necessary, if at times rather bloodthirsty, role in the overall pattern of nature. As a group, the cats are the most predatory family in the order Carnivora in that all cats are prime predators that derive their food almost completely from animal origins. In other families there are members which are partially or even wholly vegetarian, in the former case usually when times get really hard. However, this is not to say that vegetable matter is not important to cats. It should not be forgotten that most felids eat the viscera of their prey and in so doing ingest partly digested plant matter in the process.

In the wild, the predatory species serve to help their prey to retain vigor, keep the incidence of disease in check, and to remove potentially poor breeding or otherwise unsuitable individuals from the population as a whole. Cats rarely kill strong, fit specimens in their prey

The cats in the two photos above are examples of the great variation in feline coloration. The cat in the top photo shows how much can be accomplished by selective breeding, while the cat in the bottom photo remains close to the wild tabby color which some scientists believed to have served as camouflage.

MISCONCEPTIONS

One of the problems that comes from the lack of understanding of an animal's habits is that facts become distorted, and this dictates a chain of events that may have serious repercussions not only for the animal in question but for the entire environment. So strong can these false notions be that they become myth, legend, and believed fact—and as such it takes a long while for people's views to be changed. The predatory animals have suffered badly in this context; most people's views on wolves, coyotes, and African hunting dogs are classic examples of how species can be totally misunderstood. The big cats, too, have suffered in a similar manner and have been labelled as killers of domesticated livestock; however, Europeans and Americans do not need to look to the tropics to see feline examples of such misconceptions, for both the lynx and the puma are prime examples.

The puma or mountain lion (*Felis concolor*) has been hunted ruthlessly in the USA by stock breeders who accused it of mass predation on farm animals. They will cite the instances of pumas slaughtering many sheep in a single session, and they will also accuse it of seriously endangering the deer populations. In Arizona, in the Kaibab forest, pumas were all but eradicated, and the resulting explosion in the deer population resulted in an increase in disease and overgrazing to the extent that thousands of deer starved to death. So-called sportsman hunted deer and other prey species in other regions to the point that there were insufficient animals to meet the needs of the puma populations. Furthermore, poison baiting to kill off coyotes and rodents, as well as rabbits, resulted in a situation where pumas often had no choice but to attack domestic livestock or starve. Once accustomed to the easy way of life, such pumas then became habitual domestic animal killers. The result is that pumas became so labelled due to a situation that would never have happened in the first place were it not for human mismanagement of the land.

The full irony is that where predatory animals are exterminated, the resulting increase in the population of mice, rats, rabbits, and similar species is such that the cost to farmers is vastly more substantial than was the cost of any cattle

species, for if they did then overall vigor in that species would start to decline. Furthermore, it is easier to overcome a young, an ill, an old or a heavily pregnant female than it is to tackle a fit member of a herd or species. The balance between predators and prey is always carefully weighted so that both are able to survive—only when humans interfere do things start to go wrong. Beyond upsetting this balance we often create problems for ourselves at a later date, and then compound matters by our ignorance in drawing wrong conclusions from such events.

or other livestock taken by such cats or wild canids. Beyond the loss in grain, pasture, and the spread of disease, there must also then be added the cost of trying to control the bigger rodent populations—which the predators did at virtually no cost to the farmer. The story is much the same in the case of the European lynx (*Felis lynx*); where it is afforded full protection, as in Yugoslavia and elsewhere, the deer herds have actually increased in size because breeding vigor is better, and disease is controlled by such animals being taken by the lynx. Even sportsmen have come to appreciate the benefits of predatory cats and dogs on game animals.

Given access to a suitably sized mixed population of prey species, all studies clearly underline the fact that wild cats will seek to kill domesticated stock only in very rare cases—and then there is often a reason. A wounded cat may be unable to catch prey, so turns to farm stock; the same is true of aged cats. Cats avoid humans whenever they can and for this reason are only a threat to us or our livestock when we upset the balance of their world. As for the mass killings of sheep by pumas, this is explained by consideration of their basic hunting drives or thresholds; but here it can be stated that it is again directly the result of situations already mentioned—it just does not happen amongst pumas and wild herds or species because these have their own defense mechanisms that make this impossible. We have taken what defense domestic animals had away from them by selective breeding and other means.

FELID DISTRIBUTION

Wild cats are found throughout the world, with the exception of Australia, New Zealand, and various small islands. Not surprisingly, no species has actually increased its range of distribution during this century; indeed, in many cases such ranges have been substantially reduced, and in a number of instances cats have disappeared totally from former habitats. This does not imply that in every case numbers have not shown an increase compared to the disastrous position of a few years ago, since conservation is slowly helping some species to precariously hang on and even increase their woefully small numbers.

An adult puma, *Felis concolor*. For years the puma was hunted by sportsmen and by stock breeders who mistakenly saw this cat as a threat to their livestock. A misunderstanding of the prey-predator relationship has led to the demise of many species.

One glaring exception in India, which has the largest number of felid species, is the cheetah. Formerly found throughout that subcontinent,

A pair of cheetahs. The Indian cheetah became extinct soon after it was given protection as an endangered species.

many were killed for their fur, thousands captured for use as hunting cats, and even more killed simply for so-called sport. In 1952 the cheetah was finally given full protection but the last few were shot by hunters in that same year, so India no longer can boast at having the world's fastest land creature as a resident—the cheetah can attain speeds of over 100 kph (60 mph) for short distances.

The fate of the Indian lion all but followed, and even today the numbers are not considered to be safe. However, the Indian government is helping the lion by relocation policies of the villagers who live in the Gir forest, the last habitat of the lion in India. Overgrazing by domestic livestock was driving away the species which were vital to the survival of the lion.

The leopard has the largest distribution of any wild cat, though it has been drastically reduced as a result of its being hunted for its coat. Again, the numbers in India have fallen sharply and it is an endangered species in that country. Of all cats, the leopard has probably proved the most dangerous to humans, for its moderate size, immense strength, and superb climbing ability combine to enable it to approach villages, and enter them, without detection. Such a leopard may take a heavy toll on humans before it is finally caught. The more heavily built jaguar is the New World equivalent to the leopards of the Old World, in the same way that the puma equates to the lions.

FELID SIZE AND STRENGTH

The world's largest cat is the Siberian tiger whilst the smallest is the black-footed cat of the deserts of South Africa. A large tiger may have a length, not including the tail, of 280 cm (110 in) and may stand 97 cm (38 in) at the shoulders and tip the scales at over 259 kg (575 lb). That is some cat when compared to the maximum size of the black-footed cat at 40 cm (16 in) length and around 5.4 kg (12 lb) in weight. It should, however, be added that the head to rump (HRL) measurements can be misleading because they are often based on dead specimens when the head and neck are placed in an unnatural position to give maximums. In most measurements, the tail length (TL) is usually given separately.

The magnificent Siberian tiger is the world's largest cat.

A tiger cub and a lion cub.

The cheetah is the world's fastest land animal. It is capable of reaching speeds of 100 kph (60 mph). For cheetahs and for all cats, ample rest is necessary in order to achieve the short bursts of speed used during the hunt.

All cats are amazingly strong, especially in terms of their neck and shoulder muscles. This is essential, for many cats may prey on species larger than themselves. To give an idea of the power of cats, a tiger of around 202 kg (450 lb) is capable of dragging a dead cow weighing around 270 kg (600 lb) for a considerable distance; a leopard has been known not only to drag a dead young giraffe calf a for quite distance, but then to jump with it into a tree. Such a calf would be about 50% heavier than the leopard, so this is quite an achievement. However, such feats are not restricted to the big cats, for all felids have this same capacity. A domestic cat is quite capable of carrying a dead rabbit of its own body weight or greater.

DISTRIBUTION OF WILD CAT SPECIES

Africa: Small cats–7; big cats–2; cheetah–1.

Asia: Small cats–16; big cats–5; cheetah–1. *India:* Small cats–10; big cats–4.

South America: Small cats–10; big cats–1. *Argentina:* Small cats–8; big cats–1. *Brazil:* Small cats–6; big cats–1. *Chile:* Small cats–4. *Peru*–Small cats–6; big cats–1.

North America: Small cats–7; big cats–1. *Canada:* Small cats–2. *United States:* Small cats–7; big cats–1. *Mexico:* Small cats–5; big cats–1.

Europe: Small cats–2. *Great Britain:* Small cats–1.

USSR: Small cats–8; big cats–2.

Note: The difference between small and big cats is not simply based upon size; for example, the puma is classed as a small cat though it may be larger than a leopard, which is a big cat. The big cats can roar due to elasticity in their hyoid bone; small cats cannot, as this bone is fused and solid. Big cats have hair extending to the front edge of the upper surface of the nose; small cats do not. Small cats can purr when exhaling and inhaling; big cats purr only when exhaling. The cheetah has many features not found in other cats and is thus better treated on its own, though some features are more in line with those of small cats.

The margay, *Felis wiedii*, is a forest dweller native to Central and South America. It is one of the few cats that can come down from a tree as easily as it goes up.

CONSERVATION

Few people will disagree with the fact that conservation of the world's natural resources is now a pressing and obligate matter to which humans must attend. This is not only beneficial to the present generation but it will ensure that our grandchildren—and theirs—do not look back in anger at the way, through greed and indifference, we have mismanaged our planet, the more so in light of our knowledge and the resources we have at our disposal. However, talking about preservation and actually doing it are often worlds apart due to the vested interests of governments, commercial companies, and numerous other bodies of people. Whilst arguments rage, species vanish, to be seen only as paintings, photographs or stuffed exhibits in a museum. Conservation takes time and planning—but for many species, including a large number of felines, the last grains of sand are running out and they totter on the very brink of extinction.

We live in a very materialistic world which is based on always having more and more—regardless of the cost not only to the other animals that share our world, but to other peoples as well. Until we can learn to rationalize our needs to those of all others on earth, the future will never be secure for the animals—nor indeed for ourselves.

However, the word "needs" means different things to different people depending on how rich or poor they are. It is unreasonable to expect half-starving tribespeople to understand the need to conserve the game animals in their territory, or the predators that prey on them. It is not unreasonable to say that no female needs the fur of an ocelot, leopard or cheetah to make her clothes with—the woman has not yet lived that looked better wearing such a coat than did the feline that it came from. Logging, or deforestation, is a necessary reality in many countries, for the income from it, and the work it creates, are often crucial to economies of such countries. Deforestation is the prime reason so many animals are in danger, for it destroys their habitat and drives them further into the interior. Eventually, there is insufficient food for the numerous species, so they die out or are forced to raid farms. Birds and deer take the crops and predators take the deer—and any domestic stock as well. Where is the line to be drawn between basic needs of people and pure greed?

There is no doubt that we need to totally change our views and methods in certain areas. Replanting policies need to be based on a wider range of trees that will create forest again, not just barren acres of pine in which few animals can survive. Cleared forest should not automatically be given over to agriculture but allowed to regenerate itself by ensuring that it is not totally stripped in the first place. Many cats are extremely shy creatures, so certain territories must be kept totally free of all people other than those needed to monitor the numerous species within the area. These things are indeed beginning to happen, and this is at least a hopeful sign for the future.

In terms of agriculture, there is clearly an urgent need to educate many farmers on the benefits of not shooting any wild animal seen on their land. Indeed it is unfortunate that more governmental funds are not available in certain areas to encourage farmers not to rip out trees, hedges, scrub land and woodlands which give habitation to very many species of animals. In the USA, in Wisconsin, it has been clearly established that wolves can live quite peaceably alongside farmers without any attempts to raid their livestock—provided their own territory is not disturbed and the game animals virtually hunted out of existence. This same fact applies to all areas where wild cats are found.

Happily, even the fur traders' associations now restrict the number of species which their members can hunt, and governments are also banning the importation of certain skins; however, numerous cat species are not included within this list, so thousands of cats are killed annually to provide various items from coats to gloves, handbags, and decorative ornaments. The public could end this unnecessary and sordid trade simply by refusing to purchase any item that includes the skin of a cat in its make-up.

Finally, whilst there are a number of zoological gardens that would be better closed down, there are also many zoos that have impressive breeding records and, more importantly, house their animals in very spacious and well-planned accommodations. If you know of a good zoo in your area, support it by visiting it whenever you can. Zoos receive little or no financial help from governments, and running a zoo is a very expensive business. The modern concept of a zoo and its role in society is changing, and today more such places run educational courses for children and are trying to establish breeding programs for endangered species. The zoo may not be the ideal place for many animals, but it may well prove to be the only realistic haven for certain species until the day arrives when we can work out totally satisfactory methods of ensuring that the wild cats of the world may live in peace.

Opposite: A young cheetah kit. Most cats seem to mature from cute and cuddly into noble and dignified.

Top to bottom: African golden cat, *Felis aurata*; Chinese desert cat, *Felis bieti*; and Martelli's wild cat, *Felis lumensis*, an extinct ancestor of the cat family.

John R. Quinn '89

WILD CATS OF THE WORLD

Genus *Felis*—31 Species, 191 Subspecies

AFRICAN GOLDEN CAT: *Felis aurata*, 2 subspecies. Western and central Africa. HRL 95 cm (37 in), TL 37 cm (14.5 in). Many shades of brown through to red. Traces of spotting on legs, underbelly and some stripes on legs. Pumalike, with short fur.

BAY CAT: *Felis badia*. Borneo. HRL 50 cm (19.5 in), TL 30 cm (12 in). A reddish color. Nothing is known about its lifestyle. It is similar to other golden cats in its appearance.

LEOPARD CAT: *Felis bengalensis*, 7 subspecies. Southern Asia, China, eastern Siberia, Manchuria, India. HRL 60 cm (24 in), TL 40 cm (15.7 in). Color ranges from ochre-yellow and brown through to almost silver according to habitat. Spotted and blotched with black. Stripes to head and chest, which is white. Thick tail. Leopard cats swim well and are so graceful that they make domestic cats seem ponderous and clumsy by comparison. Adults defecate in water. They are truly superb climbers. Extensive distribution. Some are only as large as domestic cats. Have been kept for up to 13 years in captivity but have reputation for unbridled ferocity.

CHINESE DESERT CAT: *Felis bieti*, 3 subspecies. China and Mongolia. HRL 85 cm (33 in), TL 35 cm (13.7 in). This quite large cat is gray-yellow on back and sides, white to gray on underbelly. Stripes to flanks, and rings of black on tail. Its winter coat sports longer fur. Little is known about its lifestyle.

CARACAL LYNX: *Felis caracal*, 9 subspecies. Africa and Asia, extensive distribution. HRL 75 cm (29.5 in), TL 33 cm (13 in). Various shades of brown to red. Ears tufted with long hairs; eyes contract to a circle as in other lynx species. No longer common in captivity, it nonetheless is a good breeder. Adept at taking birds on the wing by huge leaps into the air. Pumalike in appearance, it inhabits desert type terrain.

DOMESTIC CAT: *Felis catus*, 9 subspecies (debatable). Worldwide distribution achieved by introduction by man. HRL 45 cm (17.5 in) to 60 cm (24 in); TL 24 cm (9 in) to 38 cm (15 in), excepting Manx and Japanese Bobtails which have either no tails or short ones.

JUNGLE CAT: *Felis chaus*, 9 subspecies. Asia and northern Africa, extensive distribution. HRL 75 cm (30 in), TL 35 cm (13.7 in). Color is yellow-gray to red-brown with agouti ticking. The ears sport small tufts and the legs and tail are striped—much more so in kittens than in adults. This cat is not unlike an Abyssinian and is known to live in abandoned human homes and near villages. It breeds well enough in captivity but is not a common zoological exhibit.

PAMPAS CAT: *Felis colocolo*, 7 subspecies. North and central South America. HRL 70 cm (27.5 in), TL 33 cm (13 in). Silver-gray through to yellow-brown with body spots, with stripes to the legs; ringed tails in brown or black. Some species have quite long hair, especially on mane and back; others are very shorthaired. They lie in open scrub country and are not especially fond of climbing. Very aggressive, they are rarely seen in zoos but have been bred occasionally. Little is known of their lifestyle.

PUMA: *Felis concolor*, 29 subspecies. North, Central, and South America. HRL 160 cm (63 in), TL 85 cm (33.5 in). Shades of brown with dark tail tip and ears. Spotted when kittens. Largest small felid in the world. May live to 20 years in captivity and breeds extremely well in confinement; is the most common zoo cat other than the lion. Good climber and one of the most adaptable of all felids to temperature range. Also called cougar or mountain lion.

GEOFFROY'S CAT: *Felis geoffroyi*, 5 subspecies. Central South America but may extend much further south. HRL 70 cm (27.5 in), TL 35 cm (13.7 in). Yellow-gray to brilliant ochre. Head bears stripes, rump spotted with black. All-black specimens not uncommon. Good climber, reputed to enter streams quite frequently. Infrequently bred or seen in collections. Avoids human settlements.

KODKOD: *Felis guigna*. Central and southern parts of South America. HRL 52 cm (20.5 in), TL 23 cm (9 in). Brown to ochre-yellow with black spots on the body, stripes on chest, and a ringed tail. A very pretty cat but rare in captivity. It climbs infrequently, and, although small, is known to raid chickens on farms. Little is known of its lifestyle. Melanistic examples not uncommon. Also called hūina.

Top to bottom: Pampas cat, *Felis colocolo*; jungle cat, *Felis chaus*; bay cat, *Felis badia*; and Iriomote cat, *Felis iriomotensis*.

Top to bottom: Mountain cat, *Felis jacobita*; African wild cat, *Felis libyca*; sand cat, *Felis margarita*; and marbled cat, *Felis marmorata*.

IRIOMOTES CAT: *Felis iriomotensis*. Iriomotes Jima, Japan. HRL 65 cm (25.5 in), TL 43 cm (17 in). Brown to yellow with rows of black spots; ringed tail. A small cat discovered in the late 1960s, it is probably related to the Asiatic leopard cats. Almost nothing is known about this species.

MOUNTAIN CAT: *Felis jacobita*. Chile and Argentina. HRL 75 cm (29.5 in), TL 45 cm (17.7 in). Silver-gray to light brown, spotted, and with ringed tail and bar traces to the face. Fur is quite dense and long. Little is documented on these cats, which are related to the pampas cats of lower altitudes.

AFRICAN WILD CAT: *Felis libyca*, 19 subspecies. Throughout Africa, extensive distribution in Asia Minor through to southern USSR. HRL 70 cm (27.5 in), TL 37 cm (14.6 in). Variably spotted or striped, ringed tail. The favorite candidate as the ancestor of the domestic cat. Lives in open terrain of arid type where it preys on small mammals and birds.

NORTHERN LYNX: *Felis lynx*, 9 subspecies. Europe, northern Asia, and North America. HRL 110 cm (43.3 in), TL 17 cm (6.7 in). Yellowish gray to cinnamon-red which is spotted on the flanks and feet. Tail tipped in black, and ears carry tufts. Head is fringed with longer hairs at cheeks and a small beard is present. Feet large and legs long. Excellent climber. Iris not greenish but yellow-brown. Much persecuted by man, it is now protected in much of its range.

PALLAS CAT: *Felis manul*, 3 subspecies. Northern parts of Asia from Iran to Mongolia, Turkestan to western China. HRL 65 cm (25.6 in), TL 30 cm (12 in). Silver-gray through to yellow-brown with dark agouti ticking, but stripes may sometimes be seen in individual specimens. Tail ringed; the ears are short and rounded, indicating its colder habitat. This is a cobby type of cat that sports longer hairs on its body during the winter period. It has adapted to live quite well in very cold climates, where it preys on rodents. It has a fierce look about it and a personality to match, as it is virtually untamable in spite of its domestic cat size. The very earliest cats known probably looked like this species. Rarely seen in captivity. Also known as the manul.

SAND CAT: *Felis margarita*, 4 subspecies. Sahara Desert, Arabia, and east of the Caspian Sea. HRL 57 cm (22.4 in), TL 35 cm (13.7 in). Yellow-brown to gray. Dark stripes to flanks in some subspecies; tail ringed with dark tip. Kittens born striped. Ears very large, skull broad, furred between pads—all adaptations to desert life. Feeds on rodents, reptiles and insects. Little is known of its lifestyle, and it is rarely kept in zoological collections. Closely related to European and African wild cats.

MARBLED CAT: *Felis marmorata*, 2 subspecies. Malaya to Borneo, Nepal to Burma. HRL 60 cm (23.6 in), TL 54 cm (21 in). A beautifully patterned felid, this species has a ground color of yellow-brown on which darker brown patches occur, these being edged with black. They give way to spots on the tail and legs, with striped blotches to the chest, the fur of which is lighter colored, as is the underbelly. Body is long, as is the tail, which is uniformly thickish. Head is leopardlike, and the ears are small and rounded. The back is always well arched when the cat is at rest. A native of jungle habitat, this species is very rare in zoological collections, and little is known about its lifestyle.

BLACK-FOOTED CAT: *Felis nigripes*, 2 subspecies. South Africa. HRL 40 cm (15.7 in), TL 17 cm (6.7 in). This is the world's smallest cat. Ground color of sandy brown which is spotted and blotched in black. The thick tail is incompletely barred with black. The head is broad and ears are small and black on their outer surface, which has a white mark—a common feature on many patterned wild species—this often being a white spot. Has extremely short breeding period due to its remote lifestyle. Virtually no record of being kept in captivity; little is known of its lifestyle.

OCELOT: *Felis pardalis*, 11 subspecies. Central and South America. HRL 100 cm (39 in), TL 65 cm (25.5 in). These magnificent felids never fail to impress those who see them. Their ground color is yellow-brown, on which are spots and patches of black, sometimes with brown centers. Underbelly is white. Tail is long, thick, and blunt-ended, and is brown-black with almost white rings. Ears small, head leopardlike in shape and marked with stripes.

Top to bottom: Pallas cat, *Felis manul*; kodkod, *Felis guigna*; Geoffroy's cat, *Felis geoffroyi*; and clouded leopard, *Panthera nebulosa*.

Above: Profile of an ocelot, *Felis pardalis*. **Below:** Keeping an ocelot as a pet should only be attempted by experts.

Ocelots have the best breeding record in captivity of the leopardlike South American cats and are unusual in having only 36 chromosomes, compared to the 38 typical for the family. They are larger than the margay, with whom they are often confused. Both sexes have strong body odors throughout adulthood. Millions have been killed for their fur; therefore, they are no longer common in the wild state. Many have been reared as pets; however, whilst tame as youngsters, this can change as they reach maturity—many such pets end up in zoological collections after badly injuring their owners or children.

SPANISH LYNX: *Felis pardina*. Spain. See northern lynx for further details, as the Spanish lynx is generally similar. It is now rare in Spain other than in the south, where it is protected within the national parks.

FLAT-HEADED CAT: *Felis planiceps*. Southern Asia, Borneo and Sumatra. HRL 50 cm (19.7 in), TL 15 cm (6 in). Dark brown ground color with faint spotted markings and a light-colored chest and underbelly. Tail is very short whilst the muzzle is long. Ears short and skull wide. Legs short. The nails are only partly sheathed and carried without touching the floor. This is a very unusual cat with modified dentition to secure slippery prey such as fish. It is quite happy to enter water and is probably a poor climber. Virtually nothing is known about its life and breeding habits.

RUSTY-SPOTTED CAT: *Felis rubiginosa*, 2 subspecies. India and Sri Lanka. HRL 48 cm (18.9 in), TL 25 cm (9.8 in). The ground color is gray-brown on which are longitudinal stripes to back and flanks, these becoming spots to the rear end and legs. Tail may be agouti, with black tip, or spotted. Underbelly and chest white and striped with brown or black. Face wide and ears short. Two white stripes extend upwards from inner eye to the crest of skull. The Sri Lankan subspecies is a jungle dweller, but that of India prefers more open country. The species has a poor record in captivity, and little is known about its lifestyle.

BOBCAT: *Felis rufus*, 11 subspecies. Northern states of USA to central Mexico. HRL 9 cm (37.4 in), TL 19 cm (7.5 in). Yellow-brown to gray, which may be spotted or not. Similar in looks to the lynx, to which it is very closely related. It is the most numerous of the North American wildcats and is very adaptable in its habitat. Its actions are much like those of the domestic cat, but its voice range is more varied and it has an unusual coughlike bark, as well as growls and hisses. Will enter water more readily than some cats. Its prey is mainly rabbits (65%) and rodents (25%), but it has been known to attack domestic stock if conditions force this.

SERVAL: *Felis serval*, 14 subspecies. Africa, extensive distribution. HRL 100 cm (39 in), TL 40 cm (15.7 in). Yellow ground color which carries spots on the body and bars or blotches to the legs. This cat has large rounded ears and long legs. Tail is ringed whilst underbelly and inner legs are white. It is a very graceful cat with an elegant neck and small head, on which the ears almost touch when in an alerted state. Servals like savanna habitats but stay close to water courses. They are excellent climbers and swimmers. After an indifferent record in captivity, they are now kept without problems and have lived up to 20 years. They are also very popular zoo exhibits, being so beautiful in appearance. They are possibly the swiftest old cats, bettered only by the cheetah.

Above: A young serval, *Felis serval*. **Below:** The bobcat, *Felis rufus*, is the most common North American wild cat species.

Top to bottom: Temminck's golden cat, *Felis temmincki*; tiger cat, *Felis tigrina*; fishing cat, *Felis viverrinus*; and jaguarundi, *Felis yagouaroundi*.

EUROPEAN WILD CAT: *Felis silvestris*, 7 subspecies. Throughout Europe and extending to western Asia. HRL 80 cm (31.5 in), TL 35 cm (13.7 in). The color is a ground of yellow-brown-gray on which are superimposed tabby markings of the mackerel type, but these may also be blotched in some specimens. Tail is comparatively short and the fur is dense, longer in the winter months. The species has undoubtedly crossed with domestics over the centuries but itself remains a truly vicious and untamable animal. Their desire for seclusion means they have not proved popular zoo exhibits. Breeding records are poor due to the lack of breeding pairs.

TEMMINCK'S GOLDEN CAT: *Felis temmincki*, 3 subspecies. Southern Asia to Sumatra. HRL 105 cm (41 in), TL 55 cm (21.6 in). A uniform red-brown color but with spotting to the legs and lower flanks; this is variable depending on subspecies. The tail is thick and the fur is short over the whole body. The head is puma-like and carries black barring as well as white streaks. Melanistic examples are known. This is a big cat that hunts chiefly at ground level.

TIGER CAT: *Felis tigrina*, 3 subspecies. Central and South America. HRL 55 cm (21.6 in), TL 40 cm (15.7 in). See ocelot for general description. This beautiful felid has in the past been classified as subspecific to the ocelot. Smaller than the margay, it is much rarer in captivity. It is a pure forest dweller but cannot climb down trees in the manner of the margay. It has been hybridized with domestic cats—these offspring were spotted. Little is known about its wild lifestyle other than that it feeds on small mammals and birds. Also known as the little spotted cat or tiger ocelot.

FISHING CAT: *Felis viverrinus*. South and southeast Asia and Sumatra. HRL 85 cm (33.5 in), TL 32 cm (12.5 in). Color is darker than in the leopard cats, which it resembles; the fishing cat is more gray and its body covered with spots which become longitudinal stripes on the head and neck. Ears are relatively short, as would be expected in a forest dweller of the tropics. This species is known to eat crustaceans and mollusks; and it "fishes," using its paws as studied in captivity. It is very aggressive, and its defense is basically to attack any potential adversary rather than to flee. Not common in captivity.

MARGAY: *Felis wiedii*, 11 subspecies. Central and South America. HRL 70 cm (27.5 in), TL 50 cm (19.7 in). See ocelot for general description, as the margay is very similar. In the wild this species enjoys protection but is still poached in large numbers. Many are kept as exotic pets but, happily, more people are appreciating the survival problems and are taking a more serious view of keeping and breeding what is a delightful species. They are pure forest dwellers and just about the best climbing cats in the world, with only the clouded leopard rivaling them in the ability to descend trees head first and hang from a branch with one leg. Also called the tiger cat, or little ocelot.

JAGUARUNDI: *Felis yagouaroundi*, 8 subspecies. Central and South America. HRL 105 cm (41 in), TL 80 cm (31.5 in). Two forms are known: one is very dark, almost black, with lighter chest and underbelly; the other is red-brown. Neither is spotted, although the kittens are. The light phase cats were known as eyras, but both forms can appear in a single litter, as well as every combination from dark to light. The body is long, the legs short, and the head round with large round eyes and small rounded ears. Tail is quite long and slim for a species that prefers the ground to climbing. They appear more like mustelids than cats. They inhabit jungle and dense cover and were, and no doubt still are, kept as pets by the South American Indians to control rodent populations. Rare in captivity; little is known about their lifestyle in the wild.

Genus *Panthera*—6 species, 45 subspecies

LION: *Panthera leo*, 11 subspecies. Throughout Africa south of the Sahara and in India, where the species is restricted to the Gir forest. HRL 190 cm (75 in), TL 105 cm (41 in). No description necessary. Two subspecies extinct in this century. The only truly social cat. Prides can be very large or very small.

CLOUDED LEOPARD: *Panthera nebulosa*, 4 subspecies. Southern China, Indochina, Formosa, Borneo, Nepal, and Burma. HRL 105 cm (41 in), TL 90 cm (35 in). Yellow to light brown with spots and stripes. Body pattern like marble, tail thick. The clouded leopard is regarded as an interim species, bridging the large and small felids. It exhibits characteristic features of both generic groups. It is the finest climber of

Top to bottom: Black-footed cat, *Felis nigripes*; Spanish lynx, *Felis pardina*; flat-headed cat, *Felis planiceps*; and rusty-spotted cat, *Felis rubiginosa*.

Above: The European wild cat, *Felis silvestris*, is believed to be an ancestor of the domestic cat. **Below:** The black panther is the melanistic phase of the leopard, *Panthera pardus*. Black panthers are often found in litters that contain normal, spotted leopards.

Above: A young lion cub, *Panthera leo*. The lion is the only true social cat. **Below:** Jaguar, *Panthera onca*.

any cat species, with only the margay coming close to its fantastic ability to move about and descend trees; it is so capable that it is able to catch birds and monkeys in trees despite its large size.

JAGUAR: *Panthera onca*, 8 subspecies. North and South America, but now rarely seen in the USA. HRL 185 cm (72.8 in), TL 75 cm (29.5 in). Distinguished from the leopards by its great size and by its coat pattern, which on the back and flanks comprises complete black circles with one, two, or three central spots. (The black circles of a leopard are rarely complete and are not as large; few of them contain central spots.) Excellent climbers, but not as good as the leopard, they are also superb swimmers. They will attack anything from small mammals, large herbivores (including horses), monkeys, snakes, to man. They are, therefore, the supreme predator of South America, with no natural enemies once they reach adulthood at three to four years of age.

LEOPARD: *Panthera pardus*, 15 subspecies. Africa and Asia. HRL 150 cm (59 in), TL 95 cm (37.4 in). No description needed. The Amur leopard of Amur and Korea sports a longer coat, as does the Persian leopard of Iran. Leopards have probably proved more dangerous to man than any other big felid, due to their ability to approach settlements unseen and to their superb jumping and climbing ability. Extensively hunted for their fur, a number of species are now endangered and given full protection.

TIGER: *Panthera tigris*, 7 subspecies. Asia, from Sumatra to Borneo north to Siberia. HRL 280 cm (110 in), TL 95 cm (37.4 in). No description required. The world's largest cat is the Siberian tiger. Almost white specimens are known and are very famous. Tigers are always popular zoo exhibits, but many subspecies are greatly endangered. Tigers fear no animal and will even attack elephants if they get desperate, but rarely would such an attack be successful unless the elephant was not mature. The main prey is buffalo and deer.

SNOW LEOPARD: *Panthera uncia*. Kashmir, Tibet, and the Himalayas. HRL 150 cm (59 in), TL 90 cm (35.4 in). This is a big cat with some small cat features; for example, it does not roar, and it crouches over food like small cats

do. These are beautiful cats which have superb jumping abilities. Some have gray coats with dark spotting, and in the winter they sport long fur. They have been greatly hunted for their fur and are very endangered. India and the Soviet Union give them full protection, but illegal shooting still occurs in the Himalayas. Small zoo populations have now been established, but greater safety measures in the wild are needed to ensure the survival of these magnificent cats.

Genus *Acinonyx*–1 species, 6 subspecies

CHEETAH: *Acinonyx jubatus*, 6 subspecies. Southern Asia and Africa. HRL 150 cm (59 in), TL 80 cm (31 in). This cat needs little description, as it is so well known. Formerly common in India, it is now extinct in that country due to hunting and the taking of kittens for rearing as hunting cats of the wealthy. Although the spotted cheetah is familiar to most people, few know about the unusual king cheetah, which has elongated blotches that, in some specimens, have joined to create stripes to the dorsal surface and long blotches to the lower flanks and legs. Cheetahs are renowned for their speed as the fastest land animal—they have been clocked at 90 kph on a Florida racetrack but are believed to be capable of just over 100 kph (60 mph) in the wild when hunting food. They do, however, tire very quickly, as such speeds really exhaust all their energy, so good rests are needed between hunts. They were probably the first domesticated cats and were used about 3000 years ago by the Sumerians to help hunt deer. They tame readily if reared from a young age. Kublai Khan is thought to have kept 1000 cheetahs for hunting purposes. Breeding, however, was not achieved until the 1950s but is now quite common in captivity.

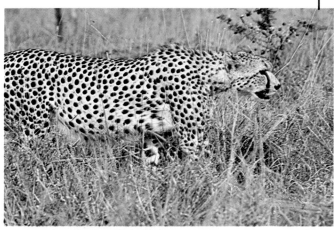

Opposite: The leopard, *Panthera pardus*, is known for its stealth and for its superb jumping and climbing ability. Like the domestic cat, some leopards carry a longhair gene. **This page:** For the most part, cheetahs are solitary animals, but sometimes males form small groups that stay together until there is not enough prey in the area to support them.

Cheetahs stalk their prey for quite some time before attacking, and they hunt only during the day. Weak prey animals—old, sick, or very young—are the most likely victims of a cheetah attack. Mother cheetahs often capture young fawns in order to teach their offspring to hunt.

KEEPING EXOTIC WILD CATS

The idea of keeping wild cats has often appealed to many people, and many species have been purchased as pets. Today this is more difficult, due to the laws in most countries which forbid the keeping of wild species unless by special license and with proof of satisfactory housing. This is important where wild cats are concerned, as many people have been badly mauled by pet cats which grow up without fear of humans or which change in their character as they mature. Even small species can be extremely dangerous, since a cat does not become domesticated just because it was acquired as a kitten—it might become somewhat tame but will always remain unpredictable.

Any person who decides to acquire a wild cat species should give this very careful thought and should ensure that he has suitable escape-proof accommodations. In addition, it is necessary to have checked with national and local wildlife services, together with townhalls, about the necessary permits.

Wild species should not be kept merely as pets but for the more scientific purposes of study and breeding. Whilst most zoological in-

For the most part, allowing a child to handle a wild cat such as a margay is a bad idea unless the animal has been completely tamed.

Ocelots, and all other cats kept in captivity, must be given an ample supply of fresh water. Suitable water containers are available at your local pet shop.

stitutions frown on the keeping of wild cat species by the public, one must remember that zoos themselves have been great consumers of wild animals for years. In addition, some private collectors have extremely impressive records of maintaining and breeding species, while some zoos may have failed in this regard. A private collector is often able to provide more seclusion for difficult breeding species and is able to study them without the distraction created by the need to exhibit the parents and offspring. In general, however, the modern zoo will have far greater facility today than the individual person, so those interested in wild species are recommended to join a scientific study group attached to a zoological garden that has a stated interest in the breeding of the rare small felid species. It is these animals that we know so little about.

Above: Some margays, with proper training, may become tame enough to share a nap with their owners.

Those who do purchase wild felids are encouraged only to have pairs, or to allow their single animals to be mated with cats of their own species—not to hybridize them with related species, as this offers no advantages in the long term. Wherever possible, wild species should be acquired from those already having breeding populations, thus reducing the need to take animals from the wild. Should these not be available, then purchase only through reputable dealers in exotic species, and check out their paperwork in respect to any cat offered to ensure that the animal has been legally imported and offered for sale.

Left: This margay has an obvious rapport with his owner. He seems to be enjoying the ride. **Opposite:** It goes without saying that a novice should never try to acquire a big cat such as a tiger.

THE HISTORY OF CATS

The history of cats can be viewed in two ways as far as domestic pets are concerned: first as a predatory group of animals, and secondly in terms of the domestication process that resulted in present-day breeds. In both instances such history is a continuum, by which is meant that it is an on-going process. In wild species we cannot see evolution taking place because of the vast time spans involved, and the only proof that it takes place at all comes from the study of fossil evidence and the deductions that may be drawn from these. However, under domestic conditions we can speed up evolution, so we are able to both see it and control it to the degree that we can selectively breed for features that we find pleasing. Such features may not actually be to the benefit of the cat, so it is important that we apply moral judgments to the selection process. However, we will first travel back in time to see the events that produced the modern day felids.

SPANS OF TIME

Paleontologists divide spans of time into a number of units based on rock formations laid down on the earth's crust. From these, fossils can be dated so that a picture of life on our planet at different times can be put together. Large spans of time are called eras. These are divided into periods, and periods into epochs. For our purposes we need not look to the earliest eras but can restrict ourselves to relatively (in terms of earth's history) recent periods. A point of interest, when evolution of animals is considered, is that the continents we know today have not always appeared either where they now are or in their present shape. Australia has been iso-

A northern lynx, *Felis lynx*. Cats are indigenous to every continent except Australia and Antarctica.

Opposite: The habitat of the Amur leopard is farther north than that of any other cat; it reaches into the Amur region of the Soviet Union.

The fur of the snow leopard is exceptionally long—two inches on the back and four inches on the abdomen. This cat is primarily a nocturnal hunter.

lated for many millions of years, progressively more so as time has marched on, whilst South America was also isolated and a land bridge, Panama, came only very recently, as periods of time go. These facts account for the very unusual animals that are found in these areas, for they were able to develop without the fierce competition found elsewhere. When the land bridge came to join the two Americas, migration went both ways, but in balance it favored those from the north, which displaced many of the more primitive South American species.

EARLY MAMMALS

All life on earth originally developed from the water that covers most of our planet. Some early creatures could live on land and in water, but they had to return to water in order to breed; these were the amphibians. The development of the cleidoic egg was a major evolutionary advancement, without which we would not be here today. It enabled animals to remain and breed on land and it resulted in the reptiles, which were to dominate the earth for about 200 million years. From the cotylosaurs (stem reptiles) were to come the dinosaurs, or terrible lizards, which themselves roamed and terrified all creatures for nearly 140 million years. However, from the early reptiles were also to come the birds and the early mammals, but of course these had to keep a very low profile indeed with so many giant lizards running around!

Some early mammallike reptiles were quite large, maybe attaining up to 1.8 m (6 ft) in length. They had hair, were warmblooded, and may even have suckled their young. However, most had died out 170 million years ago, during the Jurassic period, given the fierce and growing competition of the dinosaurs. It paid to be small in those days, and one group of the mammallike reptiles, known as Diarthrognathus, gave rise to the true mammals. Members of this group were about the size of a weasel or somewhat larger.

THE AGE OF MAMMALS

After their long rule as lords of the earth, the giant dinosaurs vanished quite suddenly—relatively speaking. We still do not know why, but by the end of the Cretaceous period they were all gone, other than for the crocodilians which have survived, in smaller forms, to this day. This happening heralded the dawn of the Age of Mammals—the Cenozoic era, which is the one we are still in. With many ecological niches thus vacant, all manner of animals appeared in order to fill them. Herbivores grew to enormous sizes, and so did the creatures that preyed upon them. One such group of the latter were known as creodonts, some of which were like giant hyenas that were larger than bears. Their teeth were modified for flesh-eating, but they still retained the capacity to chew vegetable matter. Other carnivorous animals included the much smaller miacids, a group of flesh-eaters in which the teeth modified more towards a wholly meat diet. These latter animals remained in the dense forests where they could climb trees and live on small mammals, birds and reptiles. They were not unlike the present-day civets, and had long bodies, elongate snouts, and short legs armed with claws. However, for about 16 million years, throughout the Eocene, the creodonts were the earth's prime predators, but slowly they began to wane and finally died out about five million years ago—possibly having given rise to numerous herbivores before they did so. They were not all large predators, and some may have adapted to a totally vegetable diet, as such was their dental arrangement.

Throughout the early Tertiary period there was much maneuvering amongst species to take up the vacant niches, and another aspect of evolution was also to play its role in the subsequent rise of the true carnivores.

PLANTS

Although flowering plants were evolving during the Cretaceous period, the pace accelerated during the early Tertiary, and grasses started to appear during the Eocene. This created a new food source; therefore, any species that could adapt to take advantage of this would probably find it beneficial to its own future. The result was an improved generation of herbivores, which ranged from rodents that could cash in on the actual grass seeds to the larger animals that could graze on the grasses—and act as a means

A serval. The ancestors of the modern cat species evolved to be able to catch the small herbivorous animals that were too swift for large creodonts.

of dispersal for the plant seeds. Such species were fleeter of foot than their precursors, and probably quicker witted as well, so the ruling predators of the day, the creodonts and their like, would have found it progressively more difficult to catch them. As always in evolution, one event does not proceed in isolation but immediately prompts a counteraction, so that any species that could adapt in turn would find benefit in preying on the swifter herbivores.

Evolution is a very slow process indeed, so the new herbivores did not establish themselves before other animals reacted to this fact, for the events happen together. What happens in evolutionary history is that at any one period of time

DIVISIONS OF TIME

ERA	PERIOD	EPOCH	NO. OF YEARS AGO (Millions)	DURATION
	Quaternary	Holocene	0.01-present	
		Pleistocene	0.01-2	1.9
CENOZOIC (The Age of Mammals)		Pliocene	2- 7	5
		Miocene	7- 26	19
		Oligocene	26- 38	12
		Eocene	38- 54	16
	Tertiary	Paleocene	54- 65	11
MESOZOIC (The Age of Reptiles)	Cretaceous		65-136	61
	Jurassic		136-193	57
	Triassic		193-225	32
PALEOZOIC	Permian, Carboniferous, etc.		225-600	375

there are always those species that have become highly specialized, and thus less able to react to change; those that have committed to a degree of specialization but can adapt given sufficient time; and those that have retained a very general form which enables them to more rapidly move in one or other directions, depending on the opportunities that become available. Species must not only react to each other but they must also be capable of adapting to different weather conditions and new disease organisms, and they must be able to regulate their own numbers. Therefore, we are looking at a very complex process indeed, where success or failure is measured in millions rather than in thousands of years.

It happens that the miacids were the species of the moment and were able to diversify successfully to capitalize on the changing events. It certainly seems that these small animals were ideally placed, as they were nimble in mind and limb and were not overly large. Thus they were

capable of taking the smaller herbivores that larger predators could not catch—and had a basically uncommitted anatomy that enabled them to specialize at a quicker rate than could other species during the periods in question. It should also be appreciated that all miacids did not commit to the same path of progress, for many continued to refine their ability to survive in the habitats they already occupied, whilst others chose to specialize on the insects found in the new grasslands. The overall result, however, was the creation of the true carnivores that make up the order we know of as Carnivora. As there were also small creodonts and other predatory animals on earth, the question of why some of these did not opt to adapt to the new habitats becoming available is an obvious one.

It is always easier to draw conclusions from events that did happen than from those that did not; but, this stated, the most accepted view is that the creodonts were slow of movement and of brain and could not adapt quickly enough, or rather that the miacids adapted more quickly, depending on the view you wish to take. Having gained the initial advantage, events clearly favored the new carnivores. Basic anatomy is all scientists have to work with, but I am sure other factors such as behavioral traits, vigor, and many other aspects worked together to favor the modern carnivores. In simple terms, the ruling predators, like the dinosaurs, had run out of adaptive capabilities, so their days were numbered. We do not, of course, know whether they did totally die out, for some may well have become the ancestors of species still living on earth in a much changed form.

Adult tiger and cub. Cats have never been plentiful enough to become a major food source for other animals.

THE EARLY FELIDS

The evolution of many species of animals remains a mystery to us largely because the fossil evidence is far from complete. This is certainly the case with felids, and it is made more difficult because most small cats live in forest habitats, which are not the most suitable places for preserving the remains of animals. A further complication is that it has to be decided when is a cat not a cat? Recognizing a felid now is not difficult, but as one goes back in time, things are not so easy. Slowly but surely the features become less obvious, and eventually one might as easily be looking at a civet, a mongoose, a stoat, a fossa, a dog, or even a hyena—for each of these arose from stock that was common to all modern carnivores. Remember, part of our ability to recognize a cat is based on muscle propor-

53

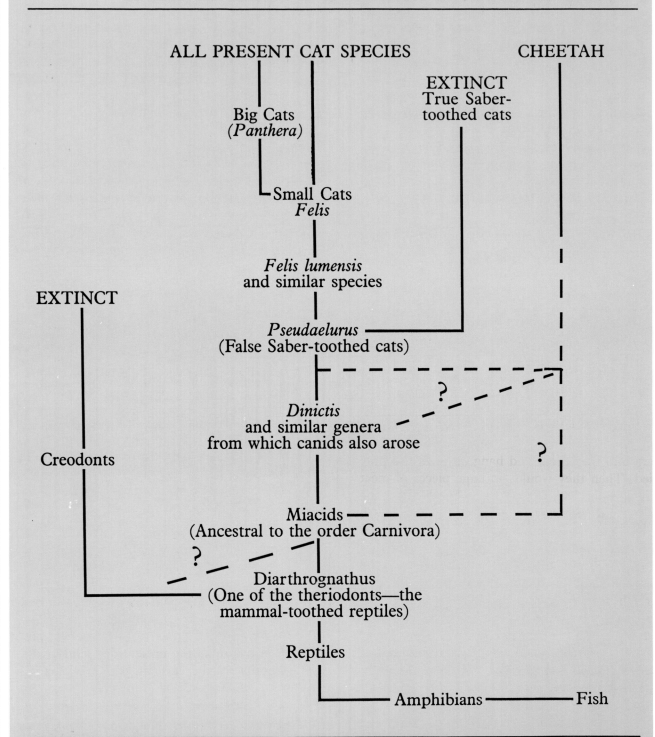

A SIMPLIFIED EVOLUTIONARY HISTORY OF CATS

ALL PRESENT CAT SPECIES   CHEETAH

EXTINCT
True Saber-
toothed cats

Big Cats
(*Panthera*)

Small Cats
Felis

Felis lumensis
and similar species

EXTINCT

Pseudaelurus
(False Saber-toothed cats)

?

Dinictis
and similar genera
from which canids also arose

?

Creodonts

Miacids
(Ancestral to the order Carnivora)

?

Diarthrognathus
(One of the theriodonts—the
mammal-toothed reptiles)

Reptiles

Amphibians —————— Fish

Evolution is a continuum, and between each of the groups above will have been thousands of individuals—each showing almost imperceptible changes but which resulted, collectively, in the transition from one species or group to the next.

tions, coat color and patterns, and the amount of fur on the tail—but we do not know, purely from a fossil skeleton, what these features were like, so a degree of guesswork must be employed. The bone structure itself was also evolving, so even this cannot be said to be clearly that of a dog or a cat, only in the case of much more recent examples.

We can thus say that the earliest carnivores, based on present-day families, started to evolve about 65 million years ago in the early Tertiary period. Of the many species then seen, one group we call the miacids roamed the earth about 50 million years ago. From these were to develop major felid groups which we refer to as the true, or false, saber-toothed cats. The saber-tooths had greatly enlarged canine teeth that protruded from the upper jaw. They were probably somewhat slow moving when compared to modern cats, and their method of feeding is still debated. Some authorities believe they were essentially carrion eaters, taking over the kills or leftovers of other predators. This hardly seems in keeping with such outsize dental work, for it is highly unlikely that they could cope with bones, and, as they appear to be the major felids of their time, the opposing view is more logical. They attacked large herbivores but did not kill by nape bites; instead they would stab their daggers into the throat and hang on until the prey died. Then they would rip large pieces of meat from the body but would not be able to cope with bone, so would leave good pickings for canids and for hyenas.

These true saber-toothed cats were around for a long while, for though they declined and came back again in modified forms, their full span stretched from the Oligocene through to the present period—the last species, *Smilodon*, becoming extinct during the last Ice Age—about 15,000 years ago. There were a large number of true saber-toothed species, each specializing in different types of prey, so it is not surprising that the true cats were not able to develop beyond relatively small sizes. However, they were in the wings and developing more and more features that would enable them to cope better with the ever faster moving game that was becoming established on the plains, which the saber-tooths were not able to catch.

A leopard cat, *Felis bengalensis*. The Pseudaelurus felids gave rise to all present-day cats except the cheetah.

THE TRUE CATS

The false saber-toothed cats shared with the true saber-tooths a common ancestor in the form of a group of felids known as Pseudaelurus. Such cats were clearly more felid than the earlier forms and had developed the stabbing teeth that were to be so conspicuous in the saber-tooths. They were also digitigrade in their stance, and they gave rise to all the present-day felids, with the exception of the cheetah, which is clouded in mystery in terms of its origins.

The earliest known present-day cats were the lynx and the puma, and these had become evident by the Upper Pliocene, about three million years ago. They inhabited much of North America and spread to Europe. The smaller species of cats were still not conspicuous (in terms of fossil evidence at least) until the very late Pliocene, though they are seen in early deposits of this period in Europe. It would seem that the species we can recognize today developed through the now extinct *Felis lumensis* (Martelli's wild cat). This species was evident in the Old World, both in Africa and in Eurasia, from about three to four million years ago; and from it, or related species, were to emerge all of the present-day small wild cats. These were seen by one to two million years ago, and it is from these that the big or roaring cats were to develop. The clouded leopard is regarded as an example of the transitional form from small to large, for it displays features common to both. The South American cats are still a bit of a mystery in their origins, but it is thought that they arrived there during the last Ice Age, and it is speculated that the Iriomotes cat of Japan may represent a link between the cats of the Old and New Worlds.

The late appearance of the big or roaring cats on the world scene is somewhat surprising, but is believed to be linked to two factors. First, it required the evolution of very fast prey—which implied a lighter protective coating of flesh. These also developed horns, which would have given the saber-tooth a lot of problems—if it could catch them—because for as long as they kept their heads down the big cats would find killing them difficult. However, the small cats utilize both throat and nape bites, the latter dislocating the vertebrae of the neck. This would be a risky procedure for a saber-tooth, as its teeth could easily be damaged if it failed to find the intervertebral spots. Small cats thus grew larger without a disproportionate increase in the size of the canines; speed, however, was probably the determining factor.

RELATIONSHIPS OF FELIDS

Possibly more than the average carnivore families, the cats are moved from one genus to the next with regularity. No one can decide how closely they are related to each other, and the latest sciences, such as blood-testing techniques or chromosome counts, have resolved nothing. Most species have 19 pairs of chromosomes—a diploid number of 38—but five species have only 36. Certainly the present position of lumping all the small cats into the genus *Felis* and the big cats into *Panthera* has only the benefit of convenience, and no doubt both genera will (once again) be subjected to much revision in the years to come.

An interesting aspect that has come out of comparative chromosome numbers is whether they indicate an advanced or primitive state, or whether they are incidental to this aspect. If a low count, as in felids, foxes, viverrids and others, indicates advancement, in that they have been derived from centric fusion of chromosomes from a higher earlier number, then these species have virtually run their full course of evolution and will be unable to make many more adaptations—they have reached their peak and have committed themselves to the limit.

On this basis, then the dogs, wolves, and bears, with a high count (78), are relatively primitive and thus have a much greater capacity to adapt to changing conditions. On such an evaluation, then, cats have changed little for about a million years, having peaked during the late Pleistocene; dogs are thus still progressing. A speculative thought is that if the cats are less capable of change, this possibly accounts for the fact that during the thousands of years they have been domesticated, they have shown little change in relative size or shape. Conversely, dogs have undergone considerable change and can be seen in a great variation of size and form. However, whilst each theory has its supporters, there are as many that remain unconvinced that low chromosome numbers restrict adaptation. Therefore, until we know a great deal more about such matters, these remain useful debating subjects.

It is a sobering thought that we humans will place enormous values on a building, a painting, or a similar item that at best goes back a few thousand years, yet we will show such indifference to a species whose pedigree goes back in a direct line of descent for around 600 million years. Many species may well have died out without man's help, but the most precious items we have on earth are the species that, like ourselves, have made it to this point in time—surely a bond worth preserving?

Opposite: Tiger taking a swim.

The leopard, like the lion, tiger, and cheetah, has proven to be a popular zoo exhibit.

DOMESTICATION

Before looking into the history of pet cats, it is perhaps worthwhile to discuss the question of domestication, for this has bearing on our relationship with cats and has influenced the way cats have been regarded over the centuries.

The fact that a cat may be kept within a human environment does not make it a domesticated species, and this subtle difference between the popular or dictionary definition of the word and that used in the zoological sense should always be borne in mind. Tameness is not to be confused with domestication—any wild animal can be tamed to a greater or lesser degree (as in zoos or private homes), but this does not make it a domesticated animal. The ability to breed a species under captive conditions is again not a suitable definition of domesticity, even if it is coupled with tameness, but is merely the first stage of the process. True domestication can only be reached when a wild species is selectively bred to the degree that physical, anatomical, and behavioral changes are such that the resulting individuals would be incapable of surviving were they returned to the wild state from which their original wild forebears came.

By using this definition, then, it can be seen that many dog, rabbit, guinea pig, bird, and fish breeds are good examples of full domestication—along with popular farm stock such as sheep, cattle, and their likes. In terms of cats, then, the majority of breeds cannot be fairly described as being fully domesticated, for most would experience little difficulty in returning to the wild state—and I do mean wild and not the semi-feral existence seen in the streets of our concrete jungles. Cats are thus still undergoing the domestication process and, happily, have made little progress in this direction over the centuries. This gives them their unique place amongst the pets we keep.

It is this very fact that endears cats to many people, and likewise gives non-cat owners or lovers the fuel to say that cats are antisocial and unreliable pets. It is the independent nature of felines that has made domestication such a long process, and this has been shaped by the way the vast majority of species live out their lives—in relative isolation.

A professional animal handler with her pet ocelot.

A female (left) and a male (right) lion.

THE BEGINNINGS

We do not know exactly when the first cats commenced an association with humans—nor indeed where this took place. However, we can draw certain conclusions from what we know of prehistoric life and of the domestication of other animals. Domestication is brought about in the first place by a need to retain a food source in the vicinity of people as they travel into areas that are not rich in available wildlife. Africa south of the Sahara, most of Europe, and the whole of the American continent, as well as the Indian subcontinent, are rich in wild species, so that there was not the same need for domestic species in these lands until settled populations grew up that were larger than the food supply available.

By contrast, the nomadic peoples of the Near East travelled through inhospitable country and quickly saw the benefits of capturing and rearing wild species suited to this role. It was found that sheep, goats, and wild pig were easily controlled if reared from a young age, so it is hardly surprising that these were the first species to become domesticated, commencing from about 8000 BC. With herds of easy prey moving through their territories, it can be seen how natural it would have been for wolf species to latch on to such a food source and follow nomadic man. In Europe, as well as in North America, man would also have gained benefit from capturing young wolves and rearing them in homes because of their guarding and hunting uses. The dog thus arrived on the domestic scene at much the same time as sheep—possibly at a number of locations in the northern hemisphere at about the same period. As nomads found land to their liking, they started to settle down and form communities, and this created a need for ever larger meat supplies; domestication of cattle via the wild aurochs of southern Europe and Asia was thus in evidence by about 6500 BC. It is probable that the various game fowl followed—ducks, geese, and jungle fowl. In the vast open steppes of Russia, herds of wild horses roamed, so these were to become the last large species of wild animal to be domesticated and distributed on a global basis (camels and llamas being restricted in such a distribution).

Each of the species thus domesticated by hu-

Above: Puma.

Above and below: Jaguars.

mans have certain common denominators with each other, and these are as follows:

1) They are herd, flock or pack species.
2) They quickly lose the desire to escape the human environment.
3) They are not a problem to control.
4) They are all herbivores and can be utilized by man in one or more ways—meat, transport, clothing, etc. (except the dog, which is a carnivore).

The wolf, being a very socially organized animal, fitted into human camps with no problems simply because, if taken as a cub, it would come to regard humans as pack members. It will be noticed that cats do not fit into any of these categories; the European wild cat (*Felis silvestris*), even if acquired as a kitten of a few days old, is virtually untamable and will be gone at the first possible opportunity! Another carnivore, the ferret, has been domesti-

European wild cat.

cated only because its wild ancestors, the polecats (genus *Mustela*), could be easily contained in hutches; it is thus also a species still undergoing full domestication.

To early man there were just two types of cat: those that were a danger to himself and his stock—the big cats; and those which avoided him and his whole way of life—the small cats. He hunted the first type for obvious reasons, and also for the attractive coat. He generally ignored the second group, both because they would be difficult to catch (indeed even to see too often) and because he had little need for them anyway; there is little point in feeding an animal that has no purpose behind it.

However, as man settled to develop an agricultural way of life, things started to change because he now attracted to his fields and grain stores that most ubiquitous group of mammals—the rodents—and these started to arrive and take up residence by the millions. As they did so, they attracted small felid species, which no doubt started to live within the vicinity of the fields. These cats would become familiar sights to humans and, as they neither bothered us nor took from us (other than the occasional fowl or two), their beneficial ability to kill rodents would have been quickly appreciated. It also happens that the felid species in the area of Asia Minor were of a less aggressive nature than those of northern type, and therefore had a greater ability to adapt to this new environment.

The earliest records of felines within human camps date back to about 7500 BC in Jericho, so we may assume that the familiarity role has had quite a long history. However, only when settlements grew to large sizes and kept larger stores would the cat population become obvious by their presence. Where there are rodents there will be disease, so this again favored the toleration of cats in the area. We can reasonably suppose that cats had become quite commonplace by about 2500 BC in and around the biblical lands, but we have no evidence that they were being selectively bred or indeed kept within the confines of homes, though the latter is likely, but on a loose basis.

A lioness transporting her cub. Lions and other big cats were hunted by man—they were never seen as potential helpmates like the wolves.

Black panther. Many ancient cultures revered the cat. For example, Egyptian gods took feline forms, Tibetans worshiped the guardian lions, and African tribes made leopard and panther masks.

THE EGYPTIANS

Although the beginnings of feline domestication may well have been going on in numerous areas at much the same time, it is usually some event of great moment that draws our attention to a subject, whereafter references start to appear with greater regularity. In the case of cats, it was the establishment of a cat cult in Egypt about 1500 BC that clearly underlines the fact that by this point in time cats were being kept within households and were greatly respected to the degree that when they died they were buried—or rather mummified—with all the ceremony that was accorded to humans. The Egyptians made many artifacts to act as representatives of the cat goddess Bast, Bastet or Pasht. The goddess took the form of a cat-headed woman, whilst the sun god Ra was depicted in the form of a cat. The god of war, Sek-

met, was depicted as a lion, so that cats in one form or another were very important to the Egyptians at various periods of their civilization. To injure a cat was a serious offense and to actually kill one was punishable by death if it had been done out of malice.

The very large number of drawings and artifacts, and mummified remains of cats in Egypt is sufficient to prove that the cats were in a state of domestication, because such numbers of the latter would not have been possible from wild sources. Furthermore, we know that by this period the Egyptians, Assyrians, and other peoples had developed considerable breeding skills.

A shipment of cat skulls and bones from one find weighed 19 tons; when it was received in England it was crushed for use as fertilizer! From that shipment, a single skull remains and is in the British Museum. This was at the turn of this century when many items were being sold without thought to their value to science and archaeology. At a later date, a further dig near Gizeh revealed 190 skulls dating from 600–200 BC. These were studied by Morrison-Scott, who published his account of them in 1952; in it he found that all but three were comparable to that of the species *Felis libyca*, the African or Kaffir wild cat. The others were *Felis chaus*, the jungle cat.

He also commented that the cats were generally somewhat larger than *libyca* but smaller than *Felis chaus*, and they were given the subspecific name of *Felis libyca bubastis*, the latter word being for the center of the cat cult in Bubastis, the capital of Libya at the height of the cult, which was probably around 1000–400 BC. The Egyptians were not disposed to export their cats, but, even so, a number did leave that country by one means or another and were sold in neighboring countries.

THE SPREAD OF THE CAT

Because Asia has more wild felids than does any other part of the world, it is difficult to say whether the semi-domesticated cats of Egypt were taken eastwards by traders or whether the peoples of southwest Asia were already domesticating cats concurrently with the Egyptians. The species *Felis libyca* is distributed from Africa to China and from the Soviet Union to Sardinia in its many subspecific forms. The Chinese are thought to have had cats within the home environment from about 1000 BC, but some authorities disclaim the dating of references and believe a truer date may be from 200 BC to AD 200. Given that dominant spotting was recognized in Chinese mice by about 1100 BC, it would be reasonable to suppose that if mice were domesticated by these extremely clever people by that date, as were goldfish, then cats may well have been kept by them too; they did, after all, have as many problems with mice and other rodents as the Egyptians did. Likewise, cats are believed to have been common in Indian households from as early as 2000 BC. Even if this is considered a somewhat optimistic date, it is quite feasible that by 1500–1000 BC, cats may well have been a familiar sight in households, or at least in the immediate vicinity of them. The fact that the Egyptians held the cat as sacred, and therefore made many references to them, should not cloud the strong possibility that other peoples recognized the virtue of cats at much the same period, but did not regard them so highly that they were glorified in art, pottery or the likes. Where attention was focused was on other species of animals, such as cattle, snakes, elephants, fish, and even mythical creatures, which to these peoples were far more important than the humble cat.

Again, whether of local origin or imported from Egypt, probably the former, we know that cats were kept in Turkey by about 600 BC, for artifacts showing women suckling felids have been found in the area of Hacilar. The obvious reasons for women suckling the cats was because either the kittens were taken from the wild at a very early age, or because the Turks appreciated that if a cat was to be encouraged to stay within the home environment, then it was essential for it to be socialized at the youngest possible age. From Turkey, the spread westwards would have been through the Balkans into Italy, as well as via sea routes through the Mediterranean that connected Africa, Asia Minor and Europe.

The early promotion given to cats by the Egyptians would have accorded status to them. This is of importance in their later domestic role, for the Romans, whose impact on the world is with us to this day, were greatly influ-

Asia has more wild cats, including the tiger, than any other continent.

enced by Greek and Egyptian cultures. It was the Roman families, following in the wake of their legions as they marched to conquer France, Germany, Spain, Holland, and England, that would have taken their cats with them and established felids in northern Europe as very much part of a domestic and agricultural way of life.

The subsequent rise of the Spanish, Dutch, French, and British Empires ensured that cats would reach the New World and Australia, as well as being re-exported to countries from which their forebears most likely came. Wherever ships went, so cats would be taken in order to keep down the mice and rat populations that were always present, and which would otherwise have taken much of the food carried for the crew and as part of the cargo.

As ships started to circumnavigate the globe, so an exchange of cat genes took place as European cats mated with the local races in far off lands. In this way longhaired cats from the more northerly areas crossed with the shorthaired varieties common to more tropical and temperate climates, and thus the full range of colors and markings seen today in cats came about in their genetic state. Matings would have been largely on a random basis, as the development of breeds is a very recent happening—in spite of the claims sometimes made by breeders of given varieties that such cats have a long and illustrious pedigree that extends directly to the cats of ancient Egypt! If such people fondly believe this, then I fear they are guilty of self-deception.

Broad types, longhaired, shorthaired and foreign, have been in evidence from the earliest times, but breeds, by any present-day definition, did not exist prior to the late 1800s. The development of consistently similar individuals—breeds—coincided with the rise of the so-called middle classes that were a direct result of the Industrial Revolution. At that period there was an explosion of interest in the natural sciences, and it was only then that controlled breeding programs were put in hand to isolate given desirable features. I do not say that fixed types have not been produced at different points in time by either religious cults or wealthy individuals, but these have been lost in antiquity, and there is not a shred of evidence to connect these, or the sacred cats of Egypt, to any present-day varieties, only in the general sense that all cats have a basically common ancestry at some point in the distant past.

THE BAD TIMES

Generally, cats were treated reasonably well for many centuries. Attitudes ranged from the sort of indifference still seen to almost worship of them much as was practiced in Egypt, and at later times in Asia and elsewhere. However, during the Dark or Middle Ages of Europe, a sinister and intolerant attitude was to sweep through the lands. It was fired by the Church, which considered anything that challenged its authority as being the work of the devil. Early in this period, things were just fine for cats, to the degree that to injure or kill one resulted in a quite hefty fine, for the mousing value of cats was given a premium. The definition of a hamlet usually included a cat amongst other livestock. A cat was considered good luck if it crossed your path, especially a black one.

However, by about AD 1300, the rot started to set in and attitudes changed with a ven-

The noble tiger is certainly one of the most beautiful creatures on earth.

Asiatic lions, *Panthera leo persica*, male and female. The Asiatic lion is still very rare, although its numbers have increased.

geance. The Church, concerned always about exerting its growing powers, was the instigator of this change, for it feared that its authority was being challenged by extant and earlier pagan beliefs and religions. In Germany, the clergy blamed the outbreak of a disease on the arrival of a witch and her cat in the area, and the result was that black cats were burned and thrown from belfries. This attitude then gained momentum, and for the next 400 years being a cat, especially a black one, was not the most desirable state. Great purges took place, and cats were subjected to horrendous cruelty. It was thought that a cat could turn into a witch, or a demon, and it was believed to have many supernatural powers that it invoked once the hours of darkness came. Superstition is a very powerful force, especially amongst illiterate peasants, which most people were in those days.

Cats were dipped in oil and burnt alive, skinned alive, roasted, drowned, beaten to death with sticks, and placed into sacks to be thrown onto the fires that consumed those found guilty of witchcraft or heresy. Others were tried in courts and then dressed and hanged along with their owners who had be found guilty of devil worship. Whilst cats suffered the brunt of such deaths, they were by no means the only animals so treated, for goats were also associated with devil worship and were likewise killed. Even pigs were brought to trial and deemed guilty if they were unprepared to speak in their own defense. Such was the mentality in those frightful times.

However, not all cats were so treated, and those living in the open on farms were left to continue their role as controllers of the mice and rats. The cats belonging to influential people were also largely safe from accusations of being familiars of witches or disciples of the devil. Ironically, rather than remove the image of mystery and supernatural powers that surrounded the cat, the Church actually perpetuated it by

Cheetah.

focusing attention on the cults. Coming from such an influential source, people believed that what they were told was thus the truth, and the myths became embedded in the minds of the simple folk and were exported around the world in the years that were to follow—even into this century they have persisted in parts of the USA, Britain, and elsewhere.

THE RETURN TO FAVOR

Happily, as Europe started to reawaken during the 17th century, old purges, though still seen, were largely fading away, and the Church's punitive powers therefore started to fade. Cats were again to be welcomed into the homes as cherished pets, and artists featured them within family portraits. Poets wrote about them, and even the clergy started to keep and love them—including the Pope. Naturalists started to take an interest in them and studied their wild relatives in the countries around the world. Many people, including Winston Churchill, left legacies to ensure that their cats would be well provided for following their own deaths. One way or the other, household cats have been subject to the full spectrum of human emotions. However, the scars of the bad years have left their mark, and even today there are many people who fear cats.

Whilst our attitude toward cats may have ebbed and flowed over the centuries, the cat itself has remained what it has always been—an animal of great beauty that has retained its independence and ability to walk alone on the wild side whenever it so chooses.

THE FUTURE

Tomorrow's history we are making today, and whether the cats of the future will be the creatures of natural beauty we now have, or whether they will merely be a collection of feline degenerates quite incapable of surviving without us, will be determined by the attitude of the public, the cat judges, and the breeders. If cats follow in the footsteps of many dog breeds, or popular pet birds, or goldfish varieties, then I fear for their future. It is one thing to try to produce new and attractive coat colors or patterns, or to

A tiger cub.

create new breeds showing somewhat different features, but matters change when we start to go beyond these perimeters.

When breeders try to modify natural feline anatomical features or perpetuate degenerate mutations—as is seen in the Manx and Sphynx breeds—then they are starting on a downward spiral in which the objective is to produce the bizarre and the grotesque for no other reason than to pander to those people who take pleasure in owning anything that will draw attention to themselves. Undue modification of the jaw, excess coat, or lack of it, are undesirable features for a cat. What is more, many mutations often go hand in hand with unseen internal changes that only become evident at a later date.

Wild cats and domestic hybrids are generally said to have more vigor than pedigreed cats that have been extensively inbred.

Presently, other than those breeds cited, the pure breeds of cat are not unduly altered from their wild cousins. The Persians, or longhairs as they are known in Britain, are possibly the ones now reaching the limits of modification of jaw and coat, and therefore need to be carefully bred so that exaggeration is not increased. In this aspect, both the governing bodies and the judges must have the courage to react when they feel things have gone beyond acceptable limits. Sadly, in other exhibited pets, the record is that the standards themselves are modified to fit the changing fashions in a given animal breed, rather than the ruling bodies standing fast. One can only applaud those ruling bodies that have rejected degenerate varieties from registration, for this shows moral responsibility for breeding only sound felines, rather than so-called exotics that merely illustrate the fact that it is possible to establish undesirable features if we have a mind to—and then spread them into other varieties.

THE MIND OF THE CAT

Over the years, much study has been devoted to the dog, so its thinking and traits are well documented. The same is not so true of cats which, to a large degree, have been overlooked. This is partly because cats are more secretive in their ways, and partly because, having no role in life other than that of general rodent killer, people have never considered it important to understand too much about a cat's way of thinking. The cat was there, it did its job, and matters were left at that. As a result, there are many misconceptions about cats and a tendency to apply various quite incorrect labels and conclusions to much of their behavior.

Cats are very easy animals to live with—another reason why so little effort has been made to understand them, for they do not represent any sort of danger to humans in the way that a large dog may if it is on the loose. However, because of these various comments, it is also a fact that much of a cat's undoubted potential has been overlooked, for we have never attempted to educate its mind in the way we have with dogs or horses, as prime examples. The cat has adapted to become a superb pet, but is this its limit?

In coming to understand the cat, we should not endow it with human traits or morals, nor view it as a variant on the dog theme. By studying the behavioral patterns of its wild precursors and cousins we can then see how these have become changed—and are continuing to change—as cats become more and more domesticated. We can understand why a cat does what it does and reacts the way it does to the world around it.

INTELLIGENCE

Cats are extremely intelligent animals, for they quickly learn many things which are to their advantage; these vary from how to open cupboard doors to how best to get their owners to react to their needs at any given moment in time. They will learn to respond to basic instructions—usually negative ones—and quickly become familiar with their own names, especially at meal times, when an instant and posi-

A four-year-old Margay. All cats are highly intelligent animals.

tive reaction is assured. They do not take kindly to discipline, which is certainly not a tool in any trainer's kit bag, least of all with felids. That is not to suggest that a tap across the backside now and then will not draw attention to your own needs of the cat at given moments—but the cat should never be struck in true malice or temper because it is quite unnecessary and merely underlines the owner's inability to communicate with animals.

A cat does not respond to instructions in the same way as a dog, and the reasons for this have nothing to do with intelligence, but are in the social make-up of the two species and in the roles each has been kept for. The process of domestication is also involved, as is the ability of the trainer, so it can be appreciated what a complex matter it actually is. A dog is a social animal that has evolved to live in a community—the pack—where it must accept discipline from higher ranking dogs. Its survival depends on its ability to work with its fellows in hunting prey, in caring for the young, and in living generally in association with others. When wolves first associated with humans, it would have been noticed how the wild instincts of these could be controlled and put to use. A few thousand years of perfecting such techniques has resulted in the dogs of today, many excelling in specific roles. We merely directed the hunting instinct into the channel we required—retrieving, herding, scenting, and so on. A mixture of discipline and reward were all that was required on our part for the dog to be motivated to respond. It thrives in a group, and, therefore, in a domestic situation we merely become other members of the pack.

The cat, on the other hand, is the complete opposite. It evolved to live alone, hunt alone, and fight its own battles. It had no dependence at all on its own kind, other than on the occasions when it needed to find a mate in order to perpetuate the species. When you are a loner in a hostile world, keep to yourself, learn to avoid larger predators, and trust in nothing but yourself are very sound pieces of advice that became ingrained in the feline nature.

Given this aspect, it will be appreciated that it is not possible to suddenly shed a way of thinking that has taken a few million years to shape.

Cheetahs. Cats respond to outside stimuli differently than dogs because they are, for the most part, independent and self-reliant.

In relative terms, the cat has had very little time in which to adjust to a human, thus social, way of life; further, in that little time, it has not been required to channel its intelligence into any specific tasks, and for most of its domestication to this point it has largely been left to continue using its own natural abilities to survive, with just a few individuals being given the full comforts of a domestic situation. Remember, we are talking about many millions of cats over the years, the majority of which have not enjoyed a life of luxury with humans.

We know the cat has the ability to do many of the same things as a dog; indeed, given its more flexible body, it is potentially capable of doing more. That it does not should not be taken to imply that it is not as intelligent, as is sometimes inferred. It is obviously restricted in some ways by its small size, but this could actually be a bonus in some instances—coupled with its flexible body, keen eyesight and superb hearing. As strange as it may seem, a cat would be excellent for aspects of rescue work, detection—in fact any role where nimble body and good climbing ability could be utilized. As it is, it is restricted to performing a few tricks such as jumping through fire hoops, backward somersaults and hurdling, to illustrate that its potential is there once humans are able to work out better ways to motivate the cat with techniques that are not based on our knowledge of training dogs.

The cat does not think in communal terms but only in terms of what is directly applicable to its own well-being—in fact, so does a dog or any other animal. However, during the process of domestication, a species changes in certain of its behavioral traits and certain of its faculties become dulled. As this happens, its natural intelligence can be diverted into a useful role, if required, but in any case it makes the animal much more tractable; it is more able to respond to communication because its mind is more relaxed. This is an interesting aspect for cat owners, for it explains, in part, why certain cats are very domestic and why others seem much more independent. It will also illustrate just why a cat is such an interesting companion—its potential is totally unexplored.

Leopard. The cat's climbing ability and overall agility inherited from its wild ancestors make it capable of learning a variety of behaviors.

DOMESTICATION AND ITS CONSEQUENCE

It has been established (Herre and Röhrs in Grzimeck, l976) that the brain weight of domesticated species decreases from the same species in the wild state—at least it does so in the higher mammals. In the case of the cat, the decrease is 23.4% compared to that of the dog at 31.1% and the pig at 34%. These decreases are largely in the forebrain, and the effect is a reduction in the senses of sight, hearing, and smell. However, other changes also take place, and amongst these are those associated with the endocrine organs. In effect, the brain does not induce the flow of adrenalin as much as in the wild species. This makes the animal less excitable and thus less aggressive. It reduces the desire of the animal to escape, but it does not reduce the animal's level of intelligence. It may dilute other traits of the animal as well—the hunting instinct, for example, and sexual competitiveness. All animals are not affected to the same degree, for it is a greater or lesser situation. However, the more domesticated a species becomes, the more these aspects hold true and intensify.

Now, given these facts, let us speculate a little. If the brain is not devoting so much of its efforts to "wild" aspects of the species, then it is more able to concentrate on educating itself in the sense that it is more receptive to our efforts to communicate, and thus is able to learn things at a much faster pace than can its wild relatives. Essentially, it is adapting to the new habitat in which it is living. As humans have educated our minds from being primitive peoples, we too have seen a decrease in our senses, retaining only sight, possibly, at a good level, but we need our sight, so this is not surprising.

If a species is to be receptive to learning, then it must first be given a role into which that learning can be applied; thus we see the varied ways in which dogs and horses are used. We think a top sheepdog rounding up and penning sheep is clever, but the actual work involved from the dog's viewpoint is the easy bit. Its intelligence is shown by the fact that it has learned to understand what we want it to do. If those individuals that show a good capacity to learn are then selectively bred for their role, they will get better at it to the point that it becomes an inher-

ent part of their nature—we arrive at specialists just as we do in our own society. Many breeds thus have a strong predisposition towards given roles, be they herding, guarding, retrieving and so on.

Given this aspect, what has happened with cats over the years? The answer is nothing! Cheetahs were trained for hunting purposes, but not on a selectively bred basis, because the breeding of these unusual cats only became possible in recent times. Cats have thus been left to utilize their considerable intelligence purely to become pets that sit on one's lap or chase rodents around. They are then described as being untrainable. Some are not even good mousers either, because, as mentioned, hunting desire is also diluted during domestication.

Even pigs have been given more consideration in terms of roles in which to funnel this "spare" capacity produced during domestication, and they have been used in parts of the world for guarding and have even been used for shepherding other farm livestock! But we all know that pigs are very intelligent animals, so this is not really surprising. A further factor that may have inhibited the cat's position is that the dog had a few thousand years' head start; thus, as they were easier to train anyway, no one really thought in terms of educating the mind of the cat.

The problem this creates is if we continue with our present attitudes toward the cat, its mind will not be given the opportunity to progress, and we will become even less inclined to attempt to communicate with it other than in a very basic manner. The exhibition side of the hobby does nothing at all for the mind of the cat, for it merely concentrates on outward appearance, and most of our efforts seem to be directed towards producing more varieties rather than cats that are able to display the true potential of their mental powers whilst still retaining the grace and beauty that nature has endowed them with.

Cats are not easy to train, both because they are by nature loners and because they are not as domesticated as are dogs or horses. This throws down a challenge to our ability to communicate with them, but maybe one day in the not too distant future, a number of breeders may start

Lion cub. The brain weight of a domesticated animal differs from that of its wild relatives. The senses are affected, and the aggression of the animal is reduced.

to work on the long process of educating the mind of the cat, and in so doing put in hand a progressive trend that will see cats as being able to do things that presently most people would say was beyond their ability.

INSTINCTS

Instinct is a natural ability to do something without having to think about it; it is an automatic process of the brain. For example, many cats have shown the ability to find their way back to former homes—their preference sometimes being for territory rather than owner. How this is achieved we still do not know, but it is not by applied thinking but simply because the cat uses its powerful sense of direction. It is thought that it navigates by the position of the sun in relation to the horizon and travels in a zigzag manner, readjusting its course as it goes along.

Another instinct that has given cats a less than endearing reputation is that concerned with hunting. Cats are labelled bloodthirsty killers, sadistic creatures that kill for the pure pleasure of it. I know of no animal that ever kills for pleasure, this being an example of applying human traits to animals. The felid researcher and cat lover Paul Leyhausen has devoted much time to the psychology of cats and has studied the hunting aspects in some detail. The conclusions reached explain why a puma will wreak havoc in a sheep enclosure and why a cat appears to be "toying" with a mouse or bird.

When a cat is hunting it goes through a number of stages—first, it must wait until a suitable victim comes along, then it commences the

A sleeping lion cub. The cat's need for sleep may make it appear lazy to people familiar with the dog's activity level. However, the cat hunts with short bursts of speed and must reserve energy.

stalk, then the attack, followed by the lethal bite, and finally it eats the prey. Each aspect of the process has a different threshold of motivation. When the cat eats the prey it is easily satiated, so there is little motivation to eat once a suitable amount has been devoured. However, before it can eat it must first bite the prey, so it needs less motivation to do this than it does to eat. To bite the prey an attack must be launched, but all attacks do not result in a bite, so the motivation to jump must be somewhat lower than that needed to bite. The motivation level falls at each stage, because at each of these stages the chances of a meal at the end decreases—the mouse sees the cat and runs away, the bird takes off, and so on.

In the wild, a cat must therefore be prepared to commence its hunting repertoire very often, for the less times it commences the less likely it will be able to progress to the next level of the hunt—its chances of surviving will thus reduce in ratio to this aspect. If a cat (or a fox or a wolf) is thus placed into an unnatural situation, it will then go through each of its hunting drives until the threshold for that stage is reached. The puma in the wild state would never find a situation where the prey just stood around unable to escape, so it reacts to its natural drives. In the wild state no predator has anything to gain by killing more than it needs; overall, this would reduce its survival chances, because in some instances it may actually itself be injured in such encounters.

This explanation puts much of a cat's actions into the correct perspective. It toys with mice because we have fed it, so that aspect of the hunt has been satisfied, but it will still be motivated to go to the next stage down—catching its prey. The lowest threshold of all is that for waiting for prey to come along, or to looking for such prey. These drives need virtually no motivation, thus the cat is quite happy sitting about or quietly walking around investigating everything. Dogs do not wait for prey; they go out and look for it, so they are, by nature, more inclined to the active end of the spectrum. Patience is thus a natural trait in all cats, for it conserves energy, which is needed for explosive bursts, not for staying power as in dogs.

Cats that have not been so highly domesti-

Head study of a puma.

cated as others, such as your regular street cat compared to the highly bred prize Persian, have retained much stronger hunting instincts and want to be off looking and catching critters. The Persian is less inclined to this, and is quite content to stay within a smaller territory and restrict its urges to hunting a ball of wool or even imaginary prey. This is not to say that all Persians are so affected by domestication but that, as a general rule, this is certainly the case. A mongrel cat that does not retain its more wild instincts has little chance of survival and can be regarded as being less domesticated—which in turn does not imply being less suitable as a pet, for we are talking about relative states within a species that, as a whole, is domesticated.

Another aspect of a cat's instincts is related to its ability to forewarn of impending disasters. From its earliest association with humans, the cat was believed to have magical powers because it would seek high spots in the house prior to flooding, or would refuse to enter dwellings prior to earthquakes and so on. Superstitions thus arose around the cat, but these happenings are easily explained in a rational manner that has nothing to do with magic, a sixth sense, or nine lives. The cat's sense of smell and hearing are so much superior to our own that it would detect earth tremors, hear rushing waters, or smell smoke long before a human could, so it instinctively took the course of action it felt was most beneficial to its own well-being.

SOCIABILITY OF CATS

The majority of cat species—indeed, of most carnivorous animals in the widest sense of this word—are basically non-socially organized because, as predators, it is a more conducive path to take in survival terms. If we think solely in relation to the small felids, it is easy to see why this should be so. The topography of an area may be very open and arid, or it may be dense jungle, or a mixture of types. Regardless of this aspect, the fact is that in each instance there would be no gain, from a cat's viewpoint, from forming groups for two basic reasons. First, the area may not have sufficient prey to support more than a few cats, or, if it has, the wild precursors of the domestic cat were not large enough to gain any significant advantage from hunting as a group—it would not unduly increase the number of prey available. Given the hunting technique of most cats, it would actually hinder matters because it increases the chances that their prey would spot one of the felids—this applies whether in open country or forest habitat.

However, cats must socialize to a degree, otherwise the species would not perpetuate itself, and if prey is numerous in an area as well, then the cat population as a whole will increase. In such situations it is inevitable that cats will meet each other, and when this happens they must, over a period, develop some basic ground rules that enable them to co-exist without fighting on sight. In the wild, what happens is that the cats will move around a given area but have their own territory within it. Such a territory will be heavily marked by scenting, clawing trees and by rubbing their faces against rocks, tree stumps, and similar objects. Obviously, the further away from a territory a cat moves, the less it is able to mark its perimeters. It will vigorously defend its territory but will be less inclined to fight as it moves away from this and into another cat's territory. There will thus be a number of areas that are common to each resident cat, and when two cats meet, they will each go through a ritual of "bluffing" to establish superiority over the other. If this fails, combat will result, and, providing one of them is not actually killed (which is rarely the case), then thereafter when they meet the loser will give way to the victor. In this way a whole system of hierarchy develops in an area and enables all the cats to live in reasonable harmony with each other.

Of course, such a system is never static because, as cats age, their position will be challenged by younger, stronger cats, and an especially tough male may move into a new area for one reason or another and thus take over the top spot by shear muscle power. An injured cat may drop down quite a few rungs of this ladder, but, once back in shape, will quickly re-establish its former position. Such cat populations never reach the state where there are lots of cats all likely to meet at once, because before that stage is reached, the prey becomes thin on the ground, so some of the cats, usually the lesser ones, will move on to find new hunting grounds. A fine equilibrium is always maintained in nature between predators and prey.

This state is seen in domestic cat populations, but is intensified both by domestication making the cats more tolerant with each other and by the large numbers of cats. Basically, to survive, they must adopt new rules to take account of their increased numbers and their smaller territories. You will see this social organization within your own group of cats should you have more than one, and certainly so in the overall neighborhood organization. Sometimes one cat seems to pick on another habitually; there is then the temptation to think in human terms and call the cat a bully and reprimand it for such actions. This will not stop the behavior permanently, but only at that moment. In addition, it may actually result in the increase of the dominant cat's hostility to the other. Cats and dogs do not have ethics but have evolved to survive by nothing other than basic aggression and power. This is crude and basic, but it is highly effective and has worked to ensure that only the toughest, hardiest and fittest members of the population survive to perpetuate the next generation.

It will be appreciated that much of the unsociability of cats is removed if there is no problem with the food supply, so that, under domestication, cats are slowly adapting to their new environment and in so doing are developing new patterns in their social organization. A cat will quite happily form a strong bond with a dog, a

A cream longhair. Like people, cats often show a decided preference for certain members of their household.

rabbit, or any other animal of its own or larger size. However, it is never wise to chance cats alone with those pets which are smaller than themselves. Cats have been known to live with mice, hamsters, and small birds, but this is not without a goodly degree of risk—a cat could kill or badly injure such an animal without even intending to. Further, the hunting instinct, though subdued, has not been removed altogether, and what starts as a game could easily change during a moment of over-excitement.

Needless to say, cats will form very strong bonds with humans and with their own species. They do show preferences in both, and they may develop stronger attachments to certain members of the family and to other cats in the household than to others. One would usually as-

sume that this reflected the extent to which the person was involved with the cat, but whilst this is often the case, it is not always so. One person may handle a cat less frequently but more gently, with the result that the cat prefers that person. Some cats will react better with children than with adults. Within their relationships with other cats, those cats introduced to each other as kittens will invariably have stronger friendships than when introductions to other cats are made in later life. A kitten may well develop a friendship with an adult cat that becomes a sort of uncle or aunt, but two fully grown cats introduced to the same household rarely become as close as those that grew up together—they merely come to accept the presence of other cats without ever letting matters develop beyond that.

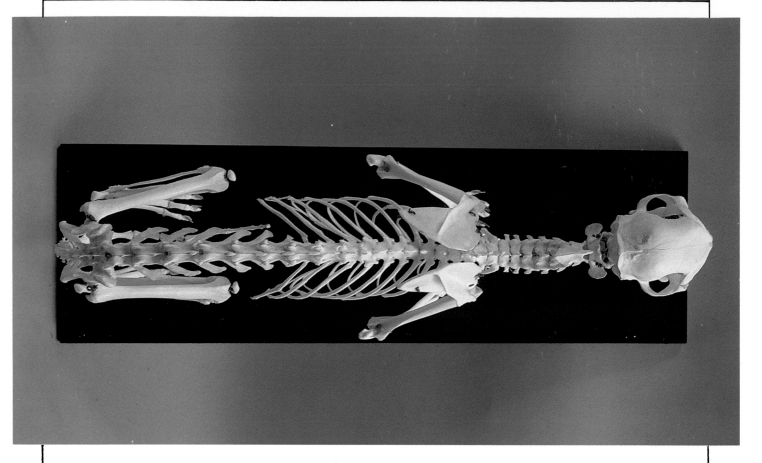

Above and Below: Model of a cat skeleton, top and side views. One of the feline skeleton's most important features is the flexible backbone.

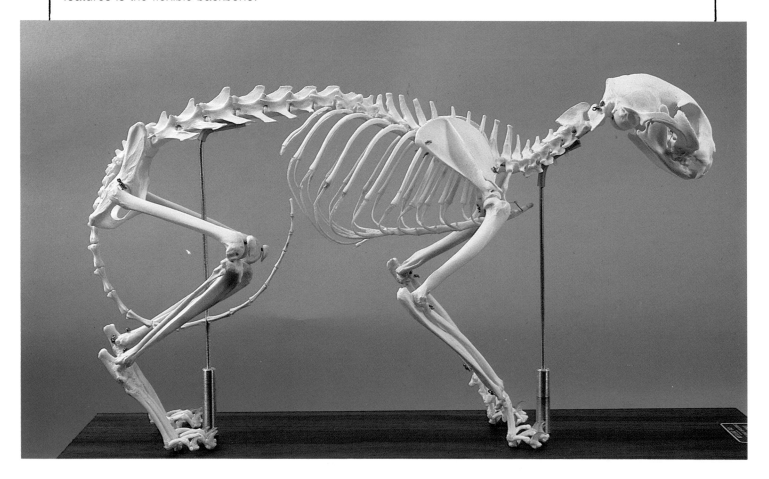

FUNCTIONAL ANATOMY

Here the overall form and function of the parts of cats will be reviewed in some detail. However, the detail will only be sufficient, hopefully, to be of interest to the average cat owner so they can see just how cats have developed their anatomy in order to fulfill their predatory role in life.

The first thing we can perceive in domestic cats is that there are essentially three basic types:

1) The cobby, somewhat short-legged and flat-faced varieties. These may have long dense fur, or it may be short and dense.

2) The slightly taller and more balanced cats which are longer on the leg and have a more pronounced foreface. Like the first types they have more or less round faces, and some may sport long coats, but these never become as profuse as those in the first group.

3) The more lean and racy-looking breeds. These have wedge-shaped faces and bodies which lack the depth of the first two types. Their fur is short or long, but the ears appear larger in proportion to their heads than in the first two groups. When they have long fur, it is never profuse and it tends to soften the face shape and to give the cats a less racy shape.

The first and third groups are the ones which have moved away from the average proportions found in the wild felids from which cats developed, but the amount of such movement is actually relatively small if one compares this to that displayed by dogs, rabbits, or horses, as popular examples of how domestication has changed size and shape in a species.

SKELETON

The feline skeleton, in most respects, is very similar to that of all other carnivores, the differences being found in the skull and in the relative lengths of the leg bones. The skeleton can be divided into two basic parts, the axial and the appendicular. The first named comprises the skull, the vertebral column, and the thorax (head, back and chest); the appendicular skeleton comprises the limbs together with their means of attachment to the axial skeleton (legs, shoulders, and hip bones). The number of bones in each region of the body is given below, together with those of the dog, the bear, and the hyena as a comparison; to complete the comparison, man's are also included.

Cat: cervical—7; thoracic—13; lumbar—7; sacral—3; caudal—14-28. *Dog:* cervical—7; thoracic—13-14; lumbar—6-8; sacral—3-4; caudal—14-23. *Bear:* cervical—7; thoracic—14-15; lumbar—5-6; sacral—4-6; caudal—9-11. *Man:* cervical—7; thoracic—12; lumbar—5; sacral—5; caudal—3-5. *Note:* Tailless cats, such as the Manx, may have no caudal bones; the Japanese Bobtail may have a few.

The backbone of a cat is very flexible, thus allowing the cat to wriggle through very narrow gaps; it is especially so in the vertical plane, which accounts for the cat's sprinting ability. It is able to arch the backbone considerably more than a dog, and at high speed all four feet are clear of the ground. There are eight phases involved in the movement of a cat which follow a pattern of power and recovery of the limbs. The manner of locomotion is that the left foot

reaches forward and is followed slightly out of phase by the right hindlimb; the weight is then transferred to the other forefoot, which is then followed, again out of phase, by the opposite hindlimb. Thus the limbs move in a diagonal manner. As the cat picks up speed, the actual time taken for the full phase remains about the same; it is the distance covered that is increased. The limbs reach forward as far as they can at full gallop, and the hindfeet touch the floor in front of the forefeet. Propulsion is provided by the rear legs, and the weight of the body is taken by the front feet, which actually have a slight retardation effect on overall speed. At walking pace all four feet may touch the floor together, but as the pace quickens, only three, and then two, strike the floor together. By the time the cat is reaching top speed, just one foot takes the weight. The domestic cat can probably achieve about 42 kph (25 mph), which is somewhat slower than a slim, reasonably sized dog and is less than half that of the world's fastest mammal, the cheetah. However, cats are able to avoid dogs because their pick-up speed is much faster, so they are able to sprint to safety.

Because cats have no, or very little, need for lateral movement of the limbs, they have no collar bone, this having been reduced to a small piece of cartilage tissue. The rib cage is deep rather than wide, both to help the cat to get through narrow openings and, of course, to reduce resistance to wind when running. The cat's center of gravity is slightly towards the head end of the body, and the tail is the means by which the cat is able to counterbalance movements that would otherwise make the cat less stable when running or negotiating difficult obstacles. If the cat is walking along a narrow branch, any tendency to lose balance is countered by the tail being placed in the opposite direction at the required height.

Opposite: The forefeet of the cat are compact and have retractable claws.

The forefeet, or paws, are modified both to aid running, by being compact, and to aid holding onto prey, by having retractable claws. The muscles hold the claws in their sheaths when at rest, so the cat only has to think of these consciously when it wishes to extend them. The claws are essentially tools for securing prey or for climbing, but, of course, they can also be used to good effect for defense or when attacking prey that proves to be more difficult than was perhaps envisaged—the hindclaws then being used to rip at the prey. The shape of the claws, and the fact that the paw has little mobility, mean that whilst being a super tree climber, the cat is quite the opposite when it is time to come down! This is affected in a most undignified backward manner, with much head turning to see how near the floor is getting and thus a spin and jump attempted. As a point of interest, the snow leopard and margay are both superb climbers in both directions. The margay can all but run down a tree head first, and both are capable of hanging by a single rear foot from a branch. How? Their feet can rotate through about 180 degrees and almost become hands. They are also unusual in that they can drop onto prey species from above. All others cats, including the domestic, only attack when two or more feet are firmly planted on terra firma.

THE SKULL

The skull of the cat differs from most carnivores in that it is shorter and more rounded on its dorsal surface. The roof of the cranium comprises an almost smooth curve, so cats tend to have less pronounced-stops than dogs but more of one than carnivores such as ferrets or weasels. The maxilla bone is greatly reduced; thus cats have no muzzle as such. In turn, the mandible (lower jaw) is also short and accommodates less teeth than in the dog. The vertical part of the mandible is known as the ramus, and at its base is a projection called the condylar process which connects the mandible with the cranium box. Being short, the cat's mouth can open much wider than can a dog's; this is important in allowing it to sink its teeth into its prey and then hold on. The muscles of a cat's jaw are extremely strong, so that it has a powerful bite.

The cat's teeth are very sharp, as they are designed to cut and slice, not to crush.

THE TEETH

A cat's teeth are designed to bite and cut rather than to crush. The canine or "eye" teeth are well developed, and the molars and carnassials have high ridges which interlock with those of the opposite jaw to form sort of mini-guillotines. Cats do not crush their food like dogs, but rather chop it into small pieces. Because of this fact you will notice that cats always bite into meat with their heads to one side so they can slice it with their carnassials.

Another interesting point is that the small felids always eat hunched over their food—never like a dog with forelegs stretched out. Only the big cats can eat in this latter manner, and this is again linked to the teeth. The small felids must be "over" their food so they can slice it, while dogs and the big felids can hold the meat with their paws and, using their strong neck muscles and incisor teeth, pull meat from the bone.

Cats have difficulty dealing with bone because they cannot crush it; dogs and hyenas have powerful crushing molars for this purpose. The canine "dagger" teeth of cats are thought to have been developed to deal with very specific prey species; their size is such as to be able to better enter the vertebrae of prey and sever the spinal chord. This would mean a very precise bite, which avoids the risk of damaging the teeth if they bit the bone rather than intervertebral spaces. However, the cat is able to "feel" with its teeth, as improbable as this may seem. The teeth have numerous sensory endings in them, so the cat will quickly readjust its tentative bite until it finds the right spot—it then sinks home the teeth. In actual fact this is probably an advanced variation to that used by the now extinct true saber-toothed cats who, in their many forms, showed great variety in their canine teeth, which ranged from serrated edges to long rapier but smooth-edged teeth—each designed to cope with a particular prey species.

Cats have two sets of teeth during their lives, these being the milk or baby teeth and then the permanent ones. The former are not shed before the latter appear, for a cat must always have its canines and carnassials from the time it is able to eat solid foods. As a result, all cats go through a period when they will have two sets of canines and two sets of carnassials. The permanent teeth usually grow just behind or at the side of the milk teeth, which are shed once the permanent teeth are strong enough to be functional.

The dental formula for each set of teeth is as follows: deciduous or milk teeth–I 3/3; C 1/1; PM 3/2; 1/2 jaw = 26. Permanent teeth–I 3/3; C 1/1; P 3/2; M 1/1; ½ jaw = 30.

The formula quoted is typical for cats as a whole, but certain species may have premolars missing, and this is also true of domestic breeds. The largest tooth in the upper jaw is the third premolar whilst in the lower jaw it is the molar.

THE SOFT PARTS

Having briefly looked at the significant features of the cat's skeleton, the functional anatomy of what are termed the soft parts can now be considered. Only those of special interest will be discussed, for many of the cats internal organs are similar in most respects to those found in all mammals. However, one point is worthy of commenting on in respect to the digestive tract. In wild cats, the intestine is relatively short because the amount of vegetable matter consumed is small and already pre-digested (by the prey of the cat); during the process of domestication to this point it has been noticed that the intestines of house cats have become longer—reflecting the adaptation to a less carnivorous diet, one that shows an increased consumption of plant tissue. The cellulose in this is more difficult to breakdown, therefore requiring a longer period in the now longer intestinal tract.

THE TONGUE

The tongue of a cat is multi-purpose, for it serves as a spoon to lap up liquids, as the means of taste to decide whether or not to continue eating that on offer, and as a feline brush and comb to groom the fur with—most important to all small cats. It is anchored on the floor of the mouth by muscles which connect it to the mandible. The surface of the tongue is rough, which can be felt if your cat licks you—a rare honor, as cats are not like dogs in this. This roughness is due to the tongue being covered by many backward facing papillae, a number of which contain sensory taste buds. The papillae help the cat to detach meat from the bone and to remove debris from the cat's fur. There are salivary glands under the tongue and in other parts of the mouth, and the sight and taste of food prompts these to release this liquid, which is mostly water in content, and helps to make food more easily swallowed.

THE NOSE

The nose of a cat is a highly sensitive organ that, like many parts of the anatomy, serves a number of purposes. The exterior openings are

The rough surface of the tongue of a cat is a most important feature. It helps the cat in eating meat from a bone and is an important grooming tool.

85

Smell is an important sense to a cat, but it is not as important as sight during a hunt. Cats do rely on scent, but not as much as dogs.

surrounded by an area of hairless skin in all small felids and are strengthened by cartilage tissue. The opening can be adjusted by the cat in order to increase or decrease the apertures. Behind the nostrils is an area of nasal chambers which is rich in blood vessels covered by a mucous membrane. Part of this mucous membrane is concerned with the sense of smell, whilst the remainder is a means of breathing in air. Within the nasal cavities are millions of nerve receptors which transmit messages to the brain, telling the cat many things about the composition of that being sniffed.

A cat's sense of smell is about four times better than that of a human, whilst that of a dog is about six times better than that of a cat, based on the number of receptor nerves known to exist in each of these species. Actually, it is very difficult for humans to set up tests to establish many of a cat's senses, including that of smell because, with our own senses being so inferior by comparison, it is difficult to measure results in a satisfactory manner. For example, we rely purely on our sight, initially, to determine likely partners of the opposite sex, but in the wild a cat may not have the opportunity to see a potential partner and is totally dependent upon its sense of smell to convey information about such. Males and females leave their own identity card via body odors and scent glands. Cats will sniff each other's heads and, especially, backsides—we find this somewhat offputting, but it tells the cats where each has been and even what they have been doing, and is a natural part of their socialization pattern. As a result, a cat will often face its backside to its owner as part of its "getting to know you" ritual!

A cat relies far more on its sight when searching for potential prey, but, nonetheless, smell is still important in this area, for it will often lead the cat to a prey area in the first instance; then sight takes over. Cats always carefully sniff their food before consuming it, as this tells them whether or not it is to their liking—likewise they can smell the odors given off by tablets, which is why they manage to ignore, or carefully spit out, medicinal tablets. You cannot smell such things, but, being aware of this fact, isn't it surprising that more tablets are not coated with an enticing aroma?

Note the dagger-like sharpness of the cat's teeth.

The sense of smell is, of course, very crucial to cats in their mating behavior and, in this connection, it is thought that the Jacobson's organ is important. This is a small pouch, lined with sensory cells, which is situated in the roof of the mouth just behind the teeth. It is associated with the process known as flehming—when the cat lifts its upper lip up and seems to be in a sort of semi-trance. It also seems to induce saliva, which indicates that it is also connected with the sense of taste. It is not fully understood in mammals or in reptiles and is poorly developed in humans. It seems to be especially activated when the cat, usually males, are sniffing the urine of females, and no doubt tells them of the sexual state of the queen. The fondness for catnip of cats is probably because this smells similar to an ingredient within the secretion given off by a female in estrus—thus toms will get especially excited by catnip toys.

Within the nasal chambers there are also many hairlike cilia, and these trap dust particles which are periodically released into the mouth either to be swallowed or vomited out—usually the former. These cilia also warm incoming air into the nasal chambers, which is one reason why cats with very short faces will suffer more from chills than will those having a longer bridge of the nose. The reverse takes place in hot climates when the air is cooled in the nasal chambers.

THE EAR

The sense of hearing in cats is extremely good and, along with dogs, civets, raccoons, and many other carnivores, is considerably better than that of man. However, this superior hearing is related to the prey species hunted, for it is obviously important for any animal that hunts those species which emit high-pitched sounds to be capable of hearing them. The ear is composed of three basic parts, these being the outer, middle, and inner ear. The outer is in the form of a funnel known as the pinna. This can be moved about through a 45° angle in order to help localize a given sound. It is covered with hair on its outer surface but less so on its inner sides. It is not a simple trumpet shape but is more complex, and it leads, via a channel, to the

middle ear. This is commonly referred to as the "drum" and is composed of three small bones called ossicles which lie in the middle ear cavity. These bones are connected via membranes to the vestibular or oval window, and beyond this is the inner ear. In this there is a series of semicircular canals connected to a fluid-filled sac, and leading to this is also another apparatus known as the cochlea, a much convoluted structure that also contains fluid. From this lead the many nerve endings that transmit the sound for the brain to decipher. The ear also controls such things as balance, in association with the eyes. The whole of the ear structure is very complex, for it has to cope with sound waves of a considerable range and intensity. Even while the cat is asleep, the ear continues to function to quite a high degree, which is why cats quickly wake up at the slightest of sounds.

The human ear can hear sounds over a range of about 8½ octaves, but the cat's covers about ten, this being an octave higher than that of the dog. This reflects the fact that cats and similar rodent-eating animals must be able to detect the slightest rustle or squeak, and it accounts for the sometimes unusual habit of a cat investigating the floor or wall of a room—we sense nothing but the cat can hear the movement of mice or other animals that may be living unseen behind walls or below floors. The cat can even hear beetles if they make too much noise! When it is considered that the domestic cat's hearing is so acute, imagine what that of the wild species of small felids is like—it is around 20% better than that of our pet cats.

THE EYE

The last of the sense organs to be discussed is the eye, which is a most important structure for most mammals. In cats it has developed to enable all felids to see extremely well during the hours of darkness, yet still be able to see very well during the daytime. The outermost part of the eye is, of course, the eyelid, which contains numerous hairs in order to protect the eyeball from debris. Behind the lower eyelid is an opaque third eyelid, or nictitating membrane, which also serves to protect the eyeball from debris by moving over it. You will often notice this

A three-month-old blue point Siamese cat. Hearing in cats is much more developed than it is in humans since, by necessity, cats need to hear the small prey species on which they subsist in the wild.

in the corner of a cat's eye, especially when it is not feeling well.

The surface of the eye is kept moist by liquid released from the lacrimal gland, which is situated above the eye; this liquid exits via small ducts in the eyelid. When the cat blinks, a regular distribution of lacrimal fluid over the entire eye surface is ensured. The fluid leaves the eye by means of a small tube which empties into the nasal chambers; if the tube should get blocked, or if excess fluid is released to combat an irritant, then the fluid flows over the eyelid, resulting in what we term a "weeping" eye.

Light enters the eye through the transparent cornea, a fibrous substance that becomes white other than at the front of the eye. When it totally covers the eyeball itself, it is then known as sclera. Behind this, at the front of the eye, is a fluid known as the aqueous humor and behind this, held in place by ligaments, is the lens of the eye. The main body of the eye is filled with a viscous substance know as vitreous humor, which is fed by means of many blood vessels. Surrounding this, thus laying under the sclera, is tissue known as the choroid, and on the inner side of the choroid is the retina of the eye. Within the choroid layer itself are a number of reflective cells known as the tapetum lucidum, and it is these that give cats, dogs, and many other animals the well-known "nightshine," which is created when the animal's eyes reflect light back to the observer. What happens is that light which passes through the receptors of the retina, and which would normally just be absorbed in the tissue beyond this, is reflected back through the retina for a second chance of stimulating receptors. If it fails to do so, it returns back out of the eye as light and takes the color of the pigment in the tapetum, be this brown, yellow, or green. Of course, so much of the reflected light does stimulate the receptors, thus increasing the cat's night-time vision.

The extension of the choroid at the front of the eye is known as the iris, and the center of this, in effect a hole, is called the pupil. The size of the pupil is regulated by the iris, which opens or closes depending on the amount of light being received by the lens. In cats, as the pupil closes, it forms a vertical slit. In very bright sunlight, it all but closes in the center and is a little more open at the top and bottom of the slit. There are, however, one or two wild felid species in which the pupil closes to become a small circular hole.

The final anatomical aspect of the eye which is of note is that the retina contains within it many structures known as rods and cones. The former are concerned with night vision and color whilst the latter are connected with day vision.

Compared with the human eye, the cat has a larger lens and pupil, relative to overall eye size, in order to allow in as much light as possible, but the rest of the eye is not proportionately larger; otherwise no benefit would be gained by the increased lens size. Being larger, the lens is nearer to the retina than in man. This necessitates a different curvature of the lens in order for the cat to focus. In animals, the lens changes shape in order to focus; this is achieved by the ligaments. A camera or a microscope, by contrast, has a lens that can be moved forward or backward to achieve the same effect.

Sensitivity to light: A cat can see about six times better than a human in terms of its night vision. This was established by training cats to select food from behind illuminated panels; the cats were still making correct selection well after the human test controller was able to distinguish a light source. This does not mean that cats, or any other animal or bird, can see in total darkness, but that they can use whatever light there is to better effect, and there is always some light even on the darkest of nights.

A calico female Scottish Fold. The Scottish Fold is somewhat more prone to ear infections than other breeds, but its sense of hearing is believed to be normal.

Since cats are primarily nocturnal animals, their eyes are quite sensitive to light.

Field of vision: The position of a cat's eyes in relation to the skull determines the field of vision; it also determines to what degree the cat is able to focus both eyes on a subject—this being most important in a predator, which must be able to judge distance very well. This aspect is known as binocular vision. All cat species have their eyes well forward in the skull, which gives them a good field of vision as well as a high degree of overlap/binocular vision. The human has even greater binocular vision but, as a result, a reduced total field; the dog has less binocular vision than the cat, but its total field is somewhat better. Under domestication, certain cats, and many dogs, have increased the binocular aspect as a result of changes in the shape of the skull resulting from the reduction of the foreface.

The pupil of the cat's eye can contract into a vertical slit when the amount of light is great.

Comparative fields of vision: *Cat:* Total vision—230°; Binocular vision—110°. *Dog:* Total vision—250°; Binocular vision—70°. *Man:* Total vision—190°; Binocular vision—120°.

Note: In domestic breeds of dogs, such as the short-faced breeds, and in some longhaired cat breeds (e.g. Persian), binocular field vision is increased, but with a reduction in the total field of vision. All values are approximate.

Color vision: For many years it was thought that only the higher primates—man, apes, and monkeys—could see in full color, but as more research was undertaken it was established that many animals have excellent ability to distinguish all the colors. The cat has proved difficult to test because it appears not to be especially concerned about color (the same is also true of the dog). The fact that cats have cones in the retina of the eye does not automatically mean that these are associated with color, for they are also the cells that control the ability to see in different levels of illumination intensity. However, after very careful training methods it was estab-

An odd-eyed white Persian. Blue eye color in cats is sometimes associated with deafness. This is not to say, however, that all or even most cats with blue eyes are deaf.

A Himalayan cat. For years it was believed that cats were colorblind, but most experts now believe this is false.

A cream male Persian. The function of a cat's whiskers is not fully understood, but it is known that they have a great deal to do with the sense of touch.

lished that cats and dogs can see colors, but the fact that it took such a long while to establish this tends to suggest that colors are not high on a cat's list of priorities. However, as evolution is not disposed to giving animals abilities that are not needed, it is probable that cats use color more than is currently thought and that it is humans that are in error in testing motivations and techniques.

OTHER ANATOMICAL ASPECTS

The bodies of all carnivores contain numerous glands that seem primarily concerned with secreting fluid which acts as both a lubricant and as a means of leaving scent markings. The surface area of cats is large in relation to their size, so thermoregulation is achieved simply by the surface area being cooled by the ambient temperature of the atmosphere, which is normally lower than that of the blood temperature of cats. However, sweat glands in the paws, together with loss of heat by panting, are back-up systems that cope with the heat loss that is needed following muscular activity—such as running.

Whiskers: The full function of whiskers is not totally understood, but they are generally believed to be concerned with the senses. Vibrissae, as they are technically called, may help the cat when it moves through undergrowth while hunting prey. In such situations its eyes will be wholly focused on the prey, and it may be that the whiskers help compensate for side vision thus lost; they immediately tell the cat if they happen to touch an object, such as a branch or leaf or such, and the cat is then able to adjust its position so that its head or body does not disturb the object. Cats can move their whiskers into different positions—up or down, forwards or backwards—and, apart from those on the sides of the face, the cat also has them above its eyes. It is thought that they may also be found amongst body hairs but in a much finer state—not as stiff. In some carnivores, sensitive hairs are found on the wrists, but I have found no reference to them being so placed in felids, though it may be possible that they simply cannot be distinguished from other hairs.

Carpal pad: The pads on a cat's feet all touch the floor except for two on each of the

Whiskers help the cat to maintain silence, when stalking prey in the wild, by letting it know the position of an object that will make noise if touched.

front feet. One is the pollical pad of the dewclaw on the inside of each leg, whilst the other is the carpal pad found to the rear and somewhat up the leg. Its function is not known, but the general view is that it may aid in braking or stabilizing the cat when it jumps from a height. Such pads are found on dogs and hyenas, and they do not appear to be positioned in many species to be effective braking aids, so one must assume they are vestigial remnants from an earlier evolutionary time when these animals were more plantigrade. Thus the carpals would have been much closer to the floor—for whatever purpose they may have had. They are certainly interesting anatomical parts worth speculating about.

THE CAT'S VOICE

Cats have a considerable range of vocal sounds which, though common to many species, vary amongst individuals. Some cats, such as those regarded as foreign, are capable of some very eerie sounds rarely heard in other breeds. Attempts have been made over the years to interpret feline calls, but nothing has ever come of them. An owner soon learns to distinguish between the request meows and those uttered when the cat is not happy about something. If a cat gets excited over a bird or other possible prey which it cannot get at because it is inside the house looking out of a window, it will often utter a sort of chirping call which is much softer in tone than its normal sounds. Another sound a cat will make is the "thank you" it will deliver when it has been let in after scratching or calling from an outside door. Not all cats respond with such appreciation! A cat wishing to go out will indicate this in many ways, but combined with these will often be yet another vocal sound which is quite different in its tone and delivery than other calls. If one takes the trouble to listen to a cat, it will be found that it can impart quite a lot of information.

Cats vary considerably in the extent to which they use their voices, for some are extremely quiet whilst others constantly chatter in one form or another—we have cats that will only say things once, whilst others will quite literally complain non-stop until they prompt an action

Although the purr is its best known vocalization, the cat is capable of making quite a few sounds.

from us! As a general rule the cats of foreign type are far more vocal than the British or American Shorthair type, with Siamese being the most talkative of all, with a whole range of little sounds they use during the course of a day.

In the wider field of cats there are those, such as the lynx, which possess a "bark" that often surprises those not familiar with it, whilst the puma, which cannot roar like the big cats, nonetheless has a very distinctive short and quickly repeated, very characteristic call. At the top end of the felid voice range is the mighty roar of a lion which, in its wild homelands, can be heard for a number of miles, so powerful is it. As one can differentiate between birds by their song, it is quite possible that this might also be feasible with cats.

A trio of tabby kittens. Before purchasing a cat, do some serious soul-searching and research. Be fair to the cat and to yourself.

PURCHASING A CAT

It is an unfortunate fact of life that a great many people decide to keep a cat as a result of an on the spot momentary decision—perhaps a friend offers a kitten no one else wants. Sometimes such cats are lucky, as some owners suddenly find that they really do love cats; however, often the association is temporary and the result is another feral cat doomed to spend its days trying as best it can to get by on scraps and leftovers from garbage cans. This text is written for those people who wish to become responsible cat owners and therefore will wish to speculate on the numerous options and considerations to be taken into account when purchasing any form of animal life.

Cats make truly delightful pets, but the concept of cat ownership must be a two-way association. Therefore, the first aspect that must be considered is the practical question of which homes are suitable for keeping cats—irrespective of the fact that the would-be owner is a confirmed lover of animals.

Cats are well suited to just about any type of home from a houseboat to a palace—if they have the freedom to explore and to keep their sense of independence, they will be happy.

PET OR BREEDING

Given that the home is indeed such as to gain the approval of the feline, then the next question is "What is the cat required for?" Obviously, it is wanted as a pet, but maybe you would like to breed and exhibit one or more cats. Or maybe you just like the look of a certain breed that is illustrated in this book. If the cat is to be purely a companion, it does not have to be purebred, as mongrel and mixed-breed cats will make just as fine pets and will be far less expensive to purchase. They come in just about every possible coat color and pattern and have the benefit of hybrid vigor, an aspect that means they are usually tougher and less prone to illness. This said, few domestic cat breeds have any particular health problems because they have not been "messed" with by humans to the extent seen in dogs.

If the cat is required as a potential show exhibit, then clearly its quality will need to be of a good overall standard, and its paperwork will have to be faultless; otherwise its show and breeding worth will be restricted.

If you wish to acquire a cat simply for companionship, consider a mixed breed. They make wonderful pets and are very reasonable in price.

AGE TO PURCHASE

In general, a kitten is easily the best option. Apart from the fact that one misses out on a great deal if this stage is by-passed, it is also easier to train a kitten into your household routine than it is in the case of an older cat. However, a potential breeder would be better commencing with a young adult, for in this way its quality is proven and not hoped for! Many a classy looking kitten failed to reach the high hopes its owner had for it. However, a young adult of proven quality will, of course, cost much more money, so the available budget might be a controlling factor in this matter.

In the case of a kitten, opinions differ sharply on what is a good age to purchase. There are two aspects to consider. First, from the cat's viewpoint, if it is taken from its mother at a very early age, say six weeks, then it will miss out on the teaching aspects of its mother and the warmth and comfort she would be giving it until it was fully independent at about three months of age. The opposing view is that the earlier a kitten is socialized to humans, the better pet it will make. This is not, however, always true, as we have hand-reared kittens where circumstances warranted such, and one such kitty has grown up to be anything but a lap cat and has retained a very strong sense of independence.

The experienced cat owner is probably able to rear a very young kitten without undue problems, but if it is to be the family's first felid, then the recommendation of the Governing Council of the Cat Fancy in Great Britain should be kept in mind: no kitten younger than ten to 12 weeks of age should be permitted to go to a new home.

A kitten that is purchased at too young an age will not have had a chance to be properly socialized or weaned from its mother.

Opposite: A Persian kitten. The best time to purchase a new kitten is when it is eight to ten weeks of age.

MALE OR FEMALE

The male cat is known as a tom whilst the female is called a queen. From the viewpoint of the pet owner, it is not important which sex is acquired, for both make affectionate companions. If they are to be kept just as pets, then whichever sex is settled upon should be surgically operated upon at the appropriate age so that the cats do not produce unwanted litters of kittens, thus adding to the already high population of such cats. Cats so treated are termed altered. This operation does not in any way affect their subsequent life. In the case of toms it is essential for another reason, which is that they spray a very powerful and, to humans, unpleasant liquid when marking their territory—your home!

I do stress that if the cats are strictly pets, then do have them desexed, as this saves you, and a number of neighbors if your cat is a tom, from many later problems.

Sterilization: The castrated tom will be less inclined to fight all the neighborhood cats and will not spend the night out on the tiles waking everyone up! The operation is simple and is performed when the male is about nine months old. It is not advised to do this earlier, as the genital organs will not be fully formed. Toms so treated are termed neuters.

For the female, the operation can be done at about four to nine months of age and is a more complex operation. Both ovaries are removed, as is the uterus (or much of it). Such cats are referred to as spayed. In both cases the kittens should not be fed or given drinks during the 12 hours that precede the operation. A return visit to the surgery may be required around ten days or so later for the stitches to be removed, though the use of dissolving stitches is now more widespread. Occasionally, a female may be retained overnight for observation following the initial operation.

The feline pill: A contraceptive pill is available for females that is sometimes used by breeders who may wish to postpone breeding activities, for one reason or another, until a later

Sterilizing your cat will prevent it from siring or giving birth to unwanted litters. Too many unplanned breedings have resulted in an abundance of stray, half-starved cats.

Kittens are capable of entertaining themselves for hours.

date. However, excess use of the pill, or injections, is associated with negative side effects, including increased likelihood of uterine disease, so one should always discuss the matter with one's vet and take the advice given.

ONE CAT OR TWO

Cats are especially suited to people who may be away from home for much of the day and equally so to those, such as the elderly, that leave the house only infrequently. In either case, two cats are always better than one, as they provide twice the enjoyment, provide company for each other, and, being small animals, their upkeep costs are not expensive. Although it has been pointed out that cats are more able to tolerate life with few friends, remember also the comments about the effects of domestication that is changing the nature of felines.

It is always better for two kittens to be acquired at about the same time, for a stronger bond will develop between them than if one is purchased some months later. If your budget only runs to a single pedigreed cat, why not have a mixed breed as a companion for it, as such a cat will cost very little money at all. It is also worth stating that in the event that you

A pair of red spotted shorthairs. Two cats are, for many households, better than one. A pair of felines will keep each other busy and will provide hours of enjoyment for their owner.

Be sure to purchase your cat from a pet shop or reputable breeder. Too many kittens from unwanted litters are sold to unwitting people; often, these kittens are the product of one or more sickly parents.

were unfortunate enough to lose, through illness or accident, your pet cat, then the fact that there is a second feline will, to some extent, reduce the pain of sorrow, for you will still have the other one wanting your attention and affection.

WHERE TO PURCHASE

Although there are numerous potential sources of obtaining a kitten, the two obvious options are from a breeder or from the pet shop. The pet shop is the most convenient place from which to purchase a cat; however, keep in mind that pet shops cannot possibly stock all breeds of pedigreed cats. If your local pet shop does not have the breed of cat that interests you, they may be able to help you locate a breeder known to specialize in the variety required. An animal welfare society can be a good source for mixed breed cats—your pet shop or veterinarian will provide you with their addresses.

The breeding cat: Before actually investing in a cat of breeding quality, the prospective owner should visit as many cat shows as possible, as in this way one will not only meet numerous breeders but will also come to appreciate at least some of the finer points of the breed under consideration. Another advantage of visiting shows is that all of the colors available in that breed will no doubt be on display. It is certainly an advantage if you can locate a breeder in your own area, as in this way you can keep in touch with such a person; this will have numerous benefits in the future.

The pet cat: The advantages of purchasing a pedigreed or mixed breed kitten from a pet shop are that the owners have good experience with kittens, carry a range of products especially for cats, and are not just looking to sell you a cat at any cost, as some backyard breeders might try to do. The pet shop owner wants your repeat business on food and equipment and has a vested interest in wishing to ensure that you remain a very satisfied customer.

An aspect not always appreciated is that when visiting a lawyer, an accountant, or a doctor, the advice given must be paid for, but from a pet shop the professional advice is totally free!

HEALTH CHECKS

Before actually concluding a purchase, the prospective owner should stipulate that this sale is subject to a satisfactory health check of the kitten by a veterinarian not earlier than 24 hours before the kitten is due to be collected. This is regardless of whether purchasing from a breeder or pet shop, for disease is not a respecter of reputations, though obviously it is less likely to be found on the premises of those who are attending to good husbandry as they should. No one should object to such a request, but if they do you should look elsewhere for your kitten. Naturally, you must pay this extra veterinary cost, but it is a wise investment.

Should you not request such a veterinary examination, then the kitten must be very carefully examined either by someone you know who is familiar with cats, or by yourself, but I do stress that this is the least favorable option if you are becoming a cat owner for the first time. Nothing is worse than to have one's excitement dashed when a kit becomes ill or dies early in its

It is always a good idea to have your new pet thoroughly examined by a veterinarian.

life simply because one rushed into purchasing an unhealthy cat.

All being well, you can look forward to about 14 to 17 years of companionship from your cat, though some have reached the grand old age of 30, but this is unusual; the world record I believe is 36 years of age, which really is old for an animal of such small size.

PREPARING FOR A KITTEN

The arrival of a kitten into a household is an exciting time for the whole family, and, in order for this to go as smoothly as possible, it is always better to purchase needed items in advance, as this saves a last minute rush, when you might not be able to obtain quite the accessories you had hoped to find. The range of products your pet shop will carry for cats is very extensive today, and the following list is divided between those considered to be essential and those which are useful extras if the budget is sufficient for them.

Essential items: Litter tray and scoop; scratching post; food and water bowls; brush and comb; cat collar and disc; carrying basket; food.

Optional items: Cat flap; play pen; cat toys; cat bed; heating pad.

The litter tray should be large enough to still be used once the cat has grown up, and a bag of litter will be required; in an emergency, should you run out of litter, clean garden soil can be used and is preferred to sand, which can both stain and be an irritant. Scratching posts come in various styles, but one that is fixed in an upright position is recommended. Hanging a ping-pong ball from such a post will help it double as a plaything, and it will also encourage the cat to use the scratching post. Cats are not as destructive to their food dishes as are dogs, so any type will do. However, for long wear and cleanliness, earthenware (crock) pots are still hard to beat. Aluminum can be kept spotlessly clean; there are even models with footplates that the cats stand on to make a plastic cover lift to expose the food!

Collars, leashes, and other equipment are available at your local pet shop.

The range of cat grooming equipment is vast, but a bristle brush is better than a nylon one, as the latter tends to create static electricity, thus prompting the hair to "fly away"; this is more noticeable in the longhaired breeds. Double-sided combs are useful, as they have a fine comb on one side and a medium to coarse comb on the other. The cat collar should have a somewhat loose band on it so that the cat can wriggle out of it should it get caught up on a branch. The disc should carry the address of the owner.

Carrying crates or baskets also come in a great variety of styles and sizes from plastic through to reinforced fiberglass. The latter type is normally the most costly but is an excellent investment because it will stand up to considerable wear. A carrying crate of good size is advised so that the cat as an adult will have enough room to stretch in. Such crates will be needed when taking the cat to the veterinary clinic and when going on journeys. They double as cat beds, and kittens can be safely placed in them during the first few nights. The addition of a blanket and a cuddly toy, or their feline companion kitten, will help provide a cozy and secure place in which to sleep. Place some newspaper on the floor of the crate and leave this exposed at the back end, as the kitty will no doubt relieve its bowels overnight.

Finally, do not forget to have a small stock of food on hand. The person the kitten has been purchased from may give you a diet sheet; but if not, be sure to ask exactly what the kitten has been feeding on, as it is better to continue with this during the first few days, until the kitten has settled in, when you can modify the diet with products you prefer—or simply continue with what the kitten is familiar with.

OPTIONALS

A cat flap or door might be considered an essential by some owners, as it gives the cat the freedom to come and go as the mood takes it. Models are available that enable the owner to adjust them to operate one way only—either in or out. This means that if the cat is out at bedtime, you can prevent its entry with some critter you would rather it did not bring in. Likewise, if reversed, the cat can come in during the night but not go back out.

Play pens are useful for very young kittens— you may not want them running around whilst you are cooking, or you may have a toddler who might be too rough with the kitty whilst you are not there to supervise the kitten and child.

There are many toys produced for cats, but those of thin plastic construction are to be avoided; if the kitten swallows a bit from such a toy, it could create an internal digestive blockage or cause the kitten to choke. Cats love things that are suspended and swing on the end of secure string, and they enjoy clambering up and down as well as in and out of things, so any playthings which incorporate these facilities will be much used. Even if you have a carrying crate, a cat bed might still be purchased, as this can be more attractive and comfortable for the cat. Fiberglass is again a good choice, as it is easier to clean than is wicker, and creepy crawlies do not like any form of synthetic resin products, as they provide no means of hiding in crevices.

If you live in a cold climate and have little or no overnight heating in your home, a heating pad can be useful in the early weeks of a kitten's life, as it must be kept warm and is still accustomed to sleeping with its mother and littermates. Various models of pads are available.

When purchasing a bed for your kitten, it is a good idea to make sure it will be big enough for him when he is fully grown.

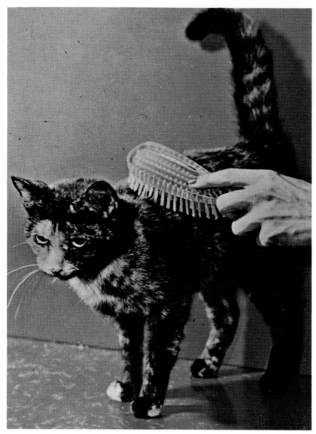

A tortoiseshell shorthair being groomed. Different types of brushes are available at pet shops.

COLLECTING THE KITTEN

It is always better to collect a kitten as early as possible in the day, as this gives it time to settle in and explore its new home before nighttime. The carrying crate can be used to house the kitten on the journey. Have this well lined with newspaper, as the kitten may well be sick on its first outing. A damp cloth will also be useful for wiping its face and paws after such a happening. If the journey is of a long duration, do take a few breaks so the kitten has a rest from the momentum of the car. It may appreciate some milk or a very light meal, but it probably won't be hungry.

Once you reach home, food can be offered, and thereafter the kitten should be allowed to have a sleep in quiet seclusion. When it awakes it can then be allowed to explore its new territory. If you have young children in the family, it is most important that they are instructed not to be rough in their handling of the kitten, and on no account should they be allowed to disturb it when it is asleep. It is surprising just how inconsiderate some parents can be on this matter, as one sees poor little kittens being pulled about by children whilst their parents seem oblivious to this very bad handling situation. If proper care cannot be exercised with children and pets, then the family should refrain from keeping sensitive creatures.

As it is very young, a kitten will require frequent "cat naps" and will have no control over its bowel movements—this comes as it grows older. A kitten is usually trained to a litter tray by the time the new owner takes over its care, but if yours is not, simply lift the cat up and place it into its tray the minute it starts to urinate or defecate; after a sleep and after a meal are prime times. The kitten will seem concerned just prior to relieving itself; it will cry and probably paw at the floor—a sure sign it wishes to empty its bowels. Never scold a cat for errors on this matter, as it will simply not understand; just place it in its tray and it will quickly use this in the future. A cat will not use a fouled tray, so it is important to remove soiled litter at once.

Winners of a cat/owner look-alike contest.

If taking your kitten to its new home involves a long car ride, be sure to make a few stops. The momentum of the car takes its toll on a young, frightened cat.

A good diet is a necessity for your cat's health and well being as well as its good looks.

NUTRITION

The attitude of different people to feline nutrition is as variable as the health of the cats they keep. Some people have no understanding at all of the basic needs of a cat and assume that "food is food," so anything will do. At the other extreme are those who react to every advertisement that manufacturer s place in magazines to promote their product. So concerned are they that their cat might be missing out on something that they pile on every known additive on the basis that if more than is required is given, then this should be to the cat's overall benefit. Ultimately, both attitudes will result in unhealthy cats—one from deficiency and the other from problems created by excess.

The key word in any form of livestock management is balance. This is not difficult to achieve, because no animal's make-up is so finely tuned that food intake must be a precision situation—the species could not survive with such rigid requirements. What is needed is the application of common sense and an appreciation that a cat is a prime carnivore that needs a diet which is essentially based around the flesh of other animals. A knowledge of the actual constituents is a useful aid in planning a feeding regimen, but it is by no means as vital as is sometimes stated, for it has only been during the last half-century that scientists have begun to study the composition of foods in any detailed manner.

Kittens are usually weaned from their mothers by the age of eight weeks, although she might start giving them adult food sooner than this.

The feeding of cats in this day and age is so simple because of two inventions, the sealed can and the can-opener! The major food companies invest substantial sums of money into researching the dietary needs of our pets, so, given this fact, there is no reason why any cat owner should experience problems over nutrition.

If you keep more than one cat, be sure all are getting enough to eat.

However, there are still places on earth where pre-packed cat foods are either not available or are very costly, so all cat owners will profit from a discussion on the many aspects of a cat's requirements, as this will enable them to make judgments on how they feel their particular cats should be fed.

THE ROLE OF FOOD

Food is used in the body for numerous purposes which may be divided broadly into the following categories:

1) For building bodily tissues. Food is broken down into its basic constituents which are then rebuilt into the sort of tissue required by the different parts of the body, such as muscle, bone, skin, soft bodily organs and so on.

2) For fuel. During the breaking down, or oxidization, of food, energy is released. This energy is needed to propel the animal, that is, for locomotion. It is also required by the internal organs so they can perform their own functions within the body.

3) For insulation. In order to protect the different body parts that are at risk of damage from external conditions, a layer of insulating material, fat, is produced. This is found just below the skin, where it is thus also able to help regulate the body temperature by reducing the effect of cold climates.

4) Energy reserves. The fat layer is also used as the first available source of energy should food become unavailable. This is vital in many wild species who store food, via fat layers, to enable them to survive over winters when snow covers the ground. All food in excess of bodily and energy needs will be stored as fat.

5) Metabolic processes. Whilst the body is able to synthesize many of its requirements that enable it to function, there are other needs that cannot be made from within. These must be made available from the food that is consumed. Without these, the specialized organs of the body malfunction, and this affects the working order of other parts of the body in a sort of domino principle basis.

A lovely bicolored shorthair.

QUANTITY REQUIRED

The question of how much to feed a cat, or any animal, seems to be difficult for many newcomers to pets to understand. On numerous occasions I have been asked to comment on the state of a given dog, cat, or other pet which did not seem as healthy as the owners would have wished. "Why is it so thin?" was a common question, and the answer was so obviously apparent that one had to be amazed that the question should ever have arisen. In such instances the pet was simply being underfed, and after further questions it became clear that they had read or been told that the pet should eat no more than this or that amount per day—and this is thus what the animal had been given. Now we are talking about sensible adults who were clearly intelligent and were concerned for the welfare of their pet, yet they appeared to experience a mental blackout where feeding was concerned! Here we see the classic case where common sense should have prevailed, for I am sure they did not feed their children or themselves according to what others said or what they read in books in respect to food quantities. The fact

A kitten will require a good deal of food in order to keep pace with its growing body.

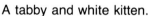

A tabby and white kitten.

that the pet was "always hungry" should itself have provided the answer to the problem.

In 35 years of keeping many animal species, I have never weighed out a food ration other than to purely establish, out of curiosity, how much was actually consumed by different individuals in relation to their size and activity levels. The one thing this established was that one cannot lay hard and fast guidelines down in respect to what a given cat will require to keep it fit and healthy. With this said, the first-time cat owner needs some advice, so approximate quantities will be quoted. First, let us consider just why cats must be considered on an individual basis.

Size: As a general rule a large cat will consume more than will a small one, but, as with each factor, this must be related to all other conditions, so that it is quite possible for one cat to eat more than another which is larger than itself.

Kittens that are orphaned at a young age may be forced to adapt to a semi-solid diet sooner than usual.

This does not necessarily make it a piggy eater, though, of course, such cats are not uncommon as household pets.

Activity Level: The more active a cat is, the more energy it will burn, thus the more raw materials it needs to replenish that energy.

Age: The age of a cat will directly affect its feeding needs because it will affect other factors. A kitten requires a progressively larger food supply the nearer it gets to full maturity, because during this period its body is still growing. At the same time a kitten is often unusually active and is burning up foodstuffs at quite a high rate. Once maturity is reached, the food intake may actually fall back slightly, because, on the one hand, the cat may not be as active, and

on the other it is not adding to its bodily size. Thus the adult cat needs only to replace tissue that is worn out by activity. Most people regard a cat as fully mature by about one year of age, but this is rather on the low side, for cats still fill out in bulk, if not in height, for some months after this. I would regard a feline as mature only when it has reached two years of age, at the earliest.

As a cat becomes very old, it is much less active and is not able to replace worn out tissue—at least not to the degree it could in its younger days. Its food intake will thus drop quite a bit in some cases, though not in all. A pregnant female is, of course, feeding both herself and her growing kittens in the womb, so she will require progressively larger amounts of food until the kittens are born and have reached two to four weeks of age, after which her intake will usually start to drop back to her normal level.

Illness: During an illness, few cats will consume normal rations; this is because their activity level drops sharply and the "energy" food is not needed at the same rate. Appetite drops as well so that the various systems are not being overloaded at a time when the body is concentrating its forces against the illness. At such

Older cats often do not get enough exercise, thus many of them become overweight.

times the cat will draw from its fat reserves. Once the cat is recovering, everything reverses, as it is a case of all systems go. The fat needs replacing and the activity levels start to increase; therefore, the cat often requires larger than normal rations to recover to its former bodily status.

Temperature: Cats living in cooler climates will generally require more food than those living in warm situations. This is because they need a somewhat thicker layer of insulation against the cold, and because a certain amount of the food will provide energy for keeping the body warm. One method of keeping warm is shivering, because this prompts muscular action which, in turn, generates heat. However, energy is needed even to shiver, and this comes via the food. You will probably never see your cats shiver; this is because they can cope with quite low temperatures, provided that they have a coat suited to this—Siamese and Oriental breeds are less well equipped to cope with the cold than are the short or longhaired breeds traditional to colder climates. However, if the former are kept indoors most of the time during bad weather, they should have no problems.

Parasites: Parasites, by definition, live off the food or bodily tissues of their host. The more parasites a cat has living on or in it, the less of its food will be available for its own needs. The most obvious parasitic group that consumes a cat's food is that of worms. High infestations will mean, initially, that the cat will always be hungry but will not gain weight; indeed, it may lose weight, showing, at the same time, an abdominal swelling or "potbelly," this being the worms themselves. After the initial ever-hungry stage, the cat will reverse and show little interest in its food, as this will tend to induce vomiting. Obviously, matters will not improve until the worms are removed by treatment, after which the cat will then require larger than normal rations.

Genetic Variance: I have added this because it can be viewed in two ways. First, two similarly sized cats may be of different breeds; therefore, their body structure and weight may be quite different and their respective bulk weight will need a different amount of food to sustain it. Secondly, even within the same

Cats that live in cool climates require more food than those in warmer places because their bodies need more fuel to keep them warm.

breed, two individuals whose lifestyle is all but the same may show quite contrasting habits in terms of food intake. One cat's overall system may simply be less efficient than that of another, and this will mean that it needs a greater amount of food to achieve the same activity and growth levels as another can in the same situation.

If one takes all of these factors into account, it can be appreciated that a cat's food needs may not only vary considerably from one to the other, but they continue to change over the lifetime of the cat in order to allow for both old age and the general ups and downs of life. Given this, it is quite pointless to feed a cat based on a set weight of food. It must be fed by taking account of these numerous aspects, and this means its rations will go up and down, within obvious tolerances, not just from year to year but indeed from month to month, according to the conditions under which it is living.

So far in the discussion we have only considered the conditions that will affect the food requirement, but this still leaves one very major consideration, and this is the food itself.

FOOD QUALITY

Food is like most other things in that it is available in a number of grades based on its properties and relative scarcity. For example, compared to the available plant life on our planet, and the cost of its propagation, meat is both a rare and costly commodity. As a result, the majority of mammal species have developed the ability to digest plant material. A number of animals have, however, evolved to live by eating the plant-eaters, and so a chain of life is created. At the top of that chain are the obligate predators such as the cats. Their entire bodily system is designed to cope with a high protein diet, which is reflected in the much smaller intestines they have. Protein is far more easily broken down into its constituent chemicals than is plant tissue; it also contains certain chemicals, in the form of amino acids, that are not found in plants.

Feeding a cat a low protein diet is akin to burning on an open fire a fuel designed for a solid fuel enclosed burner. It will not do the job correctly. However, a cat is more pliable than a stove, so it can cope with other fuels if it has no other option. Thus, in southern parts of Europe and in much of Africa and Asia, cats are given basic diets of rice or cereal crops, to which scraps of meat are added if the cat is lucky. The result of such a regimen is a thin and unfit cat which exhibits obvious signs of vitamin and protein deficiency.

The quality of a food will directly control the quantity required by the cat, because cats do not eat for eating's sake—they do so to fulfill a fundamental need. Once that need is satisfied, they cease to feel hungry and stop feeding until the food has been used up. It will take a greater amount of plant foods to satisfy a cat's needs

Food quality is of the utmost importance in keeping your pet healthy.

than is required if the cat were to be given the correct food in the first place—not that the plant food could correctly supply the cat's full needs. It can now be seen that beyond the other factors discussed, the type of food given will also have some bearing on the quantity the cat requires on a day-to-day basis. The richer it is in proteins, the less will be required in bulk weight to meet the bodily needs of the cat. Given this statement, one might at first assume that a good plate of the best steak should therefore be admirable, but this would overlook one or two aspects that are of importance.

First, when a cat in the wild state catches a prey animal, it consumes most parts of it—including the fur and the viscera—leaving only the hard skeletal bones which it is unable to crush. Even these may be eaten if the prey is of a very small species, which in the case of the smaller felids is invariably the case. In eating the internal organs, the cat thus consumes plant matter in varying stages of digestion, so its diet is totally balanced across all the different constituents of food. The liver of prey species is rich in vitamins, so only water is needed to complete the dietary need.

The second aspect of note in respect to an all-meat diet is that it is a costly way of providing fueling material burnt up on muscular activity. Food of plant origin is better suited to this, thus we arrive at the state of providing a balanced diet that will bring all factors together in the most efficient manners, both in relation to the cat's metabolism and to the owner's finances.

An attempt can now be made to quantify the amount of food per day that the average cat will require, after which we can then look at the constituents of food so that a clearer picture emerges of what must be provided in a home-made regimen.

Amounts to be fed per day in can sizes
Weaning to 8 weeks: Small can—½-1; Number of meals—4. *2-4 months:* Small can—1-1½; Number of meals—3. *4-5 months:* Small can—1½-1¾; Number of meals—3. *5-6 months:* Small can—1¾-2; Number of meals—3. *6-9 months:* Regular can—¾-1¼; Small can—1¾-2½; Number of meals—2. *Over 9 months:* Regular can—1-1½; Small can—2-3; Number of meals—1 or 2. *Note:* The above can sizes are based on the following approximations—regular 410g, small 195g.

Canned food has been used in the guidelines simply because it is a convenient and balanced preparation in which the ingredients have been formulated to supply all of the nutritional requirements of the cat, and because millions of cat owners worldwide have found using pre-packed moist cat food to be the simplest and safest way of feeding their pets. I do stress that the quantities quoted are merely guidelines and that each cat must be fed according to appetite and conditions.

CONSTITUENTS OF FOOD

All foods contain a number of broadly identifiable combinations of various chemical compounds, and these are classed as being protein, fat, carbohydrate, vitamin, or mineral, according to their make-up. Some foods will contain greater ratios of one constituent than will others, so that meat in its many forms, together with its by-products, will be rich in proteins, whereas plants, especially those known as cereal crops, will contain little protein but a far greater quantity of carbohydrates. Certain meats, such as liver and fish oils, are very rich in vitamins, as are different fruits, but all foodstuffs will have vitamins within their structure, so it is a case of how many and how much of these are present that will determine their value in a diet. Another ingredient common to all foods is, of course, water, and this may range in quantity held from virtually nil in dry seeds to about 98% in some fruits and vegetables. The body of a cat contains about 70% water, so its importance to the cat, or any animal, is self-evident.

NUTRITIONAL REQUIREMENTS

The role of food in general within the body has already been discussed, so it only remains to look at the constituents individually to complete the overall picture. Water will be considered as well, since it is fundamental to life and, from an interest viewpoint, its regulation within the body of a cat may give further support to the supposed evolutionary path of the domestic cat breeds.

The nutritional requirements for cats have been extensively studied in recent times due to their importance to the pet food industry, which has financed much of this research and continues to do so. From such collated data, the National Research Council of the American Academy of Sciences published a table of these requirements (*Nutrient Requirements of Cats*, © 1986 by the National Academy of Sciences), of which extracts are given here. To this I have added the analysis of two brands of cat foods sold in the moist, or canned, state. They represent the top and bottom, in terms of price, of the manufacturer's feline products. From this analysis, the reader can see how canned foods compare with recommended content levels.

Recommended levels as per National Academy of Sciences: Protein—28.0%; fat—9.0%; carbohydrate—00%; sodium—0.5%; calcium—1.0%; magnesium—0.05%; phosphorus—0.8%.

Levels Contained in Proprietary Cat Foods *Brand A*—Protein—62.7%; fat—28.0%; carbohydrate—00%; sodium—1.13%; calcium—1.33%; magnesium—00%; phosphorus—2.0%. *Brand B*—Protein—34.0%; fat—8.0%; carbohydrate—46.0%; sodium—0.76%; calcium—1.96%; magnesium—00%; phosphorus—1.64%.

Note: In the data provided for canned foods, the magnesium requirement was not indicated but will have been met within the ash quoted by the producers at 10.0–10.7%. Each of the figures quoted is expressed in percentages of dry matter.

PROTEIN

Protein is composed of a number of compounds known as amino acids, very complex structures arranged in chains; there are thought to be about 25 of these needed by cats. Ten of these are essential acids that cannot be produced within the cat's own bodily cells; therefore, they must be supplied via the diet. Protein rich sources are fresh lean meat and fish, which both contain about 25% dry matter protein. Hard cheeses contain 25–35% protein, whilst dried meat and fish contain up to 80% protein if they are hygienically prepared and stored. Milk is another protein rich source, as are eggs, but these are lower on the list than are meat or fish. Protein is used to build and repair bodily tissues, and amino acids are essential in the production of melanins, which give the cat its variable coat colors and patterns.

Although certain plants may be rich in proteins (for example, peanuts have a 26% protein content whilst dried peas have a 20% figure), this fact is of little value to the cat owner because no plant foods have feline palatability, which is vital in order to induce the release of digestive juices. If this does not happen, the food passes through the intestines without the proteins and other nutrients being extracted. Light cooking of meat will actually increase the rate that amino acids can be absorbed by the body, but this should be done with the meat kept moist—do not cook meat in a dry oven.

Meat given to cats should, of course, be fresh, and it should be varied as much as possible. Different meats contain different levels of given amino acids; the greater the variety of meats, the less chance that any amino acids are being omitted from the diet. Although cats are traditionally supposed to swoon over fish, the reality is that fish is not a natural food for cats and many may prove to be quite indifferent to it. However, much of this may be connected to familiarity, which is of importance to the average felid. Too much fish is certainly not recommended, for some species contain thiaminase, which destroys the vitamin B_4 (thiamine). Cooking the fish by grilling or steaming will make it more safe in this respect.

Because cats cannot chew meat, and thus crush it, it must be chopped into suitably small pieces if it is fed in its fresh or cooked state.

FATS

Fats provide the body with insulation and, in their various fatty acid states, transport themselves and other chemicals around the body in

Many cats are known to be fussy eaters; this is because taste is very important to a cat, probably as important as it is to people.

the blood. They are vital to the overall metabolism of cells, and they are the most efficient fuels available to the body, being about twice as good as proteins or carbohydrates in this function. If a cat is short of nutrients for muscular activity, it is the fat that is used up first; only when this is depleted does the protein, via muscular tissue, get used for fueling purposes. Cats have a much higher need for fats than do dogs, and kittens require a higher ratio than adult cats, which is why well-prepared kitten foods are fortified with this. Fat is, of course, associated with meat, and even very lean meat contains some fat. Mutton, lard, and cooking oils are rich in fats and may contain up to 85% of this. Milk from a cow has a fat content of about 30% on a dry matter basis. Apart from the foods named, fats can be given via butter or margarine. Since fats contain little inorganic waste matter, they do not pose undue problems for the kidneys; therefore, the fat content of the older cat can be increased slightly to beneficial effect.

CARBOHYDRATES

Of all the fueling foods available, carbohydrates are easily the least expensive—which is why they figure so strongly in the contents of the less expensive cat and dog foods. The most common form of these compounds is via the many cereal crops, such as wheat or barley, which contain very high carbohydrate levels—some over 65%. They are found in smaller quantities in the form of glycogen in proteins, and in the wild state it will be via this, and partly digested plant tissue, that cats obtain their needs. Carbohydrates are basically simple compounds made up of starches or sugars that can be readily converted for use as energy in muscular activity. There is evidence which suggests that the intestines of domestic cats are increasing in length in order to cope with the greater amounts of vegetable matter containing carbohydrates that they are fed.

Whilst these compounds can be assimilated into the body with no problem, the reason why cats ordinarily eat few vegetables is because they are unable to break the cellulose walls of plant cells. As a result, plants would simply pass through their digestive system without being affected. To overcome this, plant tissue is cooked by cat food producers, and you can do exactly the same. In doing this, the cell walls of plants rupture, thus making the cell contents available to the cat's digestive juices. The reason that cattle can cope with grass (and other plants) is because they can chew and crush it more easily; it is then partly digested in their specialized stomachs and regurgitated back to the mouth to be rechewed—chewing the cud. Other animals, rabbits, for example, release food pellets from their anus and re-eat them (giving some owners the impression they are eating defecation pellets, which is not so, as these are quite different).

Cats will rarely consume any quantity of carbohydrates unless they are made more appealing in some way—such as by adding meat extracts to them or by mixing in small quantities with a favorite meat. There is no special benefit gained from supplying carbohydrates to the diet of a cat, other than the fact they are cheap bulky foods that provide roughage that would normally be gained from the fur or feathers of prey species.

VITAMINS

Vitamins act as catalysts in so many ways within all animal bodies that it might be easier to list what they are not involved in! This is a measure of their importance, yet they are required in only relatively small quantities and are found in all foods in greater or lesser degrees. They enable the body cells to function; if they are lacking from the diet, in the cases of those that cannot be synthesized within the animal, then the effects can range from temporary illness to long-term debility and lack of development. Because vitamins are vital to normal cell metabolism, they are thus directly involved in disease, as their absence dramatically increases both the incidence and severity of illness. Fortunately, vitamins are so common that, provided that a variety of foods is supplied to the cat, it is most unlikely that the necessary vitamins will ever be deficient. However, an excess of vitamins can be as bad as a deficiency, for they can upset the overall balance of a cell and thus negate the benefits of other vitamins. For this rea-

An orange and white shorthair kitten. In addition to needing protein, cats must have certain vitamins in their diet to remain healthy.

A cat's good eyesight is affected by vitamin A. A lack of this vitamin causes night blindness, but an excess can be very dangerous.

son, unless one is concerned about a particular deficiency due to clinical signs of such, cats should not be given random supplements simply as a sort of insurance. There are certain times when certain vitamins may be recommended by your vet—perhaps during an illness, when a queen is pregnant, or for a general treatment when a cat is not actually ill but is clearly not at its best. Be advised by your vet on their use.

Vitamin A (axerophthol): This is an especially important vitamin for cats and is required in much larger quantities than other vitamins; a cat's needs are double those of a dog on a comparative basis. Lack of vitamin A results in night blindness, retarded growth in the young, and excess keratinization of the epithelial membranes of the stomach and the blood vessels. It is found in liver, fish oils (such as cod or halibut), milk, butter, eggs, and numerous vegetables. If the cat's diet is sound, the requirements will be met.

Vitamin A is a fat-soluble vitamin, thus it is readily stored in the body. Excess of it will result in lack of blood clotting, skeletal abnormality, and anemia. Therefore, do not overfeed liver, and restrict the use of cod liver oil to no more than ½ oz per week. Cod liver oil will also supply most other essential vitamins but is only needed if the other sources are in very limited supply within the diet.

Vitamin B₁ (thiamine): This vitamin is required to prevent general loss of condition and nervousness. It is important in the body to process carbohydrates. It is greatly reduced in strength as a result of cooking, when about half its amount is lost to the water or destroyed. Yeast tablets and extracts are the richest source of this vitamin, but it is also found in most foods.

Vitamins B₂ and B₆: These are comprised of riboflavin, pyridoxal, folic acid, and other compounds which are essential to cell metabolism. These vitamins are found in most foods.

Vitamin B₁₂ (cyanocobalamin): This vitamin is required to perform numerous roles in the body cells, and it affects the absorption rate of certain other vitamins. It is found in microorganisms of simple structure which occur naturally in the gut of a cat. However, any extra quantity required would automatically come via meat, milk, and yeast.

Deficiency is most likely to occur after antibiotic treatments, as these will destroy many internal bacteria which produce the vitamin. Your vet will, however, be aware of this and will advise if this is so and supply suitable additives.

Vitamin C (ascorbic acid): Essential to humans, this vitamin is not required by cats, which can synthesize it within their own bodies.

Vitamin D: This vitamin is involved in the regulation of calcium and phosphate in cells and has been associated with rickets if it is deficient; this is most unlikely in cats, as it is synthesized in the fur by the action of sunlight, and the cat will ingest it during its regular grooming of the fur. Vitamin D is also found in fish oils and in most animal fats, so bone structure problems will be the result of calcium deficiency rather than of vitamin D.

Vitamin E (tocopherol): A lack of these fat-soluble compounds has been found to cause "yellow disease" in cats, which become lethargic and find movement painful; such a condition is extremely rare and deficiency unlikely. It is found naturally in many cereals and in some meats, wheat germ oil being the most widely used source. Its absorption is halted if liquid paraffin is given to the cat—but only temporarily.

Vitamin K: This is connected with blood clotting but is not required by cats, since they can manufacture it within their bodies.

MINERALS

There are a number of minerals required in the diet; they are mainly concerned with cell structure and giving it rigidity. However, they do take an active part in most metabolic processes, and four or five of them are needed in much higher quantities than are others. The most important ones are calcium, phosphorus, potassium, sodium chloride, magnesium, iron, copper, zinc, iodine, cobalt and selenium.

Minerals are found in all foods, and the amounts required would normally be met from these. However, deficiencies are most likely to occur if a non-varied diet is given. The lactating queen needs calcium in much larger quantities than normal, for she must be able to provide sufficient milk for the kittens and, prior to this stage, enough calcium for sound bones to be formed in the growing embryo. At such times she will require extra calcium, either as prepared powder or via increased milk availability. Wild cats will, of course, obtain calcium needs at such times via the small bones of the prey they consume and via the glands of female prey.

WATER

Water, in one form or another, is vital for life itself. It must be available to cats on a daily basis and in a fresh state, even if they appear to drink very little. The extent to which they drink will reflect their diet—if this is moist, they will drink little, especially if milk is also given.

The popular example to illustrate an animal's water needs is that of comparing it to a water tank in which a given amount of water, with a variable upper and lower limit, is used. In order to remain at the required (healthy) level, the total input must be equal to the total output, and these very variable quantities must be linked or controlled from within the tank (body). If more water enters the tank than is being released at the other end, then it will fill and overflow; conversely, if more escapes than is coming in, the tank will drain. The time taken in both instances reflects the rate of the excess or loss. The input in cats, and the output, can be shown by the equation below if the cat is to maintain a stable body liquid content.

1) Water consumed = water in urine and feces.
2) Water in the food = water lost by evaporation (sweating, etc.).
3) Water produced by oxidation of food during metabolism = water lost by breathing (expiration).
4) Water lost via milk glands.

The way in which animals have developed to regulate the liquid content of their bodies has been much studied and, not surprisingly, reflects the area on earth in which they live. Camels, desert rodents, and other creatures with little access to regular water supplies retain it simply by turning down (not quite off) the output tap, rarely sweating and having fur that will not induce this latter state (overheat-ing). Some are able to store water in combination with food in their bodies (camels in their humps, some rodents in their tails, and so on). But what about cats?

Tests conducted on domestic cats have shown that they also turn down the output tap if the moisture content in their food starts to drop, or if water availability recedes. This is the opposite of the situation in dogs, which simply drink more water if the moisture content in their food starts to fall; a dog carefully controls the total water intake so that it is constant, and the output tap is related to this. The cat regulates the output to stay in ratio to the input.

In other words, if a dog is given dry rather than moist foods, it will drink its normal amount of water plus the amount that is lacking in the dry food compared to that which was in moist nutrients. The cat in the same situation will simply take in less water. It will obviously increase the quantity of water it drinks, but it will not compensate for that lacking in the food—it will simply deduct this from the output. This subtle difference allows warm climate animals to survive in adverse conditions. Of course, in the wild, the moisture level in the food does not actually drop, so it is the water drunk that can be reduced without ill effects. This is why your cat will appear to drink much less water than will your dog. This aspect lends support to the view that the domestic cat originated in warm climates, as are found in the Near Eastern countries, where water is rarely abundant. The dog is of more northerly origins where lack of water is generally not a problem, which is in keeping with its ancestry.

Opposite: The cat's need for water will depend on its diet. However, just because a cat can compensate—somewhat—for a lack of water does not mean that your cat should ever be deprived of this vital part of its diet.

EFFECTS OF FOOD TYPES ON THE WATER INTAKE OF CATS AND DOGS

Cat: *Canned*—Moisture level–83.6%; Mean water intake via food–240 ml; Amount of water drunk–26 ml; Total water intake–266 ml. *Semi-moist*—Moisture level–29.5%; Mean water intake via food–22 ml; Amount of water drunk–198 ml; Total water intake–220 ml. *Dry*—Moisture level–7.4%; Mean water intake via food–5 ml; Amount of water drunk–179 ml; Total water intake–184 ml. *The reduction of water intake is thus 31%.*

Dog: *Canned*—Moisture level–73.1%; Mean water intake via food–1353 ml; Amount of water drunk–825 ml; Total water intake–2178 ml. *Semi-moist (1)*—Moisture level–20.9%; Mean water intake via food–133 ml; Amount of water drunk–2107 ml; Total water intake–2291 ml. *Semi-moist (2)*—Moisture level–15.2%; Mean water intake via food–77 ml; Amount of water drunk–2021 ml; Total water intake–2098 ml. *Dry*—Moisture level–9.1%; Mean water intake via food–48 ml; Amount of water drunk–1894 ml; Total water intake–1942 ml. *The reduction of water intake is thus 11%.*

DEPENDENCY OF URINE ON FOOD TYPES IN CATS

Canned: Moisture level–83.6%; Total water intake per day–266 ml; Urine volume per day–194 ml.

Semi-moist: Moisture level–29.5%; Total water intake per day–220 ml; Urine volume per day–162 ml.

Dry: Moisture level–7.4%; Total water intake per day–184 ml; Urine volume per day–132 ml. *The reduction in urine volume is 32%.*

FRESH OR PRE-PACKED FOODS

Whether the cat owner chooses to feed a wholly homemade diet, a wholly pre-packed diet, or one that combines the two options, it is essentially a case of convenience. What is assumed is that the cat owner will supply his pets with a well-balanced range of those items which are basic to its needs.

The various items such as vitamins, minerals, and amino acids are not critical in the quantities needed, only within the framework that there is an upper and lower limit, beyond which ill-health is almost a certainty. However, the toleration level is such that excess or deficiency is most unlikely in a normal homemade diet provided by everyday foods used by humans. The great variability seen in the content of prepared foods underlines the fact that it is the feline body which is the supreme machine, for it can adjust to a remarkably high degree to obtain its requirements from the food it is confronted with. In this aspect, palatability is a most important aspect, so one should always attempt to provide foods that the cat finds interesting—again, this means varying the diet on a regular basis, both to achieve palatability and to establish which foods are preferred by the individual cats.

Kittens, especially, should be tried on numerous diets simply because feeding habits are formed early in life. If a cat is given only the best cuts of fresh meat, or the best brands of products, then it will show little interest in lesser foods at a later date and will all but starve itself before accepting them!

Although cats cannot crush bones, our own cats are given these on a regular basis and seem to enjoy taking the last scraps of meat from them. Chops and small beef bones left from meals are the preferred items, and the cats will no doubt gain some nutritional benefit from the bits of bone they are able to cope with. However, the biting of them also provides another valuable aspect of nutrition which is related to the therapeutic value of the eating act. Again, bones, as well as dried biscuit foods, will help to keep the teeth in a good clean state and provide essential exercise for the muscles of the jaw. This aspect is totally missing if moist prepared

Opposite: The bright eyes and full, shiny coat of this cat reflect the good diet it has been receiving.

foods are given constantly; the overuse of sloppy feeds has not a singular advantage.

Overall, prepared foods sold for cats will work out to be more expensive than fresh foods supplied from the average kitchen; nonetheless, canned cat foods have considerable advantages if they are used in a balanced manner. They will store well, they are instant, they are prepared to high standards of hygiene and, in the better brands at least, have high acceptability rate to the cats. A diet of 50% prepared foods and 50% foods from the kitchen has been found to meet the approval of our cats and is convenient to our particular situation.

The actual time that cats are fed is important only in that it should be the same time from day to day. This way the cats will arrive on time. Most cats prefer to have a little food several times a day rather than one big meal. We feed the main meat meal in late afternoon, which is supplemented with biscuit chow on a more or less ad lib basis during the day in response to the cat's individual requests. Water is always available, and milk is likewise freely available for much of the time.

Some of our cats cannot cope with one big meal at once, and the leftovers would get eaten by the more piggy members of our cat family if we did not remove them and give them to the individuals a few hours later, when they consume the balance. The majority of cats will eat only what they need, but the lazy sort of cat that sits around all day tends to eat more than it needs, probably out of boredom. Such cats must have regulated amounts if they show a tendency to overindulge. If a cat eats its meal with relish and clearly wants more, we give it more until it is satisfied—other days the cat may eat less than normal. By watching the cats eat we are quickly able to tell if they are somewhat under the weather—or if they have been supplementing their diet with mice, birds, lizards, or locusts, which are the local wild foods available to them in the garden.

You will find that some cats catch quite a lot of their own food, whilst others restrict their hunting prowess to a half-hearted swipe at a passing butterfly! As far as tidbits are concerned, the vast majority of cats do not have a sweet tooth and will not eat chocolates or any sweet item. However, such a cat does appear now and then, and, ironically, with our felids it is the one which is the most prolific hunter of them all. She will accept just about anything she is given, be it a piece of chocolate, cake, jam on toast, or whatever we happen to be eating—and she enjoys spaghetti, which none of our other cats will even consider. There is no reason why your cats should not be given tidbits of items you might be eating at the time, though many owners do not encourage this with cats or dogs. However, give these snacks in moderation.

The diet of pet cats can be as simple or as complex as the owner wishes to make it, but the essential underlying requirement is that it provide the basic needs of a predator, and, if a balanced judgment is made with this always in mind, then your cat will be assured of an excellent and satisfactory diet.

In most cases, a cat will eat what it needs to remain healthy and active. Not all small, thin cats are fussy eaters.

Some cats need to have their food intake watched, especially as they get older. Just like people, some cats like to eat more than is good for them.

Keeping a cat requires little more than simple common sense. A good diet, proper housing, and attention from you go a long way.

GENERAL CARE

One of the reasons cats are so popular as pets is that they really are very straightforward in their upkeep requirements. The main essentials are that one applies a sound degree of common sense, combined with a good basic knowledge of general husbandry procedures.

SAFETY MEASURES

A young kitten is very inexperienced in the ways and dangers of life, and, as it is a very active and inquisitive animal, it finds no difficulty in getting itself into trouble unless the owner takes appropriate steps to minimize risks. In the average home there are many potential hazards. An obvious one is when doors are left open during warm spells. Not only might the kitten wander off, but a through breeze might slam the door, causing injury to the kitten. Cats are not as bad as dogs at chewing things, but, even so, check that no electric cables have frayed ends at the socket—and unplug them if they are not in use.

Open fires should always have a fire guard around them. Open washing machine doors are an invitation to a curious kitten, who might decide to have a short nap on the clothes; on washing days it is better to keep the kitten clear of the kitchen. This latter room has other dangers, because as the kitten gets older its powers of jumping will get better. For instance, the ceramic hobs of a fireplace could easily burn the paw pads of a kitten. All fans should be fitted with guards and, when cooking a meal, it is better that the kitten is restricted to another room, as cats do have a habit of getting under one's feet at times.

For the safety of both your cat and your fish, keep the feline away from bowls and tanks or ensure that they are properly covered.

131

Climbing comes naturally to most cats but getting down does not. Try to keep your pet away from places that are high enough for a fall to cause serious damage.

If you keep any species of fish, ensure that the aquarium is fitted with a suitable canopy, as it has been known for a kitten to fall into such a tank, with tragic results. When ironing, do not allow the kitten into the same area, as it could easily knock the iron off the board by playing with the cord whilst you momentarily leave the room. Obviously, no poisons of any sort should be left where any animal or child might have access to them. If you live in an apartment, remember that a high balcony is a very real danger to a kitten. Such a balcony should be suitably screened so a kitten cannot get its body between the railings, and it should not have furniture that would give the kitten the means to climb on the top of the wall or railings. Finally, cats just love exploring cupboards or wardrobes, so if the kitty appears to be missing, check out all such places.

BASIC TRAINING

To a greater or lesser degree, all cats will respond to their names, and they can respond to a limited range of words. One that they should quickly come to understand is "no" in a firm voice. This will become a well-used word in most cat households! Cats enjoy sitting in high places, and this means they will invariably choose to recline on the tops of chairs, on windowsills, or even on high cupboards. These are quite natural vantage points for them, so if you are the sort who just does not like animals climbing over your furniture, or sleeping on it, then maybe you should reconsider owning a cat. One time when it is not advisable to suddenly say "no" to your cat is if it has jumped onto something that contains either valuable ornaments or has many loose items, such as paperwork, on it. In its efforts to quickly remove itself, the cat will invariably send everything flying! In such a situation, simply approach the cat casually and gently lift it off the table, shelf, or whatever.

Many cats enjoy sitting in high places such as shelves or window sills. Your pet will no doubt adopt such a spot for roosting.

LEAD TRAINING

Cats do not like restraint and, unlike dogs, are not at all suited to this form of training, which is totally alien to their way of life. It must be remembered that cats are not happy in open spaces and even less so if one of their main forms of defense—quick retreat up a tree or over a wall—is denied to them. Therefore, I do not recommend that lead training is done in order to provide cats with daily exercise on the average roadway. This stated, I know of numerous cats that are so trained and are taken for walks in such a manner, either because their owners travel a great deal and take their cats with them, or because they live in cities, suburbs, and apartments.

In general, the foreign breeds, such as Siamese or Burmese, seem to take to lead training better, but any cat can be lead trained if training is commenced early in its life, and if the cat becomes used to this form of walking. However, if the cat's disposition is such that it is clearly unhappy after careful training, then it is better that one does not continue, as this will merely stress the felid. All dogs can be so trained, but this is not so with all cats because they exhibit a much wider spectrum of individual personalities in certain areas, and training is one of them.

The first stage is, of course, getting the kitten accustomed to wearing its collar. Next, place a lead on the collar, but do not attempt to drag the kitten along. Let the kitten become aware of the restraint, but let it also go in whatever direction it wishes. This stage should be done in the home or yard where there are no distractions or things that might panic the kitten. Over a number of sessions, the kitten will become quite used to the situation, and gradually, over the sessions, you can exercise more control over the kitten's movements when it is on the lead. Always keep the sessions short and always encourage the cat to follow you. It should be rewarded after each training stint with its favorite tidbits—which can be used to motivate the cat to follow you. Once the cat becomes very familiar with the routine it can be taken out onto a quiet footpath, and by this process of familiarity it will eventually become as settled as it is possible for a feline to be.

The lead should be a slim and lightweight one

Since cats are territorial animals, most of them do not like to leave their home base. Therefore, walking a cat in the same manner as a dog is generally not feasible.

available from your pet shop—the sort used for toy dog breeds are fine. Even better for a cat would be to obtain a soft harness, for with this the cat can be lifted up very rapidly if the need arises, and is far less likely to slip its collar and be off if startled by a dog or a sudden noise. Do remember that cats are very territory minded; the further away from your home they are taken, the more unhappy they are—unless, as stated, they are regularly taken on such trips. The key to success in any form of animal training lies in the patience of the trainer more than in the animal's capabilities, for most predatory species are of a high intelligence. Discipline is not a good trainer; affection, patience, and motivation are the important prerequisites.

GROOMING

The extent to which a cat will require grooming depends upon the breed; Persians and other longhairs will certainly require daily attendance, whereas shortcoated breeds require little more than a quick "polish" to keep their coats looking just fine. This aspect should be considered when choosing a breed, for if a Persian is not groomed daily it will quickly become an unsightly mess, and many an owner has wished he had chosen a shortcoated variety—especially if one has rather limited time to devote to this.

The best place to groom the cat is on a patio or in a utility room, but many owners attend to this on a table or on their lap. If you use a table, spread some newspaper on it, both to stop the cat from sliding about and so that you will more readily notice if any lice or fleas should fall from the fur; plain white paper is even better for spotting these unwanted guests.

Although a scratching post will eliminate most of the need for nail trimming, keep an eye on your pet's claws. Consult your veterinarian the first time you think your cat's nails need cutting, as he will advise you about the proper length and will show you the proper method for this procedure.

Longhairs: Commence by brushing the coat in the direction of its lie, as this will remove loose surface debris. Lift the cat up so it is standing in order to gently brush its underbelly. Next, brush against the lie towards the head, and then brush it back again. Now the medium comb can be used in the same manner—first with the lie and then against it. This can be repeated if a fine-toothed comb is available; finally, give the cat another brisk brushing, after which the cat will no doubt have a good shake and commence grooming itself! When grooming, always be especially gentle with both the underbelly and the tail, as these are rather sensitive areas. The face, too, should be combed with care; a stiff toothbrush is ideal for this, and any other very delicate areas, such as inside the legs.

During the grooming session, talcum powder can be sprinkled into the coat, or the powdered chalk used for show dogs and other livestock. All powder must be completely combed and brushed out. There are numerous sprays and coat tonics that can be purchased, but if the cat is receiving a well-balanced diet its natural skin oils should ensure a really fine bloom to the coat.

Shorthairs: A soft-bristled brush or a rubber-toothed equivalent can be used in the direction of the lie of the fur. Next, a medium or fine-toothed comb can be used, starting from the neck and back and working downwards. A

final polish with a chamois will give a nice shine—a silk scarf will achieve the same effect. Again, one of the preparatory coat tonics can be used if the coat lacks condition, but do remember that such condition stems from the inside and that tonics merely cover an obvious underlying problem which is usually of a nutritional origin.

Eyes, ears, and teeth: It is convenient, either before or after grooming the cat, to inspect its eyes, ears and teeth to check that all is well. Any buildup of debris in the corner of the eye can be removed with damp cloth or cotton swabs; use tepid water for this purpose. The ears should not need more than a gentle wipe with a cotton swab dipped into warm olive oil or similar lotion. If brown wax is seen in the ear, consult your veterinarian. Home remedies for this problem may do more harm than good.

The teeth should be checked and, if possible, brushed with toothpaste; however, most cats are not keen on having humans attending to such tasks and may resist in a most forceful manner. In such cases, periodic trips to the vet can be made so that built-up tartar can be descaled under anesthetic.

Bathing: Cats rarely appreciate being bathed, and some will put up such a fight that two people are necessary to carry this out! Normally, cats are very clean, so they rarely need more than a dry shampoo (available at pet shops). A dip into the bathtub or bowl (the latter is easier from the owner's viewpoint) will be a rare occasion, but because of this, either method will be a battle. A cat may become covered in a foul-smelling substance, or it may just look very dirty or need an anti-parasite shampoo because it becomes covered with lice or fleas after an encounter with wild animals.

Opposite: The luxurious coats of longhaired cats require much more grooming than the coats of shorthairs, but owners agree that their pets are worth the effort.

A group of longhaired kittens. If the coat of your longhair has become too matted to comb, carefully cut the mats out—and, in the future, try to prevent them from forming.

It is not necessary to detail the whole procedure, as we are all aware of what is involved in bathing, but a few tips will act as reminders that are important when dealing with most animal species.

1) The fur should be groomed thoroughly before bathing; otherwise tangles and mats will result and will be impossible to remove without considerable discomfort to the cat.

2) Only feline or baby shampoos should be used. Dog shampoos are too strong and are not suitable for cats.

3) Anti-tangle solutions are available from your pet shop. They reduce the incidence of tangles but do not remove the need for grooming beforehand.

4) The water used must not be too hot, so test it with your elbow before immersing the cat. It is always better to be on the cooler side than to be too hot.

5) Place cotton balls in the cat's ears to prevent any water from seeping in.

6) At all costs, avoid getting water, and especially shampoo, into the eyes, as this really will kill off the chances of bathing on a later occasion.

7) After soaking and shampooing, make extra sure all the shampoo is rinsed off the coat; otherwise, an irritation may be set up.

8) Give the cat a very brisk rubbing with the towel and dry him with a hair dryer if it will allow this. If not, make sure the

cat is kept indoors until it is really dry—maybe it can be contained in its carrying crate on a dry towel.

As cats do not like being in deep water, ensure that the bowl or sink only has about a few inches in it—the use of a spray fitted to the tap is better than using the faucet itself. A piece of rubber matting on the sink base will stop the cat from skidding and thus panicking.

Should the coat of a longhaired cat get into a bit of a state, then grooming may be too painful. Trim off any mats, but be very careful if these are close to the skin; in such cases your vet will sedate the cat and clip them off. The cat may look a bit unsightly for a while, but this is better than allowing the coat to get even worse by doing nothing, or than attempting to groom the mats out yourself and causing considerable pain for the cat.

It should be pointed out that all cats are very sensitive to coal tar products, and cresylic acid is cited as the responsible agent. Care should therefore be taken that disinfectants containing coal tar products do not get on to a cat's fur, as it could create major problems. If you are in doubt about the disinfectants you use, consult your veterinarian.

HANDLING CATS

Never pick up a kitten or a cat by the scruff of its neck. This method, with the cat's hind

When grooming your cat, remove any matter from the corners of the eyes.

Young children should be taught the proper way to hold a cat without hurting it.

feet still supporting the body, is a last resort method of securing a very difficult cat, such as a veterinarian might have to do, but it will alienate your cat from you. Therefore, always lift a cat by gently securing its neck with one hand whilst supporting its body weight with the other. Never lift the cat simply by grasping it under its front armpits so that the body is left dangling; even if the cat allows this, it does so as a mark of its affection for you, not because it is comfortable.

A kitten, and most cats as they get older, can be lifted without securing the neck by passing the palm of the hand under the chest and scooping the cat up towards your chest. Should the

Always support the cat's body whenever you handle it.

cat be of an unreliable nature, then, if it must be lifted at all, repeat as stated but secure the front legs at about elbow level; otherwise you might end up on the wrong end of a nasty scratch on the face.

Some cats like to wrap themselves around your shoulders, while others drape over one shoulder whilst you support their hindquarters. Yet others will allow you to cradle them like babies, on their backs, but this is the least favored position for any animal, and I doubt that any cat enjoys this method, even if it accepts it because it is of a very good nature. The best position for you and the cat is when it is tucked, nice and secure, against your chest so it can see what's going on, and you can use your free hand to stroke it.

It is most important that young children are well versed in how to handle kittens and cats—if not they may well one day get a very severe scratch and bite from a feline. They must be made aware that strange cats can be especially dangerous if they attempt to pick them up, as children are not always aware of the signs a cat will give as to its intentions and nature.

In general, you will become aware if your particular cat likes being handled—some just do not, and no amount of such will change this. If they are gently handled as kittens they will rarely grow up to dislike being picked up, but each must be treated as an individual and respected as such.

Sometimes a cat will object to being placed into its carrying crate or a similar confined space; if this is so, it should be wrapped in a towel first and then placed into the crate or whatever. This way an unpleasant struggle will be avoided.

CATS AND OTHER PETS

Cats have been known to form friendships with animals ranging in size from mice and birds through to gorillas and elephants, but letting them be around when the hamster or budgie is loose is not recommended. A cat may be quite trustworthy with large rabbits, especially bucks, as these may quickly strike out at an unruly cat. Small rabbits are less safe with cats unless the cat has become familiar with them from an early age. Baby rabbits are progressively less safe because of their small size. Cats and dogs can get along well together, especially if both were brought up with each other from an early age. A kitten will be accepted by a dog far more readily than will an adult cat, unless, again, the dog is used to having lots of cats around the home.

The initial introduction of a kitten to a resident dog is obviously a cause for concern, since you can never be sure just how the dog will react once it can actually get at the kitten. The owner usually has a good idea about how friendly his dog is, which will help him gauge the particular situation. On the kitten's first day in its new home, keep the dog away but give it more affection than normal. Soon it will be allowed to see and smell the kitten, which is secure in its carrying crate—this then tells the dog someone else is moving in. The next stage will be to let the dog approach you whilst you are sitting with the kitten on your lap. Watch the facial expressions of the dog, as these will invariably tell you what it is thinking! It will either have a menacing look or will prick its ears and cock its head sideways as if curious. If things look favorable, let it sniff the kitten—which in turn will probably hiss and strike out. If the dog does not retaliate, things are going well.

The final stage is to let the dog approach the kitten whilst the latter is on the floor; this is clearly the moment of truth. Be ready to step in, if things do not go as hoped, before the dog has

Many cats loathe their carriers and other confined spaces, while others will curl up in the most unexpected spots.

actually bitten the kitten. Regrettably, there is no sure way of introducing dogs and cats, because sooner or later they will have to meet. However, if you are very concerned, then it is better to keep the pets apart for a while, as this gives the dog the opportunity to become familiar with the smell of the cat and to see it about the house in safe positions—such as on a high cupboard. At the same time, the kitten will be getting bigger and better able to defend itself when they do eventually meet at ground level. The important thing is not to give the kitten too much affection in the sight of the dog; instead, lavish extra praise on the dog, who then will not regard the cat as too much of a threat to its own position. In time they will become very good friends, but only they can decide when, and on what terms, the friendship will be made.

The reverse situation is much less of a problem: a puppy introduced to a house with one or more resident cats is not at the same risk, for the cats will simply keep out of the puppy's way or hiss at it if it approaches them, ultimately boxing its ears if it does not take due warning. Cats will treat other kittens in the same manner, but slowly they will come to terms with them.

Once a bond is established, a dog will defend its feline companion very fiercely if the two are good friends rather than tolerant co-habitants of the same home. It can be highly amusing to watch a cat and dog who are big pals having a wrestling match on the floor, as neither will use their potentially dangerous teeth or claws.

VACATIONS

Provided that it is left suitable food and water in its bowls and a clean litter tray, a cat can be left for up to 24 hours without undue worry—but not, of course, a kitten which needs small, regular meals. When it comes to vacation time, then, the best option is to have a friend or neighbor come round daily to attend to the cat and to let it out or in, etc. This may be preferable to taking the cat with you, since felids are often happier in their own territory. The final option is to board the cat in a cattery; this is the least suitable option from the cat's viewpoint. In such cases, do inspect the conditions beforehand and do ensure that your cat's vaccination boost-

ers are right up to date—good catteries will insist on this anyway and will require sight of the documents. Your pet shop or vet will provide a list of catteries in your locality. Many owners decide to take their cats with them, in mobile homes, houseboats, or cars. In such situations, cats will become used to the annual trip and regard the vehicle as part of their territory. One couple we met in Sequoia National Park always took their cat on camping trips; they said it was no trouble and seemed quite happy with life under canvas.

MOVING

Moving is as traumatic for a cat as it is for humans, but it is not as bad as is sometimes believed. The cat just might like the new home better than the old one, so it should not be thought that all cats attempt to return to former houses. If the yard at the new house is better, and perhaps if there are less neighborhood cats, it is probable that your cat will give the stamp of approval to your choice. If the reverse is true, it is likely that the cat loves you more than it did its former haunts; otherwise it may try to find them again.

Some authorities recommend keeping the cat in its new home for at least a day or two following a move. We have never done this, and only once did a cat dislike our choice and return to the former home. However, it happens that this cat did not get on well with some of our others, so maybe that was the deciding factor. After a move, we let the cats have a good look around the new home, offer them a tasty meal, and then let them go out and explore. They usually do this with care—they keep returning to check if we are still there, then off they go for another look. If possible, have your cats travel with you when the move is made, as they will be far happier with this situation. Do ensure, if the journey is long, that you have considered the cats' toilet needs and thus have a litter tray convenient for them.

Opposite: An English Cocker Spaniel and his young friend. Cats and dogs can become great friends, but they should be carefully supervised until they become acquainted.

A Burmese mother with her demanding litter. Before breeding your cat, be sure to find good homes for all the kittens you can't keep yourself.

PRACTICAL BREEDING

Although the temptation to breed one's cats may be considerable, especially if they are pedigreed, this step should not be taken without considerable thought. There is little point in adding to the cat population simply for its own sake, so a potential breeder should have some objective in mind. The exhibitor of cats will be trying, by selective breeding, to improve his or her line of cats so that they are more successful on the show scene; in so doing he will gain much pleasure, as it is always more pleasing to gain wins with cats one has bred. However, this dual aspect of exhibiting and breeding takes up much time and a considerable sum of money.

Other breeders are interested in trying to improve or create new colors in their chosen breed, but this too is not without problems. Along the way a lot of indifferent cats will result, and homes must be found for the worst as well as the best of the kittens produced. It happens that if color is the main objective in a breeding program, the overall quality of conformation will invariably suffer, especially in breeds that are not very well established.

A third objective that has become somewhat fashionable is that of producing new varieties or breeds. Again, this can be a costly undertaking that initially involves retaining a goodly number of kittens. In addition, you may be very disappointed with the first and second generation hybrids. It must be remembered that once one crossbreeds, the surplus stock is not purebred and will have little or no value in the world of pedigreed cats.

Breeding can be full of pitfalls, unexpected costs, and a lot of disappointments, so do give the matter much thought in advance.

Breeding lesser known cats, such as this beautiful Korat, will be less competitive than breeding a more well known type; however, good breeding stock will be more difficult to find.

WHICH BREED

If you have previously owned cats and are sure you wish to breed, but cannot make up your mind between a number of breeds you would like to commence with, then a few of the pros and cons may be helpful.

Getting established in one of the older breeds, such as Persians, can be very difficult because, obviously, there are many very experienced people with kennels full of high quality cats. There will be no shortage of surplus pet quality cats, and there will be many owners of pet cats that have bred them in the mistaken belief that they can make money with them. This fact may make it more difficult to sell off your surplus stock—and it will hold prices down. I am not suggesting that one looks at breeding only in financial terms, but only a fool would say that cash is not an important factor, especially if you do not have lots of it.

On the benefit side of working with an established breed, obtaining quality breeding stock should not be too much of a problem, and you will not have to travel as far, or wait as long, to obtain such. There will be no shortage of good stud toms, and there will be no shortage of exhibition classes at shows for any of the popular breeds. The range of colors available will be more extensive, but so will the incidence of genetic faults.

With the less popular breeds (such as the Korat in the UK and the Egyptian Mau in the USA), obtaining good breeding stock will entail looking much further afield, which, obviously, entails greater costs. However, genetic variation will be lower, which means that the relative newcomer will have a better chance of producing cats of good type and of being capable of competing with current winners. The market for the kittens will obviously be much more restricted, so you will need to advertise in national cat magazines or in the breed clubs as well as locally. The increase, or decrease, in the breed's popularity will determine the sort of price the kittens will command. As a general rule of thumb, the rarer breeds will sell at higher prices

Breeders of Egyptian Maus and other less popular breeds often gain experience with a more well-known cat first.

Winning cats, such as this Abyssinian grand champion, are often in high demand for breeding purposes.

than will very popular breeds, but they will rarely achieve the high figures that top quality cats of popular breeds will fetch. However, as the relative newcomer is more concerned with average prices, the rarer breeds are the better choice, because one is more able to become the established breeder of the future if the breed continues on an upward spiral.

In the show world there will be less classes available to the more unusual breeds, which means competing in variety classes, and only rarely will an unusual breed take supreme honors. Many top winners in established breeds also have an interest in one of the less seen breeds, a situation quite common in most forms of livestock breeding. If you are a young person or couple just about to embark on a hobby of cat breeding, and you are prepared to work hard at it and wait some years before the big awards come your way, then choose one of the less seen breeds, but one which shows no abnormalities to its overall structure. You will find that general attitudes are more open-minded, and you will have a greater opportunity to shape the future of the breed. If you wish to pitch into fierce competition, then choose one of the very popular breeds—but you will need to have a tough frame of mind, because established breeders will not make life easy for those seeking the top spots! The White House and the Houses of Parliament are not the only places where politics are the order of the day; for, whether in birds, dogs, fish, or cats, you will find that people are people, and the more popular the pursuit, the greater the vested interests of those who have attained success.

CHOICE OF STOCK

Initially, a potential breeder should think only in terms of queens due to a number of factors. First, if a tom is to be kept, his spraying habits will be such that you will need to invest in an outdoor or indoor cattery accommodation for him. Such restrictions on the cat may not appeal to those who want their cats to be housepets as well. However, more important is the fact that for a tom to be worthwhile, he will have to have

a proven ability to reproduce his own quality—and to have established this in the first place. Usually, this can only be achieved on the show bench; therefore, if a tom is purchased and fails to make the grade at the shows, it will have no future from the breeding viewpoint in most instances. Thus it is better to use the established toms of already successful breeders. Only if the breed is so unusual that toms are not freely available is it worthwhile to purchase a male. Of course, if a breed is not yet well established in your country, then importing a good stud tom has more merit—but this is an expensive business and not generally viable to a novice breeder.

A breeding queen does not have to be an outstanding individual to become the foundation of your program, but she does need to be sound for all of her features. She should come from a stud that has a proven record of linebreeding to type. If finances allow, two queens will give you a greater opportunity to either concentrate on one line or to run quite separate, but distantly related, lines and see how they develop. The average person will no doubt begin with kittens, but, from a breeder's viewpoint, there is greater merit in waiting a while and purchasing a young adult from a good cattery. The experienced breeder will be better able to judge the female once she has matured somewhat; at that point she may even have picked up a few prizes in competition. Such a queen will, of course, be more expensive, but if she is to be the cornerstone of your future line she is a wise investment. Do not hurry the purchase of breeding stock; instead, visit numerous shows to become familiar with the breed and who's who in it.

REGISTRATION

It is essential for any cat purchased for breeding purposes to be eligible for placement on the active register of the appropriate organization of a particular country. In the USA and Australia there are a number of such bodies. In the UK there is a single registry controlled by the Governing Council of the Cat Fancy (GCCF), and it is this one which is described here. Others will differ slightly in their rules; interested parties should write to the registry of their choice in order to obtain full details.

In the UK, cats will be placed either on the active or non-active registers. The latter indicates that a kitten was sold as a pet, as the breeder did not consider it suitable for breeding purposes. Should such a kitten be bred from, its progeny cannot be placed on the active register. All other cats are placed on the active register. A kitten cannot be registered under one month of age; the upper limit for a cat is two years of age, unless the Council should accept extenuating situations at their discretion.

The breeder of your cats should supply you with at least a three-generation pedigree. This will show the forebears and indicate their registration numbers, if all were registered, and "unregistered" on those that were not. The breeder may supply you with a certified pedigree issued by the appropriate body, or you may apply for one yourself on payment of a small fee. The breeder will supply you with the transfer form so that the cats can be placed in your own name.

You are strongly advised to obtain the full regulations of the registration body, as these will inform you of many aspects the beginner might not appreciate. These include such matters as which breeds are ineligible for Best in Show awards, a factor which may influence your choice of breed; therefore, the rules of the governing body are required before, not after, you have purchased a kitten or cat. At the time you order a copy of the regulations, it is also wise to purchase the official standard of the breed, as this will be your means of reference to the points required on a quality cat of your chosen variety.

BREEDING AGE

A queen will normally have her first estrus cycle when she is between five and nine months of age, but this can vary—a kitten of three months has been known to come into heat. Likewise, estrus may come as late as 12 months, and to a degree this may be controlled by the time of the year in which a kitten was born. Cats are polyestrous, which means they have numerous reproductive cycles in any breeding season, as compared with the monoestrous situation seen in dogs. The queen has two or three breeding seasons over a single year; these are normally from January to May, July and August, or through September. These correspond to those of wild species in different parts of the world and are so arranged to ensure that, by the time the young are born and requiring increasing amounts of food, the hours of daylight are increasing and there are greater amounts of prey species, also with young to care for. Under domestic conditions, it is possible to virtually have a full year of seasons by the use of artificial daylight, a situation that exists in most homes.

During each season the queen will have estrus cycles of about three to six days in duration, and these will recur every 14 days or so. It is not wise to allow a young kitten to be mated, for, even if she becomes pregnant, it is likely that the kittens will lack vigor. In addition, the stress of the birth will most certainly stunt the full development of the female. Therefore, the earliest age at which the queen should be mated is nine months.

The male is sexually mature at about nine months old, but, as you will require the services of an experienced tom for your young queen, he will be older than this, as first he must prove his worth in exhibition and in progeny. It is a good idea to see examples of a particular tom's offspring before choosing him to mate with your queen.

The gestation period in cats can vary from 63 to 69 days, with 65 being the average. Premature births prior to day 57 are likely to be stillborn; the same is true for those over 70 days.

SELECTING A STUD

If a breeding is planned, then no time should be lost in deciding upon a suitable mate for your female(s). In order to find one, you are recommended to consult the breeder of your cats so that you can benefit from his own experience. The tom should excel in those features in which your queen lacks quality. The use of excel does not mean overdeveloped; mating with a cat that has an overdeveloped feature(s) is termed compensationary mating and is not recommended. In such a case, a female with, say, short ears, is mated to a male with rather long ears. The correct method is to mate to a male with ideal length ears, as this will keep genetic variability down for ear size; the overall breeding trend will

Although some breeds of cat mature as early as nine months of age, most breeders wait until their cats are at least one year old. In addition, some breeds are not considered fully grown until 18 months.

then be towards producing cats with better ears, without the risk of numerous large-eared cats turning up in litters. This same theory holds true for all other features, and this is why it is important to have as much background information on the male, his ancestors, and his progeny as possible. Once a male has been located, tentative dates can be arranged; they will be confirmed once the queen comes into heat. The fee should then be discussed. At this time it is wise to check whether the tom has been tested for feline leukemia and to find out how recently such a test was undertaken. The owner of the tom should correctly show you evidence that the male has received his full quota of vaccinations and boosters—and likewise you should have with you evidence that the same is true of the queen. Normally, in the event of no kittens resulting from a mating, the stud owner will allow a second mating free of charge. This is not obligatory, however, so the matter should be raised beforehand; all such arrangements are better for being placed into writing and signed by both parties. Many disputes could have been settled had this been attended to in the first place.

THE QUEEN IN HEAT

The female cat does not exhibit physical vaginal signs of being in estrus as does a female dog; instead, she shows this both by her behavior and by her rather eerie sounds, or "calls." She may become extremely affectionate towards you and will roll over and present her backside to you. She will become restless and, if you are not observant about restricting her movements, will wish to be outdoors looking for a suitable partner. She may even vanish for a few days when in estrus, so care must be exercised at such times. In addition, the queen may twitch her tail to one side and tread the floor with her hindlegs. Once she has had such a cycle it will leave a firm impression on your mind!

At this time, the queen is ready to be taken to the tom and left for two to three days. After the mating has been completed, she can be collected and taken home.

COURTING CATS

The courtship ritual of cats is both interesting and aggressive in its different stages. I will describe the behavior of wild species, because this will underline an aspect that may have importance in domestic cats where lack of fecundity is observed. Cats are induced ovulators as compared to dogs, which are spontaneous. This means that a queen does not automatically release eggs for fertilization to take place but must be induced to do so by mechanical and possibly other means. The mechanical means is, of course, stimulation by the penis of the male, but there may be psychological actions that also trigger ovulation by ripening the follicles of the ovary to the point that the eggs are then shed during coitus.

A female will normally attract a number of males around her but will not initially allow mating to take place. Instead she will lay around and watch the males battle it out for rights to mate with her. In such fights ears are badly bitten, faces scratched, and so on, and only the toughest of males remain in contention for the affections of the queen. However, it is not always the first winner of such encounters that actually mates with the female, though he will no doubt do so in due course. It is thought that by this hard process all the weak, underage, or elderly males are removed, so that only the best are left to perpetuate their genes.

The next stage is for the male to approach the queen, who will have nothing to do with such a robust romeo and will promptly hiss, spit, and strike out. Even males that are considerably bigger than the queen treat her with great respect at such times and will not attempt to press home their desires. The tom will "talk" to the queen, and after a few refusals she will eventually allow him near her; she will roll over in front of him, lay on her stomach, and raise her rear end. The male will mount her and bite into her neck, perhaps treading on her with his hindlegs. Coitus is very quick in cats, and soon the male will dismount and rest. The queen will groom herself and then invite a further mating. As the female becomes more sexually aroused, the male begins to tire, and soon it is the female who is purring and trying to encourage the male onto greater things. It often happens that at such times, in

A blue-cream longhair mother with her litter of cream and blue longhairs. It is always a good idea to study the genetics of the colors you are interesting in breeding.

the wild, other males will mate with the female, who is able to bear kittens from different males. The mating ritual may last two to four days, with a very high number of "ties" taking place over this period.

Occasionally, an apparently successful mating does not result in a pregnancy, and the female will either prolong her estrus and still be receptive to males after she is returned home, or she will come back into estrus very quickly. In any case, after a mating she will remain in estrus for a variable number of hours, though she will not allow other toms to mate with her if she has in fact conceived. A failed mating may be a psychological problem in that the queen lacked sufficient mental stimulation. A further period of time with the stud may prove successful, for it is also thought that familiarity plays a part in the whole feline courtship ritual. However, if a second mating is not productive, then another male should be found and the queen should receive a veterinary examination to check that she is not suffering from any sort of problem that might make pregnancy impossible.

PREGNANCY

Assuming that the queen is pregnant, she should be treated as normal during the early prenatal period. The signs of pregnancy and its development will proceed approximately according to the following calendar of events.

24 hours: Ovulation takes place; ova are produced and released from the ovaries.

24-36 hours: Fertilization of the ova.

14 days (2 weeks): Implantation of the embryos.

21-35 days (3-5 weeks): Pregnancy can be diagnosed by a veterinarian by palpation. The small, pea-sized embryos may be up to 2.5 cm (1 in) in length by the fifth week.

21-28 days (3-4 weeks): The nipples of the queen may become pink, especially during the female's first pregnancy.

35-42 days (5-6 weeks): The abdomen starts to become enlarged and the queen shows a gain in weight. However, if only one or two kittens are present in a large female, abdominal swellings may not be apparent until just prior to the birth of the offspring.

49 days (7 weeks): The head and body of the kittens may be discerned by careful palpation. In addition, the skeletons of the kittens can be seen by radiography.

49-56 days (7-8 weeks): The mammary glands become noticeably enlarged. The queen will be consuming up to twice her normal rations by this time, having built up to this over the previous three weeks.

56-63 days (8-9 weeks): The queen will become much more restless and will start to search for a suitable site in which to give birth. It is advisable to keep the female indoors during her last seven to ten days of pregnancy, but up until then she should be allowed to exercise as normal, as this is important in maintaining her muscle condition.

56-72 days (8-10 weeks): The big occasion should happen around the 65th day—any earlier than day 57 or later than day 70, there are likely to be either miscarriages or problem births, in which case veterinary assistance will be vital—advise the vet if no kittens have been produced by the 65th day (and, of course, at any earlier time if you have reason to suspect the queen is experiencing undue discomfort).

KITTENING BOX

About ten days prior to the expected birth, it is a good idea to provide a suitable kittening box for the queen. This should be a well-enclosed structure, as cats prefer a darkened situation in which to have their babies. Such units may be available from your local pet shop, but if not they can be made using either lightweight woods or by cutting down a cardboard box. Leave an access hole with a front lip on it and, if you live in cooler climates, a hole in the top so that an infrared lamp can be suspended if necessary; a height of one meter (3 ft 3 in) is the minimum height for this.

It may well be that the female will not agree with your choice of site and may prefer to select her own. If she does, place the box in her chosen site; if she rejects it again, it is probably because she doesn't like the box! You cannot make a female cat subscribe to your views on these matters, so your final answer is simply to place disposable material in the spot she selects and to take matters from there by trying to make this as secretive as possible for her. Sometimes cats will instinctively remove kittens a few days after birth and find another place to rear them; within reason, the queen should be given her own way.

USEFUL UTENSILS

The following items are suggested to have on hand once the births have been completed.

1) A sharp pair of blunt-ended and curved scissors.
2) Surgical gloves of the disposable type.
3) A set of scales for weighing the kittens.
4) A length of cotton.
5) A heating pad or a hot water bottle.
6) Plenty of old newspaper and old toweling.
7) A kitten feeding bottle for use if the situation warrants.

BIRTH (PARTURITION)

In the vast majority of cases, the queen will give birth to her kittens with no problems at all—and on many occasions the first the owner knows of this is upon waking up in the morning to find the mother lying restfully and the babies all snuggled up to her to feed. If you are able to witness events, they will proceed in the following manner. Parturition may be divided into three broad time stages. The first is when the cervix opens and the kitten begins its journey down the oviduct. This period may last for up to 24 hours but is usually considerably less. The female will retire to her nesting quarters and her breathing may become quicker. She may start scratching at the bedding and preparing it for the kittens, and in the latter stages she may start to pant. The second stage usually lasts for no more than 30 minutes, but it has been known to go much longer than this. However, if no births have occurred by the 45-minute mark, then it is best if the vet is notified of this fact.

Before your female is bred, you must be sure that she is in the best of health, as pregnancy, kittening, and nursing will take a lot out of her.

A few weeks before the impending labor, prepare a birthing area for your queen. This area should be warm and should contain a bed or a nest box.

During this stage the female is now able to help the movement of the kittens down the oviduct, which to this point has been by automatic or involuntary muscular action. The queen "strains" and licks at her vulva, and there will probably be a liquid discharge from the vagina containing a small amount of blood. The number of contractions increases and they are soon very frequent, and the third and final stage of birth will then commence.

A dark jelly-like mass will be seen coming from the vagina; this is the kitten in its water bag (amniotic sac). This will burst, and the kitten itself will then be presented either with some membrane still covering its head, or without it, as it may have been broken during the act of birth. The kitten may still be attached to its afterbirth via the umbilical cord, or the latter may be severed prior to birth and the afterbirth retained in the female, to be discharged prior to the birth of the next kitten. However, if the cord is still attached to the kitten, then the queen will invariably bite through this and may eat the afterbirth as well. This greenish mass is

The queen should become familiar with the birthing area prior to delivery since this is where she will rear the kittens.

actually of nutritious content; it is the remainder of the placenta, which provided the kitten with a medium for the transmission of food during its development.

Out of all births, about one-third of them will be hindfeet first. This is normally a problem only insomuch as the birth may take a little longer if it is the first kitten. It is not a breech birth, as is sometimes implied, for a breech birth is when the hindquarters are presented but the legs are facing the head. Even with a kitten in this position, the female will normally give birth without problems.

The time lapse between births can vary considerably from one queen to the next and from one breed to another, so no hard and fast rules can be applied. Sometimes a queen may give birth to about half of the litter and then suspend matters for another 24 hours; provided that she shows no signs of stress, this will not be a problem. However, after what is thought to be the final kitten of the first period, the vet should be in attendance to check over the queen, and he will then advise you if the full litter has not been presented.

Each birth is a complete entity comprised of water sac, a kitten, and an afterbirth. Be sure that each afterbirth has been accounted for; if one has been retained, inform your vet at once. The afterbirths can be removed and discarded, or the queen may be allowed to consume one if required. The number of kittens born can range from one to eight, but the average litter will be three to five in most breeds. The female has four pairs of teats, and the kittens will each fix themselves to a particular one which will be used consistently.

HELPING AT THE BIRTH

The majority of females are excellent mothers that get on with the whole process with no bother at all. However, some queens, especially those of foreign breeds (such as the Siamese), can become quite tense at this time and may even delay birth if things are not to their liking. Others may become distraught to the point that a vet may need to administrate a tranquilizer. Quiet reassurance from the owner is needed as the births become imminent. If the mother fails

A male Somali kitten.

to break the umbilical cord, you must do it for her, but do not rush at this. Instead, ensure that no membrane is still covering the kitten's face—if it is, carefully remove it or the infant may be asphyxiated. In the final one to two minutes before being severed, it is thought that an important amount of blood flows from the placenta through the umbilical cord to the kitten; therefore, it is important not to rush. However, after a couple of minutes, tie a piece of cotton thread about 2.5 cm (1 in) from the kitten's belly along the cord. Next, using the sterilized scissors, cut the cord on the afterbirth side of the knot, thus freeing the kitten from it. Some blood will flow from the afterbirth, which can quickly be removed. The cord itself will shrivel up over the next few days. Some breeders advocate cutting the cord with their fingers, but this has no merit and could even introduce bacteria, for the cord will still bleed and need tying.

The kitten can now be given a brisk toweling, which should ensure that it is breathing all right. If it is not, hold the kitten carefully up-

After weighing each kitten as it is born, place it back by the mother's side so it can begin to nurse.

side down and stroke it with your fingers after the fashion of milking a cow—commencing from its rear end. This should help discharge any mucous that might be blocking the air passage. Once the kitten is seen to be all right it can be placed with its mother. If a kitten feels very cold, it should either be placed onto a hot water bottle that has been wrapped in cloth or immersed into a container of warm water with a temperature of 38°C (100°F) so that only its head remains above water. Massage the kitten for a few moments; when it shows signs of life, give it a brisk rub with a towel and place it with its mother, or into a warm box if she is already straining with another kitten's birth.

It is wise to weigh all kittens at birth and to record their weight gain on a daily basis. This has the extra advantage (other than compiling data on a female's breeding record) that if a weight gain is not recorded, or, worse, actually goes down, then you know something is amiss. It may be the first sign of a problem before other clinical signs become apparent.

BREEDING PROBLEMS

The vast majority of pregnancies will terminate with healthy kittens, but occasionally things can go wrong.

Pseudopregnancy: In this condition, the female is convinced that she is pregnant; this motivates other, more physical processes to commence. Her nipples may turn pink, and she may even produce milk in her mammary glands. Once it is obvious that she is not pregnant, which your vet will confirm, she can be treated with hormones. She then will come back into estrus as normal. It is essential that she be treated, for failure to do so might result in problems resulting from her condition.

Illness during pregnancy: In the event that the queen becomes ill during the pregnancy, do not attempt any form of home remedy, as such a treatment may have a negative effect on the developing embryos. Consult your veterinarian without delay.

Abortion and resorbtion: A fetus may be resorbed or aborted, depending on its state of development. Vitamin A deficiency is believed to create an imbalance that prompts resorbtion early in the pregnancy as well as abortions around day 50. An inadequate or insufficient diet will increase the risk of resorbtion, as this is nature's way of controlling populations when the food supply is inadequate to support the mother and her offspring—the adult will always take prior importance in such situations. Bacterial, parasitic, and viral infections may invade the reproductive system whilst, obviously, physical conditions (such as accidents or undue stress late in the pregnancy) will prompt abortions or stillborn deaths—the Siamese has suffered more than most breeds from these various conditions.

The genetic factor is also important, not only in the problem of resorbtion but in many other matters relating to breeding and health in general. The queen may be from a line that shows a greater than normal incidence of abortion, which highlights a more complex underlying problem.

Pelvic problems: A queen may have a rather small pelvis, may be giving birth to a very large kitten, or may have sustained pelvic damage that has not shown itself at that point in time. In any of these circumstances your vet may de-

In a few weeks, the kittens will begin to take on personalities all their own. They will also be learning more and more about the world outside the nest box.

As the kittens get older, you will notice that the queen will leave the nest box for progressively longer periods of time.

cide to perform a Caesarean operation in which the kitten is removed by cutting through the abdomen and uterus. The operation does not prevent the queen from rearing her young nor from having future litters. However, the advice of your vet should be taken about this aspect, as it may be wiser not to use such a queen for future breeding, depending on the nature of the case.

Kitten stuck during birth: Occasionally a kitten may not be able to make its entrance into the world; although visible to you and in spite of the queen's straining, the kitten is jammed in the vaginal passage. After scrubbing your hands, put on your surgical gloves and try to help the queen by firmly but gently pulling at the kitten. Time your efforts to co-ordinate with her contractions. In most cases, the kitten will be born vaginally. If not, then you must rush the queen to the vet's clinic straight away unless the vet can get to you.

Postnatal problems: Should the queen start to bleed after giving birth or should any undue amount of liquid be seen from her vagina, then contact your vet immediately. Do likewise if she seems disinterested in the kittens or if, in spite of their efforts to suckle from her, one or more of the kittens starts to cry out.

KITTEN REARING

When the kittens are born, they are blind and quite helpless and can just crawl around enough to find the mother's teats. However, development is relatively rapid. The initial milk they suckle is called colostrum and is very rich in antibodies which will protect the babies from illness during the first few important weeks of life. The queen may not eat at all during the first 12 hours after giving birth but will then normally eat with renewed vigor, as she must keep up her own strength and provide sufficient milk for the kittens.

During the first three to four weeks of their lives, the kittens will receive all the nourishment they need from their mother, but after this period they can gradually be introduced to solid foods. The mother will wash the kittens continually; this will stimulate them to defecate. Your own involvement should be to keep the kitten box nice and clean and to keep a check on the weights of the kittens. Do not let children pester either the mother or the kittens at this time.

The eyes of the kittens will start to open about the eighth day, but this is very variable and may be later than this. The color of the eyes will take on the adult shade by the time they are about three months old. Teeth erupt quite early, and by the age of eight weeks the "milk" teeth will be present, after which the permanent teeth will then start to grow and should be fully developed by about the four-month mark. The kittens get better at crawling over the first 14 days, and by about this time they may just about be able to totter, rather shakily, on all four legs. At three weeks of age they will be walking quite well, though they are still a little unsteady, and just after this will also be able to run in an equally unsteady manner. However, by five weeks of age they will be running around much better and will be eager to investigate everything around them. They will play for short periods but then need to sleep. It is important that they have sufficient rest so they can put on muscle and strong bone, rather than use up all their energy running around, which will overtax them.

By the third to fourth week, you can begin training the kittens to use a litter tray by placing them in this after naps and shortly after they have eaten their first solids. They learn to use

A copper-eyed white Persian kitten. Very young kittens will need a great deal of sleep.

the litter tray very quickly—but it must be kept clean.

The kittens will no doubt show interest in the mother's food as soon as they are able to stagger over to her dish. At about three or four weeks of age you can offer them shredded pieces of lean meat or try them on the better brands of canned cat foods. They will eat very little but very often. Their mother will teach them how to wash, and she will supervise and help them out, often to their annoyance! Although many things are instinctive to cats, some behaviors are learned. Mating techniques are a mixture of both, as is the technique of using the paws for grooming.

The maternal bond of a mother is very strong early in the kitten's lives, but as they reach the age of independence, at about ten to 16 weeks (nearer to the latter), it weakens; after they reach five months of age, the queen is far less tolerant of the kittens, whom she will cuff with greater force if they persist in trying to suckle from her. In the majority of cases she will have weaned them by about ten weeks of age. The comforting action of kneading with the front feet persists throughout most cats' lives, and they will do this on your lap, or on any soft material—some cats may also develop the habit of sucking their paws, and this may also continue into adulthood.

HAND-REARING OR FOSTERING

Just occasionally, for one of many reasons, it may be necessary to hand-rear one or more kittens. This is a time-consuming operation, as the kittens will need to feed every two hours, 24 hours a day, during the first week. During week two, the overnight feedings can be reduced to every four hours. In the third week the meals can be reduced to just one overnight feed, with day feedings every three hours. The kitten baby bottle used must be kept spotlessly clean by being sterilized immediately after use. In an emergency either an eye dropper or a doll's bottle can be used.

Substitute cat's milk can be purchased; however, if this is not available, puppy milk powder will be suitable, as will evaporated cow's milk, as both contain about the same protein level as cat's milk. The temperature of the milk should be as close to 38°C (100°F) as possible. Use hot water to dissolve the powder and then cool this to the required temperature. The milk should be fed by placing gentle, steady pressure on the kitten's bottle; you do not want the kitten to be gulping the milk, as it might enter the air passage and choke the kitten.

As the kittens reach weaning age, the amount of milk given to them can be reduced, for it must be remembered that milk is not a natural food or drink for a cat other than during its infant stage, though most will readily take it throughout their lives.

Comparison of milks: The following indicates relative composition of milks of different animals. The high protein content of dogs and cats reflects their carnivorous lifestyle. The fat content indicates the amount that is required to maintain body heat. The low percentage in cats supports the view that domestic breeds originate in warm climates; the fat content in polar bears, for example, is 30%.

Domestic cat—protein–10.1%; fat–6.3%; lactose–4.4%.
Domestic dog:—protein–5.4-10.6%; fat–8.5-13.5%; lactose–2.4-4.2%.
Cow:—protein–3.2%; fat–3.6%; lactose–4.7%.
Human:—protein–1.2%; fat–3.7%; lactose–6.8%.

Fostering: If kittens are to be fostered, this should be done at the earliest possible age, for in this way rejection by the foster mother is less likely. The foster mother should be examined for signs of parasites and, of course, must have kittens of almost the same age as the orphans; in addition, she must have spare teat capacity. Place the orphan in amongst her kittens, as this way it will take on some of the smell of these; alternatively, smear a small amount of butter or similar substance on the orphan, and as the queen washes this off she will adopt the infant as her own.

Opposite: Keep in mind that mother's milk is the best food for young kittens.

Head study of a Russian Blue.

BREEDING THEORY

An understanding of the genetic aspect of breeding is not essential but is most certainly beneficial, as it can explain many things and save a breeder much time and cost in wasted efforts. Those breeders who, in past years, bred superb animals without having any knowledge of the workings of heredity did so by applying the laws of inheritance, even though they did not understand them. Applying genetic theory to a breeding program does not ensure that you will produce better cats; it merely increases the likelihood of doing so. Other factors, such as your ability to select from stock bred, the way the cats are fed, and the way they are managed, will be crucial factors that can make or break the best of genetic programs. The genes of a cat give it a very fixed potential, but whether it achieves this will be a direct reflection of external factors.

GENES

As you know, the body of any of the higher animals is composed of millions of cells, and within each cell is a nucleus, which is akin to the cell's headquarters. Within the nucleus are a number of minute bodies called genes, and it is these that are the units of inheritance. Based on the information given out by the genes, cells develop into skeletal tissue, skin, hair, and so on. These genes are held together rather like beads on a string, and the string is known as a chromosome. We do not know how many genes there are on a chromosome, but we do know how many chromosomes many species of animals have. Most cat species, including the domestic, have 38 chromosomes arranged in 18 identical pairs plus one pair—known as the sex chromosomes—in which one is much shorter than the other.

The number of chromosome pairs in any animal species is normally consistent; humans have 23 pairs, dogs have 39, and so on. The total number of chromosomes present is called the diploid number, whilst the half number of these, present in the germ cells, is known as the haploid number.

Genes control all features of a cat, from its external appearance to its internal skeleton and all of the inner organs and tissues. They also control abnormalities and have a direct bearing on a cat's ability to fight off disease. Their control over intangible traits such as docility, aggression, motherhood ability, and so on is less well understood but is believed to be considerable. It will thus be appreciated that genes are extremely important biological units.

It is often practical to use color transmission as an example of gene action, and we will do so in this short study of genetics, but it must be re-

A white shorthaired kitten.

membered that all other aspects work in much the same manner—indeed, they are often very complex, so that color is one of the more simple examples of showing how genes work.

Let us return to the pairs of chromosomes mentioned. The genes are arranged along these in a very fixed way, so that those on the opposite chromosome appear at the same location; the specific site of a gene is known as its locus. The genes that control color all appear at the same loci on each of the chromosomes. The pair of chromosomes is made up of one from each parent, so that each parent supplied a set of genes for color (and size, length of fur, and all other features). But why doesn't the number of chromosomes double up at each new generation, you may be asking?

The bushy tail of this marmalade house pet is a product of genetics.

CELL DIVISION

There are basically two types of cells in a cat's body; the normal body cells, which are called somatic, and the germ cells found in the reproductive organs. A cat grows from a single fertilized ovum at conception into a full adult by a process of simple cell division. Basically, the chromosomes of each cell divide into two chromatids, and each chromatid migrates to the opposite end of the cell. The cell then divides so that each of the daughter cells contains one chromatid from each of the original pair. These then reproduce themselves to create a pair of chromosomes as in the original cell. By this process of division, the number of cells doubles and doubles again, but always retains paired chromosomes exactly like those of the original cell. The genes of normal body cells are referred to as being autosomal or autosomes.

In the sex cells, the pair of chromosomes come together and wrap around each other, and during this process the chromatids thus cross over each other. The chromosomes then unwind and migrate to opposite ends of the cells. How-

ever, during the crossing over stage, certain genes may have changed places with the equivalent gene on the other chromosome. The cell divides so that only one chromosome of each original pair is in the daughter cell. The chromatids of the chromosome then reproduce themselves, and the cell divides so that each daughter cell contains a single chromosome; these are the actual sex cells or gametes—ova or sperm as the case may be. When a sperm enters an ova to fertilize it, the double quantity of chromosomes is restored, and the animal grows by simple cell division, as explained. The fertilized egg is known as a zygote. The fixed number of chromosome pairs is thus passed from one generation to the next without increasing in numbers.

SEX DETERMINATION

It was stated that, in the sex cells, the chromosomes are different and are thus identifiable on that basis. One appears much like all the other chromosomes and can carry genes for all the cat's features; this one is termed the X chromosome. The other is much shorter and is solely concerned with the sex of the animal and those features which affect this—reproductive organs, relative size, and traits such as sexual drives. This chromosome is called the Y chromosome. If a cat has two X chromosomes (one from each

Opposite: A pair of Persian kittens. Understanding genetics will give you an idea of the possible products of a mating.

parent), then its genetic formula is *XX*, a female, but if it receives a *Y* chromosome from its father then it will be *XY*, a tom. Within any litter, the theoretic probability is that there will be an equal number of queens and toms, for any recombination of mating *XX* with *XY* must produce 50% of each sex. However, as any breeder knows, a litter may be all toms, all queens, or any ratio in between; this is due to the random nature of gene combinations. What is important to remember in any genetic calculation is that each parent can pass to its offspring only one of its two genes for a given locus. Exceptions to this rule are possible but can be ignored for now, as they represent genetic abnormalities.

GENE EXPRESSION

Different genes have different powers of making their presence apparent, and we can use the popular example of tabbies and black to illustrate this fact. If a purebreeding tabby is mated to a purebreeding black, then all of the offspring will be tabby. This one mating can give us much to discuss. The use of the term purebreeding is important in this example because breeding a non-purebreeding tabby to a black would produce a different situation in the kittens.

Purebreeding or homozygous: A cat is homozygous for its color (or any other feature) when both of its genes at a given locus are for the same color.

Non-purebreeding or heterozygous: A cat is heterozygous for a color when its genes for color are different from each parent. If the tabby and black parents are purebreeding, and if tabby kittens are produced in the litter, then there has been no mixing of the genes. Production of a sort of halfway house, as at first might be thought, is not really possible; genes are not like paints, as they do not blend to create new colors but tend to keep their own identity.

By using letters to represent the genes, we can see just how the all-tabby litter was possible. The tabby will be given the formula *AA* and the black *aa*. The tabby can only pass on an *A* gene and the black can pass on only an *a*, so the only recombination of genes from such a mating is *Aa*—heterozygous tabbies. The tabby is assigned the capital letter because its color pattern

is known to be dominant to that of black, which is termed a recessive. Geneticists use capital and lowercase letters so that in any formula, one can see which colors are dominant to others. It can be seen that a dominant gene need only be present in single dose to reveal itself; further, there is no visual difference between the purebreeding tabby *AA* and the heterozygous tabby *Aa*; only further matings will establish the exact genetic state of the two types.

The visual appearance of a cat, its phenotype, may differ from its breeding state, or genotype; in other words, two apparently identical cats may be totally different as to how that similarity was arrived at in breeding terms. The letter *A* is used to denote tabby because the tabby color is actually the feline equivalent of agouti, the normal wild pattern seen in cats and many other animal species. There are a number of loci which control the color of a cat, and one is called the agouti locus. Should this gene mutate, then the mutant gene carries the same letter as that from which it is derived, but as a lowercase or, rarely, as a capital with a superscript if the mutant is actually dominant to the normal wild type. This way, confusion in genetic formulae is less likely than if one were to use different letters for alternative genes at the same locus.

With the basic information so far detailed, it can easily be seen that if an *AA* tabby is crossed with another *AA* tabby, then all the kittens would be pure tabby *AA*, for no other combinations are possible; likewise, black *aa* with another *aa* cat will produce all *aa* black kittens. A cat can thus be purebreeding for both dominant and recessive genes, but only when present in double dose.

Opposite: A pair of white Persian kittens. Before breeding two cats, remember that each parent can pass only one gene at each locus to its offspring.

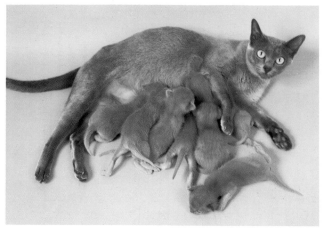

A Burmese mother with her litter. The Burmese comes in four colors: sable, blue, platinum, and champagne.

HETEROZYGOUS CROSSINGS

By pairing two of the kittens resulting from our mating of a tabby and a black, we can see what happens and, in so doing, can establish the fact that the genes have retained their own identity. If Aa is mated to Aa, then the A of the queen might unite with the A of the tom to give AA—pure tabby. However, it has an equal chance of receiving an a gene to produce Aa, a heterozygous tabby. Likewise the queen's a gene can unite with either the A or the a of the tom to give aA and aa respectively. The full set of theoretical combinations is therefore AA, Aa, aA, and aa, and no matter how many kittens are born to these parents over numerous matings, they will all have one of these four genotypes, as no other combinations are possible.

Did you notice that in three of the four possibilities, an A was present? This means that these kittens would be visually tabby. In the fourth case, however, both the genes are aa, a double recessive; with no tabby present the genes will show themselves as visually black, just as in one of the grandparents. The ratio of 3:1 is a standard expectation when two contrasting genes are paired from both parents. Another aspect you may have noticed is the reappearance of AA, purebreeding tabby. As there is no visual difference between the pure and non-pure tabbies, it can be appreciated how important it is to know the genetic state of a cat. Another way of work-

ing out theoretical expectations is to use a checkerboard diagram, as this is useful once one starts to deal with more than one pair of different genes. On the top and sides, the individual gametes are placed for each parent (one parent on the top and one down the side); it is then easy to fill in the squares with all the combinations without the risk of overlooking any.

Checkerboard diagram to show theoretical expectations of mating heterozygous tabbies.

Tabby Aa (gametes are A or a)

	A	a
A	AA	Aa
a	aA	aa

Tabby Aa

Note that Aa and aA are exactly the same and would normally be presented as such—aA would be transposed to read Aa but has been left so as not to confuse the beginner.

RANDOM COMBINATION

In all genetic calculations, all possible permutations of the genes must be taken into account, because it is a matter of chance which gametes (ova or sperms) mate with each other at the point of fertilization. It is possible, in the mating discussed, for the whole litter to be black, tabby, or any ratio of these. In actual fact, the chances are strongly in favor of tabbies—of non-pure tabbies in particular. However, whilst all of one type could turn up in a single litter, it would be found that over many litters the ratio of 3:1 would become more accurate.

A piece of useful genetic terminology is that used to describe a cat that carries a "hidden" gene in its make-up. A tabby which was known to carry black would be called a tabby split for black, and this would be written as tabby/black. The color in front of the oblique line is visual, while that behind it is present but non-visual, being masked by the dominant color. Using random combination of genes with a checkerboard diagram, you can now work out the result of pairing a purebreeding (homozygous) tabby to a tabby split for black. The result is 100% tabbies, but the ratios are different than those seen in earlier matings because 50% are purebreeding (*AA*) and 50% are tabby split for black (*Aa*). If a pure black is paired to a tabby split for black, the result will be 50% tabby split for black and 50% pure visual blacks.

With this very basic understanding of gene action, it can be seen that if two supposedly purebreeding tabbies were mated and produced just a single black kitten in the litter, this would automatically show that neither of the tabbies was purebreeding. The black kitten could only be produced if it received a gene for black from each parent. (It is assumed that no second male was involved in having mated with the tabby queen, but even if it had it would establish the fact that the queen was non-purebreeding for her color.)

TEST MATINGS

Should one have a situation where one has *AA* and *Aa* breeding stock, then it might be important to establish which were which, but this can be a long and expensive business involving a series of test matings. In such a case, one would pair the cats to a recessive black. If the kittens were all tabby, then this would suggest that the tabby was purebreeding, because if it was split for black there would have been a 50/50 chance that at least one black kitten would turn up. However, the fact that no blacks turned up would not be sufficient proof that the tabby was *AA* and further matings would be needed. It will be appreciated that establishing which is the *Aa* cat is much easier than establishing which is *AA*; this is because a single black kitten reveals that there is a heterozygous parent, whereas no black kittens proves nothing but merely suggests a probability which needs more testing.

Breeders who are just starting out often test-mate two of their cats in order to find out their probable genotypes.

It is important to remember that the tabby or agouti coat pattern is dominant in cats.

MUTATIONS

Within any species of animal there is clearly a wide range of variability for certain features, which is why no two individuals are quite the same, and this state must remain so in order for the species to adapt. Genes mutate within a species quite often, but the change such a gene brings about is so small that it is not even noticed within any given time period, but over long time spans it is responsible for speciation—the creation of new species.

However, just occasionally, a gene will mutate in a big way, and such a mutation will clearly show itself in the individual carrying it. In wild species, the common examples of this occurrence are seen in melanistic individuals, which are all black. Other common mutations are albinism, to a greater or lesser degree, and brown and blue, the latter two colors being rarer. Normally, a major mutation will not favor the individual carrying it, either because it is noticed by its prey or predator species more easily, or because it may result in rejection by its own species at times of searching for a mate—if markings are important at such times. Gene mutation has given rise to all of the colors, hair length, and bodily changes seen in domestic cats, some as original mutations and some as recombination of such mutations with other mutants. Selective breeding of variations already in existence in cats has given rise to the complete array of breeds and color shades.

When a gene mutates, its chemical composition is changed. This dictates how that gene will show itself from that point onwards. What induces a gene to mutate is not fully understood, but x-rays can produce such an effect, so it is thought that cosmic rays may be involved; in addition, mutations may occur from dietary causes or be linked to some other unknown factor. Once a gene has mutated, however, it then expresses itself in a predictable manner from that point onwards. Some mutations have appeal to breeders if they produce interesting colors, longer or silkier hair, long or short legs, and so on, but other mutations produce abnormal conditions such as freak animals with extra toes, faulty bone structure, and similar conditions. Sometimes a mutation may be totally restricted to a given feature, such as color, but others may affect other aspects of the animal as well as the color. These changes are usually internal and invariably of a negative nature, and it may be some time before the negatives show themselves in the population as a whole—by which time they are well established and more difficult to eradicate. One example of an abnormal mutation that established itself to a high degree is seen in the Manx cat, which is not a purebreeding animal but a heterozygote; in this breed, the double recessive situation is lethal. Thus mutations can be interesting to breeders but they can be equally risky, which is why experimental breeding to produce new varieties should not be undertaken without monitoring all offspring to see if there might be negative side effects. The advice of a qualified geneticist is always advisable for those developing new colors and breeds, as such a person will be aware of known risks with certain combinations of genes.

A brown tabby Manx. Manx cats have been selectively bred for taillessness. They were originally created by a mutated gene.

A pair of Manx cats, white and red tabby.

A Somali kitten. The Somali is basically a long-haired Abyssinian, and it comes in the same colors as its parent breed.

GENE LOCI

The locus or site of a given gene can be now looked at in relation to mutations. It is only when a normal gene mutates that it can actually be identified, and when this happens the locus can be named. The black gene in cats is the result of normal coloration being disturbed to the point that the yellow pigment is greatly reduced or removed from the wild agouti color. Black gene mutants are thus at the agouti locus; however, the cat has many loci controlling color, so it is possible for an individual to carry numerous normal and mutant genes at the same time. Likewise, a gene at a given locus may mutate numerous times so that at that locus there may be a number of alternatives to the normal wild type gene. When this happens, the mutants are arranged in a series based on their known or believed powers of expression in relation to each other. A cat may carry only two contrasting genes for any given locus, so it could have one for normal color and one for any of the mutants known to exist at that locus—or it could have two of the mutants, one on each chromosome.

There are known to be about 13 different loci in cats which each have mutant genes at them, so, obviously, there are thousands of potential combinations. Breeders can only work with perhaps three or four pairs at the most, and even then the potential offspring from these in all the theoretical varieties are unlikely to be seen because of the number of kittens that would have to be produced. Nonetheless, this does not negate the value of genetic theory, which can still be applied to most breeder's programs.

It is worth pointing out that the genetics of all mammals is very similar, which is hardly surprising since the genes will have a common origin at some point in the past. This means that information gained on one species may well have application to another—or give an indication of possibilities. Where an animal has a very high reproductive rate, as in the mouse, geneticists are able to explore more easily the full potential of the combinations of genes. Thus, where genetics are concerned, a cat breeder is not restricted to literature purely on cats, as information devoted to other species will most certainly widen one's total concept on the workings of genetics.

TWO GENE PAIRS

In previous examples discussed, only one pair of genes was considered, but, knowing that mutants can be at different loci, what will happen when they are present in the same cat? We can look at this by taking our previous example, tabby and black, and adding the dilution factor. Let us assume that a tabby is split for both black and for dilution (blue)—this is possible because the two mutant genes are at different loci from each other. Such a tabby will have a genotype of *AaDd*, so it looks just like any other tabby. Should it mate with a cat of the same genotype, then the position is as follows: each cat could pass on either of its genes at each locus, so the gametes possible are *AD*, *Ad*, *aD*, and *ad*. Using the checkerboard we can see what will happen.

In this example we have come up with both black and blue cats from parents that were both visually tabby, and the overall ratio is 9:3:3:1, which is standard for two contrasting pairs of genes. It can be seen that it could take quite a number of matings before a blue cat turns up, but when it does it would be purebreeding for its color. The blue tabbies have different genotypes, and if these were crossed with each other, or any combination, then the results can be calculated just as in the example—why not try a few combinations and see what sort of kittens would (in theory) result?

Another aspect can now be added to your growing knowledge of genetics, and this is in respect to formulae which involve unknown genotypes. For example, of the blue tabbies, some are *AA* for agouti but others are *Aa*, thus split

Crossing two gene pairs to show segregation of the individual genes.

Tabby Parent *AaDd*

		AD	Ad	aD	ad
	AD	ADAD Tabby	ADAd Tabby	ADaD Tabby	ADad Tabby
Tabby Parent *AaDd*	Ad	AdAD Tabby	AdAd Blue Tabby	AdaD Tabby	Adad Blue Tabby
	aD	aDAD Tabby	aDAd Tabby	aDaD Black	aDad Black
	ad	adAD Tabby	adAd Blue Tabby	adaD Black	adad Blue

for black. If such cats were produced in a real breeding program, you would not know which were which; therefore, the formula for such a cat would be shown as *A-bb*, the dash indicating that only one gene is known for sure (the other could be *A* or *a*). This would obviously affect the onward breeding of the cat until it had been established which genotype it actually was—never assume such things in breeding until you are quite sure of them, as this is how so many unexpected colors or features turn up in a program.

Using this same system, one could add yet another pair of genes to calculations—such as the one for coat length, which is controlled by another locus. In such a calculation, the letters used would be *L* for the normal length and *l* for a long coat. Of course, the checkerboard keeps getting bigger! In fact, there would be 250 possible combinations, and if just one further pair of genes were to be added, the theoretical number of squares needed to calculate all permutations would be 1024—32 squares across and 32 down! However, it should be remembered that if one is already dealing with known homozygosity, the genes for this need not be included in such boards. For example, if one was working on known shorthaired breeds, then, as long as their pedigree was not in doubt, all the offspring would be shorthairs, so *L* would not be needed, as all the cats would, of necessity, be *LL*.

At this point, it is perhaps worth making reference to the cat's bodily features. Imagine that *d* represented an undesirable feature—not necessarily an abnormality, but just a lack of a desired exhibition point. Of the 16 cats under consideration, no less then 12 of them would be carrying the fault, but it would only show itself in four of the cats, whilst only four of the 16 would actually be clear of the fault. This can be used to illustrate two aspects. Firstly, if the 12 not showing the fault were all winning cats, only one-third of them would be assured of not passing the fault to their offspring. Secondly, it can be seen just how easily a problem can spread unseen in a breed; it reaches the point where carriers are so numerous that the incidence of the fault being visible starts to increase. The same is true of genetic abnormalities, and in both cases the only way to deal with the problem is

through rigid culling of known carriers and, of course, by never breeding from cats that show a visible fault that is of a very bad nature. Once recessives are in a population they are extremely difficult to control; conversely, if the recessive is a desired feature, then it is more easily perpetuated simply because any cat showing it must be pure for the feature.

MIMIC GENES

Sometimes an apparent visible feature may appear at two different loci; when this happens the genes are termed mimics. The classic example is in the Devon and Cornish Rex breeds. On first sight one would assume that, if these cats were mated, then only rex coats could result—for the rex fur is the result of a recessive mutation. However, this does not happen—the result is all normally coated cats. This shows that the rex gene in these two breeds must be sited at different loci. You can work out the results by the checkerboard system, using the symbols *R* and *r* for non-rex and Cornish Rex, and *Re* and *re* for non-rex and Devon Rex respectively. The Cornish Rex will thus have the genotype of *Re-Rerr* (non Devon Rex and Cornish Rex at the respective loci) whilst the Devon Rex will be *RRr-ere*. All of the first generation will be *RrRere*—normal coats—but if these are then mated, rex coats will reappear in the next generation in the ratio of 9:3:3:1 (9:7 normal/rex coats). There will be three each of the two rex types plus one which combines the two.

It is wise to be aware of mimic genes, since it is always possible that they could turn up in a color. If this happened, then two cats known to be purebreeding for the same color could be paired, only for their surprised owners to find no kittens of that color in the litter that was produced—causing obvious confusion and maybe even the thought that one of them owned a sort of genetic abnormality for color production! This situation can arise when a color is known both in dominant and recessive forms. Therefore, until it is realized that there are indeed separate mutations producing the same effect, one's program can be brought to a temporary halt. If the known color was a recessive (as in the case of black) and then a dominant form appeared,

A male sable Burmese.

this would be visible in the heterozygous state; thus a line of good blacks could suddenly turn up kittens of another color though having no previous record of it. The answer for this would be one or two generations back, when a second black mutation was used which was not pure-breeding.

SEX LINKAGE

The final aspect of gene action that should be understood by the newcomer to genetics concerns the linking of a color to the sex of the cat. All domestic cat colors are autosomal in mode of inheritance—that is, they are normal body cell genes not affected by sex—except for orange, which is sex-linked. Orange includes reds, yellows, gingers, and creams, the latter carrying the d dilution gene.

With sex-linkage, the X chromosome can carry color genes, but there is no equivalent locus on the shortened Y chromosome. This fact affects all theoretical calculations, which must take the sex of the cat into account. In terms of orange, a queen can be OO orange, Oo tortoiseshell, or oo non-orange. The tortoiseshell is an interesting situation, because here the recessive single gene can actually show itself visually on a different part of the body from the orange, thus creating this unusual pattern. The male, having just one X chromosome, is therefore either orange or non-orange. Actually, tortoiseshell males are known but are genetically abnormal.

Using the checkerboard method we can illustrate sex-linkage by pairing a black female with an orange tom. The sex chromosomes will be shown, so you can appreciate how they affect the color in each sex.

A Persian kitten. The vast majority of tortoiseshell cats are females, since this pattern is due to sex linkage.

Female Black *XoXo*

		Xo	*Xo*
XO Orange Male *XOY*		*XOXo* Tortie Female	*XOXo* Tortie Female
	Y	*XoY* Black Male	*XoY* Black Male

Checkerboard to show sex-linked transmission.

The black males resulting from the mating are thus normal cats, which means they carry no orange factor in their make-up, even though they had an orange father—there can be no hidden genes on the male sex chromosomes. If the female was tortoiseshell and the male was orange, then the expectations would be 25% orange and 25% tortoiseshell females, and 25% orange and 25% black males. If two orange cats are paired, then only orange kittens will be produced because the *O* gene will mask any other colors the cats may have in their genetic make-up; when this happens the gene is said to be epistatic. Dominant white is another such gene, and is actually dominant to orange.

NON-GENETIC INFLUENCES

Sometimes a breeder can be so immersed in the genetics of color that other factors which influence color can be forgotten. Color is produced by melanins, and the way they are distributed within the hairs determines the color and pattern of a cat. Any factor that can affect the cells can therefore affect the color, as it may alter the distribution of pigments. Melanins are themselves derived from amino acids, so clearly the diet of a cat will have some influence on the shade of color a cat displays. The effect of diet is probably shown best in canaries, which can be color-fed with carotene-rich foods in order to increase the orange-red coloration; whilst this is not so obvious a factor in cats, nonetheless poor nutrition will not produce good color in the individual. Temperature is also of importance and is exemplified within the Siamese pattern. In this, the color of the points is thermosensitive, so that in colder climates the points are darker than in warmer climes. However, there will still be genetic variance within local populations, so one may still see dark-pointed cats in hot countries, and pale cats in cooler places. Sunshine has a bleaching effect on coat color, so, again, judgment of color intensity should take account of this factor when selecting breeding stock—that is, it should not be assumed that a somewhat pale individual has become washed-out due to its poor genetic state.

PRACTICAL GENETICS

It often happens in many subjects that a beginner may fail to grasp the workings of a system because of the way it is conventionally presented. Sometimes, if it is shown in a different manner, it suddenly starts to fall into place in the person's mind. Seeing genetic formulae and checkerboards does not always help beginners, for, whilst they may follow the basic theory, their minds go into neutral when numerous genes are being considered. Geneticists do tend

Persian kitten. Red color in canaries is believed to be enhanced by color-feeding. In cats this is not the case, but the health, and therefore looks, of a cat are certainly influenced by its diet.

to presuppose knowledge, and this often leaves the novice asking all sorts of questions as he reads a given text, thus creating confusion. He understands that a cat can be split for only one alternative but then reads that a cat is split for longhair, Siamese, brown, and rex as well as dilution! To show how these things are possible, I have therefore attempted an alternative presentation of calculating theoretical expectations so that the reader can see the genes in situation on an imaginary chromosome.

It must be remembered, however, that the drawings are diagrammatic representations. The loci are conveniently arranged next to each other and the colors are in alphabetical order. On real chromosomes they will not be so spaced and will be interspersed with many other gene loci controlling many other features.

The reader will also note that in the previous examples of matings the formulae were shorter than in the following examples. This is because it is assumed that any genes not noted in a formula are of the normal wild type. The Havana Brown is thus *aabb*, as this represents the mutation which reduces black at the *B* loci to brown, the *aa* mutation having removed the yellow from agouti at the *A* loci. However, the blue Persian has mutations at the *C*, *D*, and *L* loci; therefore, when considering a mating between these two breeds, it is beneficial to include the state of these genes on the Havana so that nothing is lost. Likewise, the *BB* state of the blue Persian is normally assumed, but, as the Havana has mutated here we must show the *BB* in calculations, as these will obviously affect the genotype of the resulting offspring. The beginner can calculate any matings simply by substituting the genotypes of any other breed into such chromosome representations and then checking with the effect of the mutation that is cited in order to work out what the cat will look like and what genes will be carried in a masked state. Once this is understood, then it will be found that the checkerboard system comes into its own for calculating the more complex matings.

GENE LOCI AND THEIR MUTANTS SEEN IN CATS

The components of this list are as follows: loci, symbol, alternative genes (allelomorphs), and effect on the normal gene.

A: *A;* agouti; The normal wild type gene showing a mixture of yellow with black-gray. *a;* non-agouti; removes the yellow to produce an all-black cat.

B: *B;* black; Produces black in areas of the coat. *b;* brown; reduces black to a medium (chocolate) brown. b^1; brown; reduces medium brown to a light (milk) brown.

C: *C;* full color; allows maximum intensity of black and yellow pigments. c^b; Burmese; reduces full color to dark brown. c^s; Siamese; reduces brown on the body to pale cream. c^a; blue-eyed albino; reduces all pigmentation to white except in the eye. *c;* albino; removes all pigment, producing pink or red-eyed whites.

D: *D;* dense pigment; allows full density of black pigment. *d;* dilution; alters the distribution of a black pigment to give a blue appearance; dilutes yellow to cream.

O: *O;* orange; Full intensity of yellow (called orange or red in cats); this is a sex-linked gene; removes all dark pigment. *o;* non-orange; allows any other color to be visible.

W: *W;* dominant white; completely masks the presence of other color genes and is associated with blindness and deafness.

Note: Other known mutants are not detailed but have various effects, such as inhibiting full expression of color or modifying color as in piebalds. Dominant black is believed to have died out.

PRACTICAL GENETICS 1

Simplified diagrammatic representation of a pair of autosomal (body) chromosomes.

Name of locus		Known alternative (mutant) genes at each locus
Agouti	Ⓐ	ⓐ Non- Agouti
Black	Ⓑ	ⓑ ⓑ*ⁱ* Brown and Light Brown
Full Color	Ⓒ	ⓒ ⓒ*ˢ* ⓒ*ᵃ* ⓒ Burmese/Siamese/Blue-eyed Siamese and Albino
Density	Ⓓ	ⓓ Dilution
Orange	Ⓞ	ⓞ Non-Orange (This locus is sex-linked)
Non-white	ⓦ	Ⓦ Dominant White (This gene is epistatic to all others as it will mask them)
Tabby	Ⓣ	Ⓣ*ᵃ* ⓣ*ᵇ* Mackerel/Abyssinian/Blotched (classic)
Spotting	ⓢ	Ⓢ Not fully understood—variable in action
Non-Rex	Ⓡ	ⓡ Cornish Rex
Non-Rex	Ⓡⓔ	ⓡⓔ Devon Rex
Short hair	Ⓛ	ⓛ Long hair
Non-Manx	ⓜ	Ⓜ Manx
Normal color	ⓘ	Ⓘ Color inhibitor

A cat can have only two genes at any given locus regardless of how many mutations (alternatives) are known to exist at that loci. For example, both genes at the full color locus could be CC, or they could be cc^s, cc, or c^sc, but the cat cannot be Cc^sc. In addition, at each locus, one gene must come from each parent. Each locus is an independent unit, which means that the potential permutations across 13 loci would run into millions, but, of course, at many loci the genes from each parent would be the same. There are other loci which influence color, hair length, and so on, but those indicated are the most well known to cat breeders.

PRACTICAL GENETICS 2
To show how color and hair length are transmitted.

BLUE POINT PERSIAN
(Also known as blue
Himalayan and blue
colorpoint longhair)

HAVANA BROWN

aaBBc^{s}c^{s}ddll   ←————Genetic Formula————→   *aabbCCDDLL*

Loci	Genotype	
A	*a*	*a*
B	*B*	*B*
C	*c^s*	*c^s*
D	*d*	*d*
L	*l*	*l*

Paired Chromosomes

×

Genotype

a	*a*
b	*b*
C	*C*
D	*D*
L	*L*

Paired Chromosomes

It should be remembered that on each of the paired chromosomes of the above breeds, the other six gene loci—and thousands of others that control color and other features—will be present as well. However, we are assuming that they are all in an unmutated state and do not need to be considered in calculating out the likely result of pairing these two particular varieties. Only mutated genes and their alternatives need be considered.

**Offspring
Genotype**

a	*a*
B	*b*
c^s	*C*
d	*D*
l	*L*

Paired Chromosomes

BLACK SHORTHAIR

aaBbCc^{s}DdLl

The first generation inherits a gene at each loci from each parent, and this produces the offspring indicated. However, they will also be carrying genes for the following characteristics in a hidden of masked state: brown; Siamese marking; dilution; long hair. This will mean that these cats can pass on any one of 16 different genotypes to their own offspring, not just the two they received from their own parents.

A blue point Himalayan (colorpoint Persian). Himalayans were originally produced by mating Persians and Siamese. The body type and long hair of the Persian were then set while maintaining the Siamese colorpoints and blue eyes.

PRACTICAL GENETICS 3

To show the result of pairing blue Persian or Havana Brown to hybrid black shorthair.

a		a
B		b
c^s		C
d		D
l		L

Because the genes segregate independently, the potential gametes that the hybrid cats can pass on are as follows, with any single set thus being able to pair with those of its breeding partner's genes.

1	2	3	4	5	6	7	8	9	10	11	12	13	14	15	16
a	a	a	a	a	a	a	a	a	a	a	a	a	a	a	a
B	B	B	B	B	B	B	B	b	b	b	b	b	b	b	b
C	C	C	C	C	c^s	c^s	c^s	C	C	C	C	c^s	c^s	c^s	c^s
D	D	d	d	D	D	d	d	D	D	d	d	D	D	d	d
L	l	L	l	L	l	L	l	L	l	L	l	L	l	L	l

Let us assume permutation number 5 paired with its blue Persian parent—then this is what the offspring would look like:

Chromosome from
Hybrid   Blue Persian   Visual Appearance

Genes Carried
in Masked Form

a		a
B		B
c^s	×	c^s
D		d
L		l

Offspring
Genotype

Seal Point
Shorthair

Dilution
Longhair

If that same permutation united with the genes of its Havana Brown parent then the result would be as follows:

a	a
B	b
c^s	C
D	D
L	L

Offspring Genotype

Visual Appearance

Black
Shorthair

Genes Carried in Masked Form

Brown

NOTE: Although this offspring looks the same as its short hair parent, its genotype, thus its breeding behavior, is different.

It must be appreciated that one could not specifically select permutation number five from the original litter of hybrid kittens because this particular combination of genes would not be visibly apparent and would only be known as a theoretical permutation—in fact one of sixteen, any of which the hybrid might pass on to its offspring. If knew the parentage of the hybrid, as we did in the example used, one would know that there were colorpoint, dilution and longhair genes in the hybrids make-up. Another aspect that often creates confusion in the mind of those just learning the basics of genetics as applied to cats is that in respect of tabby markings. If one looks at the simplified pair of chromosomes depicted, it will be seen that each of the two alleles of the wild type are still tabby; they differ only in the arrangement of markings. This means that all cats are tabby and always carry one of the tabby genes, for example TT^a (that is, one of each type), or two of one type, for example $t^b t^b$. It is the mutation for non-agouti that masks the visible appearance of tabby markings in the non-visible tabby colors. However, trace markings are still often seen in kittens. The extent of tabby seen in kittens is variable, because modifying genes which reduce the expressions of tabby may be selected for—and in some cases all but totally mask them. If one is aware of this aspect, then the sudden appearance of tabby tracings will be understood and not cause the breeder to wonder where the markings have come from.

CONTINUOUS VARIATION

So far, genetics has been viewed from major gene effects on the individual, but of equal, if not more, importance is the accumulative effect of genes either on color or, especially, on the conformation of the individual. When a feature is controlled by many genes, it is referred to as being a polygenic trait. Most features are, in fact, of this nature, and there is no way of knowing just how many genes are involved—they are termed modifying genes. An orange cat can range from deep, almost red, orange to the palest cream, and whilst it requires the presence of the major gene for orange in the first place, thereafter the intensity of the color is determined by polygenes or modifiers. The dilution gene is a major modifier, but many more have only a small effect as individuals but a large effect when considered in total.

The overall size and conformation of a cat is achieved by a build-up of given polygenes which can be selected for. Because they are so numerous, they cannot be expressed in genetic formulae, which is why you will find that the formulae for certain breeds appear to be exactly the same; these refer to the color make-up of the breed. Even then, such formulae cannot take into account the shade of a color, only insomuch as one can distinguish between dark and light brown—but not in shades of these.

The effect of a major gene is instantly visible to a breeder, but once it has been incorporated into the breed, its outward expression will be controlled by selection for those modifiers that tend to intensify or dilute its appearance. Therein lies the basis of breeding—the art of selection of breeding stock. Because we are talking about so many genes, and because the average breeder has limited space or finances for maintaining his cats, it is clear that there must be some degree of chance within any breeding program; however, the random element can be reduced by one's knowledge of the genetic state of one's stock.

BREEDING OBJECTIVES

It is obvious that the basic objective of any breeder is to improve the quality of the stock and, hopefully, its color as well. In order to achieve this, one's awareness of how genes work is of immense help because it underlines the need to know the genetic state of the stock as far as is possible. Where a breeder is limited is in knowing whether or not increasing the homozygosity (pureness) of the genes will be beneficial or not. Generally, it is assumed that it is beneficial, but the fact that tortoiseshells are heterozygotes, as are Manx cats, illustrates the fact that desirables may not always be best in a pure state—and can be ridden with problems if they are. If one could keep adding to the desired genes, then, in theory, the ultimate breeding population would result. However, it is known that as the state of pureness increases, so does the number of negatives, such as loss of breeding vigor, resistance to disease and anatomical abnormality.

A pair of shorthairs strolling on the beach. As the state of pureness within a strain increases, vigor is lost. That is why breeding experts outcross from time to time.

Let us assume that a given gene exerts a very minor influence, in a negative way, on another feature of the cat (which might be internal and not necessarily visible). Up to a given point, this effect may never be a great problem, but once the accumulation of many genes is reached, then suddenly a very negative situation shows itself—rather akin to the straw that breaks a camel's back. Here we have continuous variance as a problem, but the same state may be reached if a given desirable gene is also linked with a negative gene, as in the Manx. As pureness is achieved, so is pureness of the gene at the other loci, and the problem then becomes apparent.

The breeder's objective should therefore be to produce the finest possible stock without a loss of vigor or good health. There is not a lot of gain to be made from a situation where one has a few super individuals but a high proportion of "throwaways" that give you a reputation for producing highly strung and unreliable breeding stock. No one should breed like that—but some do; the evidence is all around us in many pet species, where problems such as lack of fertility, increasing illness in a line, or genetic abnormals are more common than is realized.

BREEDING PROGRAMS

Two factors are important when setting up a breeding program: correct selection of stock and sound monitoring of results. Selection is important, because a good breeder can upgrade average stock by judicious removal of cats that are not up to par. In the same vein, a wealthy person can obtain the best of cats but will not maintain quality in the line just by having money, for it is proper selection that determines success. Record-keeping is essential, as it is impossible for a person to remember specific facts on individual cats over a number of years. Quite often, tracing a problem is only possible by consulting one's records and studying pedigrees to pinpoint the cats that possibly introduced a problem.

At this juncture, it is of value to bring to the reader's attention an aspect of genetics that can easily be overlooked. It is always worth recording if a given queen is a good mother, but it should not be assumed that such a quality necessarily came from her own mother. Motherhood, and other traits in either sex, are known as being sex-limited—they are not sex-linked—so either parent may have the gene for "goodness." The sire rarely has the opportunity to show his parental abilities, but he can pass his genes for this onto his daughters (and sons). In tracing a bad mother's pedigree, it would thus be as important to look at her father's side of the family as well as her mother's.

Returning to the question of breeding programs, the best method is to stay within given family lines so that one is dealing with a reasonably restricted population of genes. This way, unknown variables are less likely to suddenly appear. The most popular method of such breeding is termed linebreeding, a less intense form of inbreeding. The opposite of inbreeding is outcross or random breeding (although this might also include a certain amount of inbreeding). The objective in a linebreeding program is to select one or two especially impressive individuals—which may be living or past cats of distinction—and increase the number of their genes within the program. This is done by mating to their known relatives, and it also includes a degree of inbreeding, perhaps involving very close matings such as father to daughter, brother to sister and other such matings. Inbreeding does not of itself mean that faults will occur, for these can only happen if the fault is already there; however, it increases the chances of the fault becoming visible, so it has the dual benefit of both fixing virtues and highlighting faults. After initial inbreeding, one usually returns to more distant relative matings so as to ensure continued vigor within the line.

Once a particular line, or strain, has been developed, then one must be very careful when introducing other cats into the program, because many years of careful selection and improvement can be undone in a short space of time if the introduced cat is carrying recessive genes for an undesirable trait. Obviously, if a cat looks good, it certainly must have the genes to give it such looks, but if they are of dominant-recessive mode, rather than of polygenic nature, you cannot be sure that the cat will pass the quality genes on, as it could as easily pass on the poor ones—whereas your own cats may have that feature in a very good state of pureness.

Top breeders will study any outside cat that looks as though it could improve their lines. They will check into its pedigree and see the quality of stock it has produced. If they feel things look interesting, then they will test mate it to just one of their cats and see how results turn out. In point of fact, a male introduced to a line may not show its worth in the first generation, so it may be necessary to have a number of matings, or to use him to cover a few queens, so that an overall judgment can be made on results. Few breeders have sufficient cats to conduct really good test programs, but, even so, one should attempt to exercise care where unknown genes are involved. If a breeder begins with two distantly related but separate lines, then it is quite possible to go for many generations without having the need to introduce new genes; one may be able to use the second genetic line of stock as the outcross to bring in vigor or other needed features.

SELECTION

There are numerous ways a breeder can go about selecting from offspring produced, and each has its merits and drawbacks. One could try to upgrade the stock for all features at the same time, which is a long process; or one could concentrate on one aspect, such as head, size, or color, and when this is improved turn to another feature whilst trying to retain the quality achieved on the first feature. In the latter, the total score method can be used as the means of selection.

Total score selection: In this method, one makes a list of the features being considered and then gives each a score out of ten. Each feature is also given a separate coefficient based on its importance to the breeder. In this way one is actually concentrating on certain features yet giving consideration to other aspects; however, it cannot be said that this method is an overall judgment because the coefficients favor certain features.

As an example of this method, the breeder might consider head shape to be more important than color, but color more important than tail length. The coefficients might thus be three for head shape, two for color, and nothing for tail length. Overall health and breeding vigor should head the list, so these would have a coefficient of maybe four or even five. There is no limit to the number of features that can be listed—the more the better. Fixing the coefficients is obviously important for retaining good balance in the system.

The kittens may be scored at different age levels so that development can be monitored as well. Each cat is scored out of ten for its features, and then these scores are multiplied by their coefficients to give a total score of breeding merit. The advantage of such a system is that it gives important favor to desired features, which a typical overall judgment would not. For example, in an overall assessment a cat may have scored well out of ten on a number of features but not so well on just a couple of key points. The total score will ensure that key features can outweigh lesser considerations because the coefficient sees to this.

As with any system of selection, it is only as good as the person making the judgments and compiling the tables in the first place. It is no good kidding oneself about a feature and giving it a high mark that a judge would not; therefore, an experienced person is needed to help construct the initial table with the breeder so that this can be done based on the cats one starts with. The success of the system will be self-evident if the results come, because this will mean that the judgments have been sound.

It can be seen from the foregoing text that genetics is both a complex, certainly at times baffling, and a fascinating subject of study. Even with the most basic understanding, a breeder is better off than if he has no awareness of the laws of heredity.

CFA judge Walter Hutzler looking over a Cornish Rex. Many serious breeders use a point system which helps them select the best offspring for future matings.

An Abyssinian participant at a cat show.

EXHIBITION

The exhibition side of the cat fancy, though large in its organization, involves only a small percentage of the cats living in a given country, but it is a very important part of the overall hobby. In the UK, for example, there are about 6.5 million household cats, but only a few thousand of these will actually be regular exhibition entrants. For the purebred cats, exhibition is the shop window of the fancy; at a show one can see all of the various breeds accepted by the given registration association. There will be kittens, adults, neuters, and these will be seen in all of their various colors. There will also be breeds that are in the process of development; such cats cannot compete for major awards, and some may not even be in competition but are presented in order to arouse interest in their type or pattern. This represents the first stages of becoming a breed.

At a cat show there will be various trade booths which sell all of the specialized equipment and products made for cats, and numerous specialty societies or clubs may also have booths at the larger exhibitions in order to recruit new members. Unlike a dog show, feline exhibitions are much quieter and do not have the hustle and bustle associated with canids; they are usually more tranquil affairs. However, in the USA, these shows are very colorful events, with all the show pens being brightly decorated in various materials in order to display the cats in the best possible manner.

Any person contemplating the purchase of a pedigreed cat is strongly advised to visit one or more cat shows before committing their money to an actual purchase. It is very much a family event, so a day at a show will be enjoyed by all and will be most rewarding, especially with the information gained.

THE FIRST CAT SHOWS

The idea of holding a show for cats was the brainchild of Harrison Weir, a cultured Englishman and in many people's eyes the father of the cat fancy. His show took place at the famous Crystal Palace at Sydenham, London, in 1871, and it proved to be a great success. In all, 170 cats were entered, including a Scottish wild cat exhibited by the Duke of Sunderland; by all accounts, this proved to be an especially ferocious feline that no one could get near, which is not surprising given the nature of these cats. Weir's own blue tabby was a winner at the show, but it was the Persians and Angoras that attracted most of the attention. A pair of Siamese were on view, as was a cat which sported white mittens, though this looked more like a Ragdoll than a Birman.

The success of the show resulted in many more exhibitions being organized, and even the famous Charles Cruft, whose dog show is now so well known, turned his talents to planning a cat show. His 1894 exhibition attracted 567 exhibits in 74 classes. After the 1871 show, another was held in the same venue later in that year and again proved a winner. This was then followed by an increasing number of exhibitions throughout the UK in the ensuing years. The idea quickly spread to mainland Europe and to the USA, as well as to other parts of the world, and the success story has continued unabated since those early days.

In the USA the first show was held in Madison Square Garden in 1895; this was an all-breed affair, but it is probable that less formal events were seen in earlier years for specific breeds. The Maine Coon, in particular, had a good following before the turn of the century but was to lose favor with the arrival of the exotic Persian

and other foreign breeds—today, however, it is enjoying a rather good revival that is well deserved.

The early shows were as much social occasions as they were cat shows, and they became quite fashionable gathering places for the gentry of the day. Lady Beresford, who owned some 160 cats, entered up to 30 of these in a single show and had a retinue of servants to attend to them. This was quite common practice in those early years, and the names of the cat owners read like a few pages straight from *Who's Who*. The fact that members of the royal family were keen cat owners clearly gave the cat fancy a considerable boost. Shows were organized on basically similar lines to those of today—they were pen shows, and the judges walked along the rows of pens in order to evaluate the cats. An attempt was made to exhibit cats in the manner of dogs—on leads—but this was an unqualified disaster. A number of toms were soon engaged in a pitched battle, and only after receiving bad scratches were these felines parted by a brave young man. A cat with a piece of its ear missing does not make the best show specimen, so the idea was quickly and permanently dropped!

Although horse, dog, and cat shows were largely supported by the upper and middle classes during the early years, this was to change as the years rolled on. More of the working classes could afford to enter their cats and proved to be as good at breeding and exhibiting as any other social group. The two World Wars obviously affected both exhibitions and the breeding of cats, but after 1945 things quickly returned to normal; the cat fancy and its show structure rapidly made up lost ground. Today, at the National Cat Show in Great Britain, an entry of 2500 cats is quite commonplace; at large European and American shows the entries are no less impressive, whilst in Australia the number of cats exhibited rises with each passing year.

Opposite: Abyssinian in a formal pose. Cat shows range in size from small, informal exhibitions to large events with more than 2000 cats.

TYPES OF SHOW

Different countries apply their own rules and procedures for the organization of cat shows, so it is not possible to consider the procedure for each registration association here. The reader should obtain the show regulations applicable to the association he plans to join. We can, however, look at certain basics which will generally apply to all cat shows; at the same time the difference between the British and American systems can be briefly reviewed.

All cat shows are indoor events, this being a necessary precaution to prevent cats from escaping. The size of a show can range from a small, informal affair at local level to the enormous exhibitions of all-breed championship status, such as those held in New York, Paris, and, of course, London. However, large shows take place in many provincial cities, so there is likely to be one within your area. A cat show will either be of championship or non-championship status, the latter being divided into either exemption or sanction shows in the UK. An exemption show is really a small local event in which certain of the regulations of the GCCF are relaxed—they are ideal shows for the first-time exhibitor, as they will introduce one to the show world at a less competitive level, where the exhibitors are largely from the same area. The sanction show is run on full GCCF rules but does not offer the coveted challenge certificates that go towards the title of champion. Likewise, in the USA, a non-championship show will be a smaller exhibition, where points towards championship status are not on offer for winners of the open classes.

In North America there are many shows, called back-to-back shows, that are held on consecutive days. Here, two shows run in tandem so that a cat can compete in separate shows on consecutive days in the same venue. This is very useful for exhibitors who have had to travel quite long distances. Each show is an individual affair, and a judge in one cannot officiate in the other on the following day.

Cat shows may be for all breeds, or they may be for longhaired or shorthaired breeds, or they may be restricted to a single breed, such as the Siamese; the latter two show types are known as specialties.

THE SHOW CAT

Provided that a cat is healthy and does not display an anatomical defect (unless this is a feature of the breed, such as in the Manx or Scottish Fold), it can be exhibited in one or more classes at all multibreed shows; even household pets have classes and their own awards system—the cat fancy really does cater to every type of feline. Pedigreed breeds with established standards will be judged against them, but this by no means dictates that only the very best of cats can be exhibited. Clearly, at major shows, only such cats will pick up a winner's ribbon, but there are many exhibitors who are regular show goers even though they never receive top awards. Their cats may pick up prizes at the smaller shows, and the owners just enjoy the whole atmosphere of the cat show and live for the day they will produce a real big winner.

Many a cat owner has started a show career with very ordinary cats, become enthused by the whole hobby, and then purchased better breeding stock in order to make up champions. The beauty of cat shows is that you can compete at many levels according to your ambition and reason for attending shows. The important thing is that the cat is healthy and is a sound example of its breed. Some cats have no standard and are entered into assessment classes, where they are judged against an unofficial standard; these are developing breeds. Household cats are judged on overall health, type, and the beauty of their color and markings.

SHOW CLASSIFICATION

Every cat show is composed of a number of classes which cater to the various individual breeds, their colors, their age, their sex, and whether or not they are sexually entire or whether they have been desexed (that is, altered cats). A typical classification will be as follows.

Championship classes: Male Open; Male Champion; Male Grand Champion. Female Open; Female Champion; Female Grand Champion. Neuter Open; Neuter Champion; Neuter Grand Champion. Spay Open; Spay Champion; Spay Grand Champion.

Non-championship classes: Male Kitten; Female Kitten; Household Pet Classes; Assessment Classes; Club Classes; Miscellaneous Classes.

Within the championship classes, that for open male, for example, will include classes for each breed and for each color within the breed. This is repeated for open female, and so on. A show might schedule many hundreds of classes if it is an all-breed championship exhibition. A smaller show will have fewer classes and will group the breeds by not splitting them into their individual colors.

Within the non-championship classes there will be all types of groupings; some are restricted to members of a particular club, whilst others are restricted to people from certain distances from the show venue. There may also be numerous novelty classes, for example the kitten with the prettiest expression, or the cat or kitten with a pedigreed companion entered in the championship section. Wins gained as kittens do not count when entering adult classes and do not qualify towards the title of champion.

DEFINITIONS

In the following listing I have taken various definitions used by cat associations in the USA and in the UK; these will give the beginner a useful idea of what is meant in the cat fancy in respect to cat shows. The list also includes definitions used by some clubs in given classes at their own exhibitions.

Cat: Nine months old and over (UK). Eight months old or over (USA). A domestic feline of either sex, neutered, or spayed.

Kitten: For show purposes, a cat over three months old and under nine months old (UK). For show purposes, a cat under the age of eight months but over four months old (USA).

Altered cat: A cat that has had the testicles (in a male) or the ovaries (in a female) surgically removed.

Neuter: An altered male.

Spay: An altered female.

Breed: A subpopulation of cats that differs from other cats with respect to certain genetically determined characteristics which all members of the defined subpopulation share in common. These characteristics are described in the written standard of the breed. *Source*—The International Cat Association (TICA), USA.

TICA judge Gloria Stephens looking over a tabby Maine Coon kitten. In the UK, the kitten class is for cats between three and nine months of age; in the USA, it is from four to eight months.

Breeder: The person who was the owner of the dam, or who was the lessee of the dam in a lessee agreement on record with the secretary at the time of mating. *Source*—American Cat Association, USA.

Aristocrat: A cat with one or two challenge or premier certificates but not yet a champion or premier (UK).

Junior: A cat under two years of age on the day of the show.

Senior: A cat over the age of two years on the day of the show.

Debutante: A cat that has never previously been exhibited.

Maiden: A cat that has not won a first, second, or third prize.

Novice: A cat that has not won a first prize.

Limit: A cat that has not won more than four first prizes.

Visitor: An exhibitor that lives beyond a given distance from the show venue (the distance varies depending on the club sponsoring the show).

Radius: An exhibitor living within a given distance of the show venue (the distance depending on the show in question).

ENTERING A SHOW

Before a cat can be exhibited in a given show, it must be registered with the association under whose rules the show is to be organized; however, this requirement does not apply to household pets. Other classes of cats, such as developing breeds, may also be excluded from this regulation depending on the association concerned.

In the USA, a kitten must be four months old before it is permitted to enter a show venue; in the UK the age is three months. A list of shows organized by a given association or its member clubs is available from the association or from its member clubs. Exhibitions are advertised in the various cat magazines, and a show will normally be advertised at local level, though by this stage entries will usually have closed.

To enter a show, an exhibitor must write to the organizing secretary for a schedule and an entry blank. The entry blank will indicate the closing date for entries, which is usually about two months prior to the actual show in the case of a large all-breed affair. The association usually fixes a minimum number of classes that a cat can enter (in the UK this is four), one of

Two calico Cornish Rex females eyeing each other from their show cages. At large shows, classes may be divided by color and sex—within a breed—as well as by breed itself.

which must be an open class if the exhibit is eligible for such. The blank, when completed, is returned to the organizer together with appropriate fees, and it must be signed and indicate, where applicable, the cat's registration number. Failure to complete these aspects will result in delays, which may prevent you from meeting the closing date. When completing a form, exhibitors should never forget to list all clubs of which they are members, as this would preclude them from winning any special club awards given at that show—most frustrating if your cat had beaten the specials winner but was ineligible to take the prize on a technicality. Once the blank is received by the show secretary, you will be notified of your benching number and given any other instructions applicable to the show.

cats are exhibited in carrying crates. A cat may be entered into a show as "not for competition"; this is usually done to promote new breeds. The exhibitor is not obliged to state why the cat is not competing, but entry fees still have to be paid. For sale notices can be applied to any cats in competition, but the show organizers must be advised of this via the entry blank.

Each association lists, within its show rules, the exact requirements for entry, which will normally include such aspects as the cat having been vaccinated against major feline diseases at least 21 days prior to a show. Some shows will not allow a cat to be exhibited if it has been benched at another show within four days. Declawed cats are invariably not able to enter shows, and pregnant or lactating queens are also

Many people have found that exhibition is a thrilling pastime that the cats enjoy as much as the owners.

All shows run under GCCF rules in the UK, or under the various American registrations, must provide proper benching or penning facilities; these are either special cat pens or chicken coops. At some shows you may request to be benched next to a friend, and you may request to be benched in a non-smoking area. Such requests do not apply in the UK. In those countries where pens are not normally provided, the

ineligible for exhibition. Cats coming from homes or catteries where fungal or infectious diseases have occurred within 21 days of a show are always ineligible for entering a venue. There are, in fact, a great many regulations, and no prospective exhibitor should be without the appropriate show rules. These cost only a very modest sum from the association or ruling body of registrations.

THE SHOW DAY

The show day is a long and tiring affair, especially for the owner, as one must be up early in the morning to pack all the day's necessities into the car. The cat must be transported in a carrying crate into the show venue. Once at the show, the cat will be inspected by a veterinarian, and, if all is well, the cat can be taken to its pen. In the UK, the exhibitor will be given a identification tag which must be fixed around the cat's neck. In the UK, no pen is allowed to be dressed in any way that would make it identifiable, and judges are instructed to walk straight past any such pens. The regulations state that "each exhibit must be provided with a sanitary tray and a clean white or near white blanket without distinctive markings or edges. Cellular blankets are not allowed."

Staying with the UK, the rules continue: "A hot water bottle may be concealed by the blanket, but no other articles or decorations may be placed on or in the pen until judging has been completed. The only exception to this rule is that a container with water must be placed in the pen." Food containers may be placed in the pen after the time announced for the admission of the public. If used earlier, food containers must be removed before judging commences.

In the USA, pens can be decorated provided that no decoration extends beyond the limits of the pen itself, and no awards gained at other shows may be affixed to the front of the pen. The reason for the different rules on either side of the Atlantic is that in the UK, the cats are judged on site at their pen, behind closed doors—the exhibitors are not allowed into the show hall whilst judging is being carried out. The judge passes along the rows of pens and inspects each cat, which is taken from its pen by a steward. In the USA, the cats are taken to the judge, either by the exhibitor or by a steward, and the public and exhibitors are allowed to

TICA judge Pat Smith examining a torbie (patched tabby) Maine Coon. On the day of the show, try to make the journey as easy as possible for your cat.

TICA judge Marjorie Hanna checking the head shape of a brown tabby male Maine Coon.

watch the whole process. I should perhaps mention that at the National Cat Show of the UK, the public is allowed into the hall whilst judging is taking place, which makes the latter rather difficult. In Australia, the British system is used, but experiments with American style ring judging do take place.

Once the judging has been completed, the cats must remain in the show pen until the allotted time for removal. If a cat is taken from the venue before the scheduled time, it will forfeit any awards it has gained during the show; if none have been won, the exhibitor may still be disciplined by the association. In certain cases early removals may be sanctioned by the show committee, but these are less common these days—after all, the public pays to see the exhibits, which is not possible if a number are removed before the announced show closing time.

At a show, neither visitors nor exhibitors should handle other people's cats without permission. Disease is easily spread in this manner,

so if an exhibitor will not let you touch his cat, it is not a case of his being unfriendly but of simple precaution—you may have handled many other cats before or during the show. Children should be well drilled on this matter; in addition, they should never be allowed to roam around a show venue unsupervised unless they are old enough to understand these instructions. A show will normally commence about 10 am, with vetting from about 8:30 am, and it will close around 5:30 pm.

JUDGING CATS

All cat judges are highly qualified; in the USA they must pass examinations before they are accepted. There may be specialty judges or all-breed judges. The former are restricted to certain breeds whilst the latter can judge any breed. In the UK, judges do not have to pass examinations but must progress to their status on experience. A person is first required to

Awards will vary from show to show. Winners may be presented with ribbons, trophies, plaques, or some combination thereof.

serve a period as a steward, after which he becomes a probationary judge and, when sufficient experience has been gained at this level, is then promoted to the rank of judge. The maximum time allowed for one to be a probationary judge is four years, and failure to gain promotion to full status at this time usually terminates one's status, unless special circumstances prevail.

At the show itself, cats are judged against the breed standard. A winner is required to gain a minimum number of points as specified in the standard. A judge may withhold first, second, and third prizes yet nominate fifth and sixth if there are sufficient entrants in the class. Such a decision is rare but does occasionally happen when, in the judge's opinion, none of the cats on view are of sufficient merit to justify any of the first three places. In the same way, a judge may appoint a winner even though the exhibit is the only one in its class, again, assuming that the judge is satisfied with the merit of that one exhibit.

In the event that the scheduled judge is unable to appear at a show, the exhibitors may withdraw their cats from competition if they do not wish to be judged under the replacement announced. Fees paid are reclaimable, but, in the UK, the penning fee is not.

In the USA, the actual judging can be quite a spectacle, with the judge parading along the row of exhibits, maybe hesitating at a pen and then moving on. When the winner's ribbon is fixed to the lucky cage, the crowd—and the owner—are by then really keyed up. Many an owner can be quite overcome by a win in a major competition, such is the excitement that builds up. This is the great advantage of American ring judging style—it adds a touch of nerve-tingling tension that is lacking in British shows. Again, judges in the USA really dress up for the occasion, whereas in the UK the judges all wear white overalls.

The number of cats a judge may officiate over is determined by the association. In the UK it is 90 per day, whereas it can be up to 200 per day in the USA, a very large number of cats indeed, though, of course, the American judge does have a greater time span in which to conclude his or her duties.

AWARDS

The prizes that cats compete for range from cards which state "Commended" to rosettes and ribbons won in different classes, all the way to the large trophies given for best of breed and best in show. In the open classes of the UK, provided that the breed is recognized for championship status, challenge certificates are given to the class winners, male and female; when three of these have been gained under three different judges, the cat becomes a champion. This also applies to altered cats, which become premiers after gaining premier certificates. A champion may then enter grand champion classes, and when three wins in this have been obtained the cat becomes a grand champion.

In the USA, the qualification for the title of champion varies depending on the association, but the basis is that open class winners in the different colors compete with each other for the award of male, female, neuter, or spay winner, and each receives a winner's ribbon. When a cat has earned four or six such ribbons it becomes a champion, provided that the ribbons are won under different judges—the number depending on the association concerned.

Once a cat is a champion, it may then enter the grand champion classes, where it must attain a given number of points and meet certain other criteria, after which it becomes a grand champion. Points towards this title are gained by taking one of the top five or ten places at an all-breed or specialty show—the number of points being lower at the latter than at the former. The number of champions beaten along the way may modify the number of points gained. A cat may go on to higher titles, such as a master grand champion or an international champion, again based on a build-up of points.

It should be mentioned that in the USA, awards gained with one association do not count with another, so that championship status is restricted to the association concerned. An exception to this is the American Cat Fanciers Association, which allows winner's ribbon awards gained with certain other associations to count towards championship status in certain circumstances.

A trio of Siamese—two blue points and a seal point—taking a break between rings. In the USA, no ribbons other than those won at the current show may be affixed to the outside of the cage.

Show-winning Abyssinian kitten with trophy.

HOUSEHOLD CATS

Provided that they are registered with an association, household cats may be eligible for any annual awards that are available for them, and they may gain titles on offer. A household pet for the purpose of such awards may actually be a purebred, but one which has not been registered as such. It is judged on the same basis as other mixed breed cats—for health, condition, and so on—not against the standard for its breed.

The American Cat Fanciers Association (ACFA) offers the following awards: Royal Household Pet (250 points); Supreme Household Pet (1000 points); and Household Pet Supreme Roll of Honor (2000 points). Points are allocated based on the type of show and place the cat finished in such a show; a winner receives 50 points whilst the tenth placed cat receives 17 points—assuming it is an all-breed event. This is an interesting aspect for pet cat owners, as they are encouraged to become regular exhibitors even though they do not have a purebred pet. In all cases, a household cat can only be entered into a cat show if it has been neutered or spayed, according to sex.

DISQUALIFICATION

The different registrations each list those aspects which will result in the disqualification of a cat from a show, and these will be listed in their show rules. However, a few of these are cited here as typical examples.

1) The use of any powders or sprays within the show venue is forbidden, and any traces of powder left within the coat of a cat will result in disqualification and any wins gained at the show become void.

2) No dyes can be used to improve the true color of a cat.

3) Trimming of improperly located white or colored hairs is not allowed.

4) A cat must be placid and allow the judge to handle it without risk of it scratching or biting. Any cat that is not tractable will be returned to its pen, which will have a notice to that effect placed on it; in addition, judges in other rings where the cat is scheduled to appear will be notified.

5) A cat or kitten removed from the show venue contrary to the show regulations may be disqualified; any prizes won will be void.

6) A cat or kitten showing any signs of being drugged in order to make it more tractable will automatically be disqualified.

7) Declawed cats will usually be disqualified. (In my opinion, the practice of de-

clawing cats is a barbaric act that should have no place in the cat fancy.) However, the American Cat Fanciers Association does not disqualify such cats.

8) Entire adult males must have at least one testicle (monorchid) fully descended into the scrotal sac. Cryptorchid males are disqualified (but not, of course, neutered males).

9) A cat may be disqualified if it is entered in the wrong class or if it is not the cat that was originally entered into the show.

10) A cat with more than the correct number of toes on each foot, which is five on the front and four on the back, will be disqualified.

11) Blind cats will normally not be permitted to be entered into exhibitions.

12) Any exhibitor may report, to the show manager, any other exhibitor whom they believe to be exhibiting a cat in contradiction to the show regulations. In such cases, the show manager will investigate such a protest and either disqualify the cat or rebuke the protest—in this case the person instigating the protest, if an exhibitor, will forfeit a fee.

SUGGESTED REQUIREMENTS FOR THE SHOW DAY

1) All vaccination certificates, in case these are needed.

2) Pen number and correspondence with the association for all entries for that particular show.

3) Brush and comb for final grooming prior to judging.

4) Cat litter tray and litter. Must be white in UK.

5) Cat blanket. Must be white in UK. Any color or material for the show pen, USA.

6) First aid kit.

7) Water bottle (for the cat) together with food container.

8) Hot water bottle for use under blanket if required. Show regulations do, however, require the organizers to maintain a given minimum temperature in the show venue.

Many shows now feature classes for household pets, making exhibition more and more accessible to a great number of cat owners.

9) Cat food and food for yourself.

10) Carrying basket for transporting cat into venue.

11) Collapsible trolley; very useful item if you are overburdened with equipment.

12) Camper type chair for your own use.

13) Disinfectant for wiping down the show pen, together with suitable cloth.

14) Schedule of classes (you should purchase a catalog at the show).

15) The cat! Don't laugh—this has happened on more than one occasion.

Note: Do not forget to allow plenty of time for travelling to the show, in case of breakdowns. Nothing is worse than having to rush the preparation of your cat for judging.

Silver tabby female American Shorthair. Note the bright eyes and alert expression on this cat—two important signs of good health.

HEALTH CARE

Under normal living conditions, and with a sound diet, most cats will go through life with the minimum of health problems. Of course, the probability is that they will suffer from one ailment or accident over their lives, for few creatures are so fortunate that they never become ill. Indeed, it is essential for them to be exposed to undesirable microorganisms, because this is how they build up and maintain immunity. Within the cat's environment, there will always be many potentially dangerous germs; it is the objective of the cat owner to keep the population down to an acceptable level, so that the cat's natural resistance is never overcome. This is achieved by constant attention to hygiene and by being aware of the different ways that ill health is brought about. Before discussing this aspect, it is a good idea to briefly consider what a healthy kitten or cat should look like.

THE HEALTHY CAT

A fit cat will exhibit a coat that is lustrous and full in relation to its breed. There will be no areas of broken fur or bald patches, and the fur itself will be supple and not brittle in its texture. When brushed with the hand against its lie, it should spring back to its normal position. The kitten's coat, not being mature, will not have the same high standard as the adult's, so it will look neat and smart without having the high sheen that will only come when the guard hairs have fully grown.

The eyes of a cat should be round and clear with no signs of a liquid discharge; the nose should be dry and not cracked or wet. It will generally be of a cooler temperature than will other parts of the body, but this will not always be obvious on warm days. There will be no signs of a discharge from the nose. The ears should be clean and fresh smelling, with no signs of brown wax in them, though dirt will tend to accumulate in the outer ear and will need removing.

The teeth should be clean with no indication of a build-up of tartar; if this is seen, it should be periodically removed by the vet. The teeth should also be of a level bite, by which is meant the top teeth should just touch those of the lower jaw. If the incisors protrude over those of the bottom jaw, they are overshot, whilst if the bottom teeth protrude in front of the upper teeth then they are undershot—both conditions are undesirable and regarded as faults in cats.

Other than stating that the teeth should be level, cat standards give little attention to the felid dental work, but breeders should strive to ensure that all teeth are present—normally 30 in all. It is likely that the Persian varieties will suffer the most from faulty dentition, as the reduction in foreface will invariably go hand in hand with missing teeth and a tendency to be undershot—very much more so in the peke-faced variety. The tendency to favor dish-faced cats is an unfortunate result of a fashion that takes no consideration of its effect on the cat.

The legs of a cat should be straight and show

good bone, with no evidence of bumps or similar swellings. The feet should be compact, not splay or hare-footed. The pads should be soft and show no signs of abrasions. Their color will be determined by the overall color of the cat. The nails should be barely visible when the cat is at rest but will tend to be more prominent in the foreign breeds. The abdomen should be soft with no swellings, lumps or sores; the anal region should be clean with no signs of matted fur or stains, which might indicate internal disorders.

The tail should be well furred with no visible kinks to it, though these may sometimes be felt in certain breeds. When moving, the cat should walk with grace and suppleness, showing no signs whatsoever of discomfort. Some breeds may tend to be more stilted in their hindleg action than others but never move with difficulty.

Any cat showing different signs from those suggested is likely to be suffering from ill health or from a basic deformity to its structure.

A blue-cream longhaired kitten. The coat of a healthy cat should be full and supple with no bald patches.

THE TREATMENT OF ILLNESS

The subject of disease in any animal species is clearly of such complexity that the average pet owner has no chance at all of fully understanding it—which is why people study to become veterinarians. The cat owner is better advised to concentrate his efforts on recognizing clinical signs of ill health, and on the means of preventing it in the first place, rather than in attempting to understand treatments other than for the most basic problems. Because cats are not able to relate symptoms to us, it follows that by the time we realize they are ill, the germs have a head start. If action is then delayed because the owners attempt to make their own diagnosis and treatments, valuable time is lost if they have made error in judgment. As the majority of diseases have broadly similar clinical signs, then it is very easy to make such errors—even vets must work through careful procedures before they can be sure of the cause of a problem, and often microscopy will be needed to establish this. They may use broad spectrum antibiotics to check the advance of a condition whilst tests are undertaken to give them a better guide to the best form of attacking the disease. The advice is, therefore, to leave treatments to the professionals.

THE CAUSE OF ILLNESS

There are a number of reasons why a cat can become ill, and they are all connected to the continuance of the species—both of the species of animal that is ill and of the organism that is causing the illness. The latter acts as a regulator to ensure that the former retains vigor—in other words, only the fittest survive. Ultimately, it is not in the interests of the disease germs to be so successful that the entire population of the host is wiped out, for if it was, the microorganism would itself be in danger of becoming extinct, so a careful balance exists between the prey and the host which works to the advantage of both, dubious though it may appear to us.

In the wild state, the equilibrium works because animals do not overcrowd themselves unduly and because they are not forced to live in adverse, unhealthy conditions. Overpopulation of germs is thus much less seen, and the different species each develop their own resistance to the germs within their territorial limits.

Under domestic conditions, things change dramatically, and unless the conditions are carefully controlled, microorganisms flourish and overwhelm the cat's defenses. In addition, cats may be moved from one area to another, and when this is so two things can result. First, the introduced cat may be susceptible to local germs it has never before encountered and may quickly become ill from them; secondly, that same cat may itself introduce germs to an area, and these may have a dramatic initial effect on the local feline population and an epidemic may break out. Until natural resistance to this builds up, all cats are at risk unless vaccinations are available.

It must always be remembered that disease organisms are no different, in the zoological sense, than the cats, for the former are themselves capable of building up a resistance to that which attacks them—such as antibiotics and other medicaments. A microorganism may be an individual species, but its potency within given populations can vary very widely based on the treatments it has been subjected to. Thus, that which may well cure a problem in one area may have little effect in another, which is why the unqualified use of antibiotics, where these are available without veterinary prescription, is such a dangerous aspect of home treatments.

Illness is created when a foreign organism lives in or on the body in such numbers that it directly drains the host of nutrients or adversely affects the normal metabolism of bodily cells—usually a combination of both. Again, what we may describe as a given illness is rarely as simple as a single description might suggest. A disease is a whole range of happenings going on at the same time, each one of which has an effect on another part of the body. As the body cells of many organs are linked to the alimentary canal, it is thus a common exit from the body for their waste products. Therefore, any imbalance in the normal functioning of cells is often seen by the way it affects a cat's motions. Diarrhea is well known to most people, but it is not an illness in itself but an example of that just discussed. It is the end result of a chain of internal actions that cause a softening of the feces towards a liquid state. The cat's body will always try to discharge

A pair of cream longhairs. Each population of cats has its own set of bacteria to which it is immune. Therefore, when bringing a new kitten home, it is a good idea to quarantine it from your other cats for a while.

from itself foreign matter that has a negative effect on it, and this is seen at the most appropriate exit point—be this excessive weeping of the eyes, nasal discharge, local swellings, vomiting. and so on.

Sometimes the cause of a problem may be some way from the exit point. A cat may vomit if it has a local infection in the throat, but it may also do so if there is a blockage much further down the digestive canal; it is thus pointless treating either for a throat infection or an organ malfunction if the problem is actually one of hairballs or similar physical bodies blocking the passage of food. Some of the food may get by the blockage, but only in small amounts, and this may result in diarrhea. Along with vomiting, the owner might then treat the cat for all manner of ailments that exhibit vomiting and diarrhea, and these very treatments might create the imbalance suspected, when the actual problem was relatively easily cured had correct diagnosis been made in the first place. This aspect cannot be overstressed, because so often the veterinarian's job is made more difficult simply because the owner of a cat has listened to non-qualified people's advice on what the problem was. The average cat owner is thus far better off having a cupboard full of quality foods rather than a cupboard full of medicines!

There are other factors that can cause an illness which may not be of organic origin. Examples would be genetic abnormality, poisoning, accident, or stress. Each of these can prove fatal by themselves, but more often than not they simply interfere with normal body metabolism so that organic invasion of the body in the form of microorganisms becomes possible due to the cat's lowered resistance. Again, external parasites on the body of a cat are relatively easily controlled; their real danger lies in the secondary infection they can create, either by injecting disease germs directly into the cat's blood stream, or by creating bodily lesions which become prime breeding grounds for various bacterial or fungal life forms. The treatment of these is invariably more difficult than the treatment of the original parasite.

BACTERIA AND DISEASE

The term bacteria is largely connected in most people's minds with disease and negative effects on the body, but this is not actually the whole picture and can give rise to problems in the treatment of disease. Bacteria are single or multicelled organisms that multiply, in the majority of cases, by simple fission—they divide to form sister cells which in turn divide in the same manner. By far the majority of bacteria are saprophytic—this means they live by assimilation of dead organic material, be this the animal itself or material passing through the body or within the bodily cells. As such, they do not create disease and are vital to the general well being of all life forms. Other bacteria, the minority, are parasitic and thus pathogenic—they create disease because they live on or in the host at its expense and render no beneficial service in return. Dead parasitic bacteria can thus be assimilated by the "good" bacteria, and likewise these can be attacked by the "bad."

Bacteria are so small that they can only be seen under a powerful microscope and are iden-

tified on the basis of the way they react to certain staining agents. They are said to be gram-positive or gram-negative, and antibiotics are based on their ability to kill either type. The problem is that the good bacteria are not of one type and the bad of the other, so that an antibiotic will kill the beneficial bacteria as readily as it will the parasitic types. For this reason a vet will not persist in the use of a single antibiotic, because if the parasitic bacteria becomes immune to the medicine and the saprophytic varieties do not, then its continued use will clearly make matters far worse. This general theory can be applied to most medicaments, for they will also have as much negative effect on the beneficial bacteria as they will on the parasites, which is why no treatment that fails to produce results in a given period of time should be continued. If it is, both bacteria types may well build a resistance to it and the net result is that it is achieving nothing and the illness marches on. It can thus be seen that illness is really an on-going battle that is continually being waged within a cat's body at microscopic level, and the cat stays healthy only for so long as the saprophytic bacteria hold the upper hand, thus allowing body cells to function properly.

TRANSMISSION OF DISEASE

Bacteria, together with viruses (which are really very small types of bacteria) and fungi (these are simple plant forms that may be saprophytic or parasitic), are very durable organisms, and because they are so small they are easily transmitted from one place, or host, to the other. They sometimes develop complex life histories that involve more than one host species (in which they are parasitic on one animal species but not on another, which is used purely as a means of transmission).

They are also capable of long resting periods, when they form spores which can withstand extremes of temperatures which would kill them in their active states. Winds can carry them high into the atmosphere, and thus around the world, to land and become active if conditions are right for their survival. When they reach high numbers in the host, many of them will leave, via feces or discharge from the nose, and so on, to be

Profile of a Persian kitten. If you notice that your pet seems listless, take it to the vet.

released into the air, where they may settle on a new host. Some are ingested by insects (such as fleas, flies, and the like), and these either deposit them onto the food of a potential host or they introduce them when the insect itself spends part or all of its life on a host (lice, fleas, and worms).

If they are carried by prey species of the cat, such as birds, mice, or rabbits, then this is yet another means by which they are transmitted from one animal to another. A very obvious and convenient way for bacteria to move is when humans give them a real helping hand by not maintaining good hygiene. If we do not wash our hands after handling sick cats, we can easily pass them on to other cats we have. In addition, failing to isolate ill cats will clearly be fortunate for the spread of pathogenic bacteria and their likes. Another way they can gain access to whole cat populations in an area is when we deliberately place cats from different regions together in close proximity to each other: in the cattery, the pet shop, the veterinary clinic's waiting room and, in great numbers, at the cat show. The early feline exhibitions were plagued with disease, and it was quite common for entire breeding programs to be wiped out after a cat had visited an exhibition. Happily, our knowledge of bacteria is now sufficiently advanced that we can combat these potential problem areas by sound hygienic husbandry. Risks are thus reduced to an acceptable level, but only if constant attention is paid to cleanliness at all levels of management. This is why catteries of repute insist on production of vaccination documents, as do cat exhibitions—and why they have veterinarians in attendance throughout the show. Pet shops will regularly disinfect all cages and utensils and will carefully check over all new arrivals to ensure that they are in good health. Even zoos are at risk from local cat populations, so every one of them automatically treats its various cat species, from the little ones through to the tigers, with suitable medicines and vaccinations against the major feline diseases.

Opposite: Copper-eyed white Persian kitten. Proper hygiene will go a long way toward keeping your pet healthy.

A basic understanding of bacteria, virus, and fungus thus shows that each are necessary realities of life and that we cannot protect the cat from them—nor would it be wise to do so completely. The objective is to keep them in a balanced form, for in this way the cat's natural metabolic machinery will ensure that the cat remains in good health.

HYGIENE

The subject of hygiene covers every aspect of the cat's life. Beyond washing our hands, we must do likewise with the cat's feeding utensils, which must be washed daily in hot water and a suitable detergent. Coal tar products affect cats in a negative way and should not be used for cleaning cat accessories. The availability of isolation quarters is vital when a number of cats are kept. The quarantine area should be as far away from where your cats regularly go as possible. In severe cases of illness, many veterinarians have special hospitalization units—just like humans have, and these are very useful to the owner of a few cats. Catteries should have their own facilities for treating sick felines; those who plan to board cats in such an establishment should be sure that divisions between adjacent pens are of a solid construction, not just netting, because this raises the possibility of direct contact and thus the transmission of germs.

Food: All food given to cats should be as fresh as possible, and should always be covered when it is in the kitchen waiting for preparation. Uneaten portions should either be discarded or returned to the fridge to be given to the cats later the same day. Meat should never be re-frozen once it has already been thawed, and frozen foods must be fully thawed before being fed to cats. Cats like their food at about room temperature—neither too hot nor too cold. Supplements such as cod liver oil must be kept in a darkened spot otherwise the rays of sunlight will reduce the strength of vitamins in them, rendering them useless.

It is not true that cats will not eat spoiled meat; as far as is known, every felid species so far studied will partake of carrion, but this does not mean it is healthy. Cats, like most animals, including man, will eat just about anything if they get hungry enough. Any food that you are not quite happy with should be thrown away, as the risk of introducing disease is not worth the chance. If fresh meat is given, it is much wiser to ensure that it is fit for human consumption. Meat sold for animal use only is often from stock that is diseased in some way—a high germ risk. Water should always be fresh, though sometimes its chlorine content is too high for cats and they would rather drink from puddles after rain has fallen.

STRESS

If the general husbandry of a cat's environment is sound, this is the first line of defense against illness and, with the exception of stress, other causal effects of illness will be physical—as with cuts, parasites, internal problems, and so on. Stress is much more difficult to identify specifically yet has received much attention from zoologists in recent years. Delicate species of animals, such as small birds, can die from stress within a few hours, but even large animals, such as wild cats brought into captivity, may decline rapidly in health and may die due to the stress factor. In domestic species stress is less prevalent, but is nonetheless an important factor that can reduce a cat's ability to ward off an illness.

In effect, the stressed cat consciously or unconsciously worries itself over a given situation and in so doing uses up much energy, thus depleting its body of such to the degree that it actually induces an illness. Stress can be difficult to trace because of its intangible nature—the presence of an aggressive dog next door is an unlikely cause for a cat, but is the sort of thing that illustrates the problem. A more likely source is if a cat is bullied a great deal by another cat and is confined so that it is unable to get away from the tormentor. Because stress is so difficult to pinpoint, it is very difficult to cure, so a cat owner can do no more than consider every aspect of the cat's life to see if there are situations that might create the condition. This can be so vague a condition that it is the overall environment that creates it, and in such a case then the only cure would, in fact, be to relocate the cat. Stress is clearly related to the overall central nervous system of a cat but is not necessarily of a genetic nature which has resulted from close inbreeding. Nervousness and stress are similar in many ways but should not be confused. Wild cats are unlikely to be closely bred, but they may well be very nervous when first captured—yet they adjust. A stressed cat may be quite a well-balanced animal that is suddenly bothered by something. Fortunately, if the cat is well cared for and is given much affection, then stress is not likely to be a factor to consider in the majority of cases—unless the cat is unduly confined, which is when the condition seems most likely to occur. Certain breeds are more susceptible to stress than others.

PARASITES

Parasites may be conveniently divided into two groups: those which are found externally and those which invade the inner body. The external forms can be grouped together with lesions as obvious ways in which disease gains access to the body. In all cases of treating a cat's fur with powders and sprays for parasites, care must be taken that excess is not left on the coat; otherwise this will be licked off by the cat and may have a toxic effect on it.

External parasites: *Fleas*–apart from their direct effect upon the cat, fleas are also intermediate hosts of the tapeworm, *Dipylidium* sp. Fleas are most prevalent during warm weather and are visible to the naked eye as small red-brown creatures that scurry about in the fur. They usually congregate at the base of the tail, behind the ears, and on the sparsely coated underbelly. They live by sucking the blood of their host; however, they do not complete their lifecycle on the cat but lay their eggs in the bedding, woodwork, and such places.

The feces of fleas can be seen as black clusters the size of dust. If placed on dampened white paper they will stain this red. Infestations of fleas will cause anemia, but they should never reach such proportions in the first place, as this would indicate lack of attention to the cat's fur and general hygiene. Sometimes a cat may return home with numerous fleas on it, if it has been in contact with birds or hedgehogs, and may also carry the fleas of dogs—and vice versa. Treatment is simple enough with one of the

Ebony Oriental Shorthair. Stress can leave a cat quite vulnerable to illness; therefore, if your cat seems upset by something, try to find out what that is and alleviate the situation as soon as you can.

A show cat, like this champion Russian Blue, is very likely to pick up different germs at shows. Therefore, upon returning home, a show cat should be quarantined for a few days, especially if there are young kittens or pregnant queens in your home.

powder, liquid, or aerosol acaricides, which will not only kill the fleas but all other related creepy crawlies, such as lice and mites.

It is essential that all bedding is treated as well, otherwise reinfestation will occur. Repeat treatment will be required seven to ten days later so that unhatched eggs at the first treatment have had time to hatch.

Lice–These are flat grayish creatures that usually invade the head region. They move slowly through the fur and complete their life-cycle on the host. Their eggs are elongate white cone-shaped bodies that can be seen with a hand lens on the fur, which they adhere to. Lice are less common than fleas on cats. Treatment is the same as for fleas.

Mange mite–These are microparasites (however, the ear mite is barely visible to the eye). On the body, they burrow into the skin and create rashes and hair loss, whilst in the ear they invade the skin and create a brownish wax, with which they can be identified. Irritation is accompanied by scratching, which may ultimately cause lesions which add to the problem. Veterinary preparations are recommended, as the various mite species may prove difficult to eradicate without proper microscopic identification. Parasitic baths may be required, and repeat treatment is essential to account for the complete life cycle.

Ticks–These undesirables are not common on cats but sometimes are able to avoid the cat's grooming and hang on. They quickly fill up their bodies with the cat's blood before releasing their hold, and fall to the ground where they shed many eggs to infect the next victim. They should not be pulled off with tweezers until they have been treated with iodine, alcohol, a saline solution, or similar methods of making them release their holds. Commonly known as sheep ticks, they use the hedgehog as a host, and it is often via this that dogs and cats may pick them up.

Ringworm–This is not the result of a worm's activities but is a fungal parasite. Bare areas of the skin are seen and may exhibit liquid or crusty edges. These will spread if the condition is not arrested with veterinary treatment. Soft bedding belonging to the cat should be burnt, as the spores of the fungi can live there.

Internal parasites: Of the non-bacterial parasites that may afflict a cat's internal organs, the most common are roundworm, *Toxocara mystax* and *Toxascaris leonina*, and the tapeworms, *Dipylidium* and *Taenia* spp. Other worms, such as hookworms, heartworms, and lungworms may also afflict cats but are less common. All cats have worms of varying sizes in many parts of their bodies, and the majority create no problems. However, infestations of roundworms or tapeworms will deplete the cat of its nutrition and eventually create other problems.

Worms can be seen either as long spaghetti-like threads or as segments that look like rice. They live by ingesting the food in the cat's intestines and then produce eggs which are shed in cat's feces to be picked up by another cat sniffing at these. They may also be transmitted via mice or beetles, and, once in the cat's mouth, they are swallowed and pass to the intestines. While small, they can also migrate through tissues and enter the female's uterus, thus into newly or unborn kittens. It is in the kittens that they are the most serious hazard; they will cause diarrhea and stunted development. For this reason, all queens should be wormed prior to being mated and can be treated again during pregnancy. Adult cats should be wormed about twice a year—provided that they are healthy at the time. Any worms found in a cat's feces should be destroyed by burning, and, of course, all litter trays should be regularly subjected to washing and disinfecting.

Hookworms are rarely seen in the UK but are more common in the USA and other countries. These worms actually suck the blood of their host, and blood-streaked diarrhea may indicate their presence. Your vet will identify and treat these parasites.

In all cases of suspected internal parasites, the owner can help the veterinarian by gathering a sample of the feces and urine, in suitably hygienic containers, so that these are available for microscopy if required.

Non-parasitic skin problems: Not all scratching by the cat is indicative of a parasite, for the problem may be internal; the diet may lack something, a chemical may be causing the problem, or the cat may have burnt itself without this being apparent to the owner.

SKIN LESIONS AND BITES

Both cuts and bites are obvious ways disease bacteria can enter the cat's body, so they should be treated promptly. Wounds can arise from numerous sources; examples would be from cat fights, attacks by dogs, snake bites, wasp and bee stings, or by the cat cutting itself on glass, etc. The first thing to do is to establish the extent of the damage and to restrict blood flow in the case of bad wounds. The latter, of course, must receive veterinary treatment as soon as possible, and the cat must be restrained from excessive movements; wrapping it in a towel after initially dressing the wound is one way. This will also keep it warm, thus reducing the effect of shock. It may be necessary to clip the fur from around a wound so that it can be properly cleaned and treated with an antiseptic ointment. If bandaging is needed, it should be wrapped around the wound for some distance either side of it; it should be tight enough to reduce the flow of blood, but not so tight that it becomes a tourniquet. The wound should be covered with a cotton or similar cold compress.

With the exception of snake bites from poisonous species, the vast majority of skin lesions will have a localized effect—that is, bacterial or fungal infection is usually restricted to the area of the wound. If treated promptly, skin lesions are unlikely to prove serious.

Stings: Try to locate and remove the stinger after bathing with a mild disinfectant—the bee leaves its stinger in the victim but the wasp does not. A cat stung on the mouth is difficult to treat and should be rushed to the vet, as swelling may interfere with breathing.

Bites: Dog bites should be carefully bathed with mild disinfectant and the cat taken to the vet for a thorough check-up. Broken skin, if bleeding, should be treated with a gauze bandage. Treat for shock as well—this may be delayed and become obvious some minutes after the actual attack.

Snake bites: Restrict blood flow to the bitten point—usually the limb—by the use of a tourniquet if it is known that the snake was of a venomous species; this will be obvious by rapid swelling around the wound. Apply permanganate crystals, if available, to the wound. The cat will probably vomit and will certainly go into shock. If at all possible, keep the snake (if it was killed) for identification so the appropriate serum can be given. The vast majority of the world's snakes are non-poisonous; in the UK only the adder is venomous, but in the USA and other countries with warm climates there are a number. If poisonous species are known to exist in your locality, it is wise to become familiar with their markings and to obtain specific instructions on coping with emergency cases.

Burns: These may be caused directly by fire or hot kitchen burners, by hot liquids, or by chemicals. In the latter case the cat should be very well washed with water to dilute the chemical, toweled down, and taken to the vet. In other cases the wound should be cooled by the use of a compress and then cleaned as best as one can. A thin layer of petroleum jelly can be put on a gauze pad, which can then be secured with a bandage pending treatment by the vet. A burn will automatically be germ-free so it is important not to contaminate it with dirt.

Swellings: The fact that a cat has been subject to a sting or bump may not be immediately apparent, and only when a swelling bursts and extrudes pus is it obvious something was amiss. When this happens, the wound should be carefully bathed and suitably dressed using an antiseptic ointment to prevent secondary infection.

Shock: A badly shocked cat may collapse and should be placed in a quiet, well-aerated but darkened spot. Cover it with a blanket to keep it warm, and seek the vet's advice. It will probably recover after a short while. Glucose will be helpful in recovery. Cover a shocked cat only if the weather is cold—if it is warm, no blanketing will be required, as this might actually increase heat loss.

MAJOR FELINE DISEASES

There are, of course, a great number of diseases that a cat may become ill with and here just a few of the more well-known ones will be mentioned because of their considerable importance to all cat owners.

Feline influenza (cat flu): A potentially fatal disease, cat flu affects the upper respiratory system and is caused by one of a number of viruses. The clinical signs are sneezing, coughing, runny

Siamese. Regularly check your cat's ears for parasites, especially if you live in a high-risk area.

A brown tabby domestic shorthair. Vaccines and booster shots protect your cat from the major feline diseases; they should be administered on a schedule suggested by your veterinarian.

eyes, and nasal discharge. However, these same signs may indicate only a heavy cold or other problems; only a veterinarian can establish this fact. Kittens are especially susceptible to serious illness from cat flu, so they must be protected by vaccination from about the age of eight to ten weeks—this coinciding with a drop in the antibodies the kitten received from its mother. A second injection will be required about 21-28 days later, and thereafter annual boosters are necessary. Full protection is not developed in the cat until seven days after its second dose, so during this period the cat should be kept within the confines of the home. Should a cat have had—and recovered from—cat flu, it can thereafter become a carrier and infect other cats. This disease is transmitted by close contact with affected cats or carriers.

Feline enteritis (feline panleucopenia): Along with cat flu, this is another high mortality rate disease in all felid species kept in captivity. It is highly contagious and is transmitted by direct or proximal contact with other cats, but can also be passed via host species such as the flea. Affected cats will vomit, exhibit acute diarrhea, excessive thirst, dehydration, and obvious pain. They may die within hours of exhibiting clinical signs, or they may linger on for days, depending on the severity of the attack and the cat's resistance levels. Protection from the disease is via vaccination, which can be combined with that for cat flu; it requires the same repeat dosage and boosters.

Pregnant queens can be given additional boosters to top up their levels of antibodies, which become available to the kittens via the colostrum milk of their first feeding from the mother. It will be appreciated that the signs of several major feline diseases are so general that they could indeed by symptomatic of just about any illness; this is why veterinary advice must be obtained sooner rather than later. It is wiser to assume the worst; this way time will not be lost with home treatments, especially where young kittens are concerned.

Feline leukemia virus (FeLV): This terrifying virus strikes fear into the hearts of cat lovers everywhere. Highly contagious, FeLV can cause tumors, anemia, and, of course, leukemia. Many pet shops and catteries advertise that their stock is FeLV-negative; therefore, when purchasing a cat, buy from such an establishment if at all possible. If you already own a cat, have it tested for the virus by your veterinarian.

Cats that test positive for FeLV should be isolated so that they won't spread the disease to others. Some FeLV-positive cats live for years with the virus, while others die within a few months of contracting it. A vaccine has recently been developed which protects cats from FeLV; contact your veterinarian about it and have your cat inoculated before it's too late!

OTHER HEALTH MATTERS

Respiratory problems: Other than cat flu, felines may suffer from pleurisy, pneumonia, bronchitis, asthma, or lungworms. In each case the cats will exhibit difficulty in breathing, wheezing, coughing, and possibly vomiting. Various causes can create these problems, and these include chilling, inhaling of irritant gases (including tobacco smoke), dust particles, and, in the majority of cases, different groups of microorganisms such as bacteria, fungus, or virus. Relief is obtained by drugs or antibiotics which liquefy any build-up of matter in the lungs and attack the root cause.

Digestive problems: Whilst enteritis is a major disease in cats, there are many other ailments that can become just as serious if left unattended. Afflicted cats will exhibit signs which will include lack of appetite, thirst, diarrhea, constipation, and regurgitation of food or vomiting. Often the cause may be a blockage of the intestines by a physical body such as a hairball, or something such as a piece of plastic from a toy. Hairballs are most likely to occur in longhaired breeds due to the cat's constant grooming habits. Administration of liquid paraffin (medicinal), at the rate of two to three teaspoonfuls on each of two days, should dislodge the obstruction; if this doesn't work, veterinary help will be required. Do not make a habit of using this liquid as a preventative measure because it will adversely affect vitamin absorption.

The digestive tract may be infected by many bacteria, which may be specific to it or the result of infections to bodily organs such as the liver or kidneys. In addition, clinical signs will include collapse and sensitivity when touched. Only a veterinarian can diagnose and treat such ailments.

Rabies: This very serious illness is of importance to humans because it is so dangerous. A bite or scratch from a rabid animal is fatal unless it is promptly treated, and, as a result, certain areas have very strict quarantine laws; these include the UK, Australia, New Zealand, and Hawaii. Rabies may exist in dogs, wolves, foxes, rodents, and cats, amongst other species, and is of a viral nature that affects many parts of the body, including the nervous system. Its incubation period may be up to 12 months, though quarantine is usually six months because pets are automatically vaccinated against the disease on arrival in quarantine stations. Anti-rabies injections are not required for cats that have never left the countries stated, but if you are moving from one of these countries, vaccination against the disease is advised—even if it is not a requirement of the country to which you plan to take your pets.

A rabid animal develops a fear of daylight, has great thirst, develops muscular twitches, and, most importantly, has no fear of humans and will attack without fear for its own safety. It is thus important to immediately take your cat to a vet if it is involved in a fight with feral or wild animals. Fortunately, this disease appears to be dying out as a result of the various measures taken to combat it over the years.

Post mortem: Should an adult cat or kitten die suddenly, for no apparent reason, having exhibited no signs of discomfort, it is always wise to have your vet conduct a post mortem on the cat. This may reveal the cause and may be of some significance, especially if other cats are kept in the household.

Accidents: Generally, cats are not prone to broken limbs, but they sometimes land badly from a jump and may limp for a while. This should clear up within 48 hours, but if it persists and the cat continues to limp, then a visit to the vet is advised. In the event of a cat being knocked over by a motor vehicle, it should be moved with great care to a safe place. Because of the risk of internal injury, place the cat on a stiff carrier, such as plywood or thick cardboard; this way it can be transported rapidly to the nearest vet. Try to keep the cat calm if it is able to move, and do not lift its head if it is bleeding from the mouth, as this may merely cause the blood to go back into the throat. Remove its collar if this can be done without problem. Broken bones can be repaired by your vet, but even if the damage means that a limb must be amputated, this is not the end of the world. I know of both dogs and cats that have only three legs yet have adjusted and lead very happy lives; they still manage to run, jump and play.

Feline body temperature: The normal body temperature of a cat is about 38.6°C (101.5°F), but this can fluctuate slightly, depending on the state of the cat (for example, after exercise or during hot weather). However, once it reaches 39.4°C (103°F), it may be assumed that the cat is exhibiting a high temperature and may thus be showing the first signs of an ailment. Taking the temperature is done at the rectum by means of an appropriate clinical thermometer. This is first shaken so that the mercury drops down to the bulb end, and it can then be lubricated with a suitable medium—petroleum jelly or olive oil. It is easier to attend to the actual job if somebody helps you by securing the cat by its neck or forepaws. The tail is then lifted and the thermometer slid inside to a depth of about 2 cm (¾ in), tilting it slightly so that it presses against the anal wall. Hold for about a minute and then take it out and read the temperature. Sterilize the thermometer before and after use.

Feline pulse rate: The pulse of a cat will indicate the rate at which blood is being pumped around the body—it is indicative of heartbeat. This rate may be strong or weak, which indicates the amount of blood at each pump that is being circulated. The normal pulse rate for cats is in the range of 110 to 140. However, apparent lack of pulse in a motionless cat should not be taken to indicate that the cat is dead, but urgent veterinary help should still be sought in such instances. The pulse may be taken by carefully feeling an artery just inside the rear leg of the cat at the groin.

Opposite: Although cats have the remarkable ability to land on their feet in many situations, they are not immune from accidents caused by falls.

Black and white American Curl. Experimental in most associations, this breed is selected for the curled ears. Some mutational breeds have health defects caused by their genetic state, so find out about your cat's breed before you mate it.

THE FELINE FIRST AID KIT

Whether one has a single cat or a number of them, it is always worthwhile to have various items available so that, in the event of the cat being ill or suffering an injury, treatment can be given, even if only until the cat can be taken to the vet for more thorough attention. The first aid kit should be kept handy, suitably labelled, and well out of the reach of young children. A typical first aid box would contain the following items:

1) Sharp, blunt-ended curved scissors
2) Wide and narrow bandages
3) Lint gauze
4) Cotton balls
5) Cotton swabs
6) Adhesive dressings of different sizes
7) Tweezers or forceps
8) Clinical thermometer
9) Eye dropper
10) Eye wash (human type)
11) Liquid paraffin (medicinal)
12) Styptic pencil or permanganate crystals
13) Petroleum jelly
14) Milk of magnesia
15) Antiseptic cream and lotion
16) Disinfectant
17) Anti-parasitic spray (for fleas)
18) Graduated measure for liquids
19) Surgical spirits
20) Disposable surgical gloves
21) Good hand lens

A pair of Persians. If you keep more than one cat, keep a lookout for signs of ill health. Remember that many ailments are highly contagious.

GENEALOGY OF DOMESTIC CATS

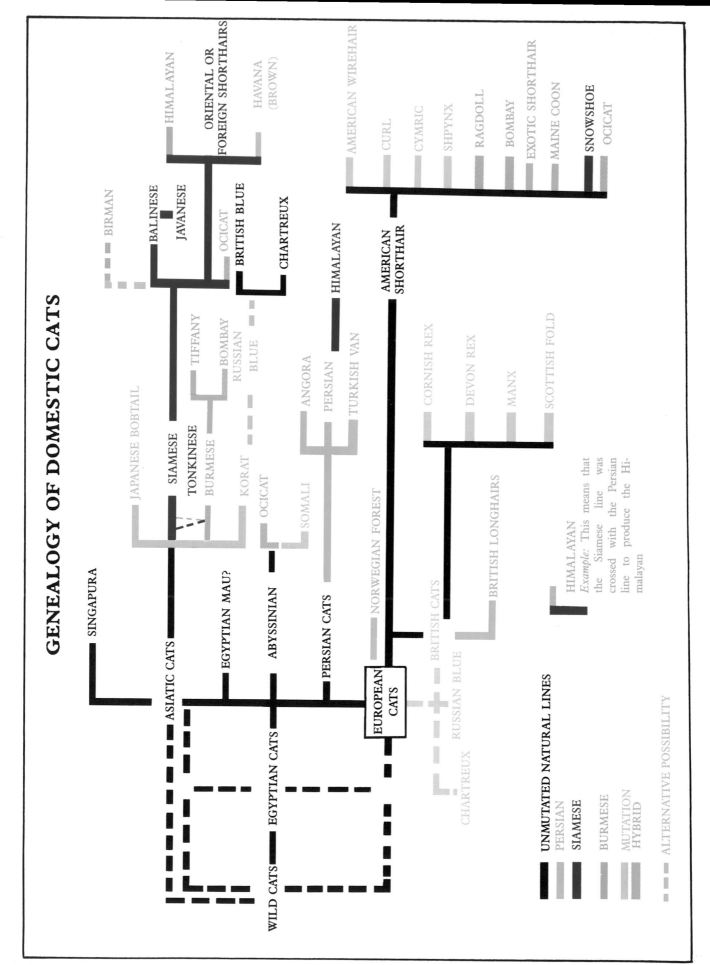

Legend:

- UNMUTATED NATURAL LINES
- PERSIAN
- SIAMESE
- BURMESE
- MUTATION
- HYBRID
- ALTERNATIVE POSSIBILITY

HIMALAYAN
Example: This means that the Siamese line was crossed with the Persian line to produce the Himalayan

DOMESTIC CAT BREEDS

To the person just entering the cat fancy, the way in which cats are classified may seem rather bewildering—the more so if they are familiar with dog groups, which follow a system based on purpose of origin and the long establishment of breeds. Cats are more akin to rabbits and guinea pigs; since they have a restricted number of bodily forms, other features are used to determine breed status, such as color, pattern, and fur length. To the dog fraternity, such features are relatively trivial matters that merely indicate the variety of a breed, but in most other domestic species they become far more important.

As a result of the way cats have developed, the term "breed" has a much more loose application in cats than in dogs, and it is this that, in part, creates the problem. It is compounded by the fact that a breed in the UK may only rank as a variety in the USA; in addition, a breed of cat which exhibits long hair is not only given breed status but its name changes as well. For example, a longhaired Siamese becomes a Balinese, a longhaired Abyssinian a Somali, and a longhaired Burmese a Tiffany. In addition, a color variety may also become a breed; the light phase Burmese, for example, were once called Malayans in the USA (some associations may still call them this).

Color itself is often transposed when it crosses the Atlantic, as the chocolate Burmese of Britain becomes the champagne Burmese in the USA. Clearly, international agreements between the various ruling bodies would be of great benefit to the cat fancy, but, alas, these are unlikely in the near future. Even when a breed is recognized on both sides of the Atlantic (which is true for most breeds), there are often clear differences—the American Burmese would often not get a prize in a British show, and vice versa. This is because the breeds themselves have developed along separate lines in the two countries.

BASIC CLASSIFICATION

Cats are divided into three broad groups: longhaired, shorthaired, and foreign; these groups can be divided further. The foreigns include the Siamese, the Burmese, the Korat, and others in which, apart from color, the overall conformation is of a lithe cat with a wedge-shaped face and comparatively large ears; it may sport a long or short coat. The shorthaired cats are essentially the same cats, in conformation terms, as the longhairs, but, of course, they have shorter coats. They are stocky cats with round faces and good muscle, and they are mostly of European origin. The longhaired cats are those known under that name in the UK, but are known in the USA as Persians. These are cats with profuse fur; other longhairs, such as the Birman, have fur that is far less dense. Still confused? Perhaps if we look at the way in which the breeds have developed, it will help to place things into a sort of logical pattern.

HOW A BREED IS PRODUCED

It will be appreciated that the term "breed" in cats is used rather loosely, as many of the breeds are actually hybrids or merely color varieties of more obvious breeds by a typical understanding of the term. Given time, the new breeds will no doubt slowly develop into more obvious types; however, it must always be remembered that the cat is probably genetically limited in its conformation, so there will always be very little difference between certain breeds—be they of the foreign type or of the Euro-American types. The present-day cat breeds have been produced in one of three ways.

Natural: Many cat books will state that "this is a natural breed"; however, this should not be taken in the literal sense, because all domestic cats are man-made. What natural means is that the breed was developed from street cats that were indigenous to a given area. In some cases, the breeds existed in purer states than in others (how pure being a bone of contention amongst those in the cat fancy). A natural cat was the product of random matings within its locality or country, depending on how precise one wishes to be in this discussion. Such cats were then selectively bred to retain or lose certain features so that, by this process, a purebreeding population of cats—a breed—was produced.

Mutation: If a mutation appears in a cat, whether it is in an established breed or in a mongrel, a breed can be created. The mutation may be one of color or one of conformation. For example, the famous Manx cat (with no tail) appeared in a litter of street cats found in Europe. It was then selectively bred in order to retain the abnormality; thus it became an established breed—its lack of tail is the crucial factor that raises it to breed status. If the mutation is one of color, again a breed can be created. As an example, the Siamese cat is well known because it sports dark extremities on its face, ears, feet, and tail. This mutation appeared on a cat of foreign origin which was believed to have come from Siam (Thailand); thus the breed became know as the Siamese. A standard was applied to the breed for type, but the crucial feature was, of course, the coloration.

Hybridization: The third method of producing a breed is by crossing existing breeds, either to create a modified overall conformation or to transfer a mutation from one breed to another. As an example, the Bombay is the result of crossing a Burmese with a black American Shorthair. The resulting offspring are thus basically black Burmese but have a less foreign look to them. They may then be bred to their own type or mated back to one of their precursors. Therefore, they are presently hybrids, but, given sufficient time, will eventually become established to the point that only Bombay to Bombay matings will be accepted. A parallel can be seen in Old English rabbits, which are also hybrids at each generation. In the case of Himalayan cats (called colorpoint in the UK and most other countries other than the USA), the Siamese color pattern was transferred to a Persian (known as a longhair in the UK). So well established is the Himalayan as a longhaired variety that the British consider it merely one of the many forms of the longhair (Persian), and it is exhibited as such, not as a separate breed. In the USA, the Himalayan enjoyed breed status for a while, but it is now mostly judged against the Persian standard for its type.

BREED HISTORIES

Many breeders will claim great antiquity for their chosen breed, and such claims will range from the credible to those which stretch the imagination and take no account of historical reality. The newcomer should take a balanced view based on probability, rather than accepting fanciful notions at face value.

A breed's history can basically be divided into two parts: first, that part which is undisputable and backed up by recorded fact, and, secondly, that which pre-dates records. Breeds such as the British and American Shorthairs, or foreigns as a group, obviously go back for centuries—indeed right back to the first domesticated cats; such origins are common to all cats. However, to imply that a breed has existed, as such, for centuries is the more debatable aspect. Consider the Egyptian Mau as a case in point. The fact that it is spotted and that the original imports to Italy were from Egypt establishes nothing. A British spotted tabby could have as much claim to direct lineage from the cats of the pharaohs as could an Egyptian Mau!

The American Shorthair is a natural breed, having been developed from street cats indigenous to the United States in colonial times.

What is often conveniently overlooked when discussing breed histories is the enormous span of time that is involved. During that period, countless wars have taken place, as have periods of high drought, complete movement of populations, and the arrival and departure of many foreigners—and their cats. Of course, there will still be an onward progression of local cat populations, but to imply that they have remained "pure" throughout the two or more thousand years we are looking at is fanciful in the extreme. The infusion of wild cat genes until very recent times—indeed to the present—is quite possible in the Near East but highly unlikely in Europe, thus the comment in respect to direct lineage of British tabbies from the cats of the Egyptians. On the other hand, there are clear instances where, through geographic or other forms of isolation, a cat might qualify for the label "breed" for many centuries even though this has not been recorded, or any standard set to breed against.

As an example, many of the street cats of Asia had (and still have) the typical head shape of foreign breeds, and it is entirely possible that if a color mutation had appeared amongst these then this might have been regarded as something special—just as it is today. Such a cat would have had value and would no doubt have ended up in the hands of a wealthy person or the local temple. The mutation would then be established and guarded as the property of the royalty or of the temple. This is how a form of isolation was created that resulted in a closely bred population, which then resulted in the movement towards breed status. Even so, such breeds were unlikely to remain in isolation for great spans of time, so it is reasonable to suppose that the purest of breeds are only of a few hundred years old at best. To think in terms of thousands of years is quite unrealistic.

Mere possession of a feature cannot be taken as a sure indication of lineage—a fact well known to zoologists—because an animal can somehow acquire a feature that makes it look like another. In terms of domestic cats, the Himalayan is a clear example. It looks and breeds like the best of pedigreed Persians, but we have already shown that it is a crossbreed of the Siamese. Comparison of present-day breeds to historical statues or paintings may give a clue to origins, but they should certainly not be regarded, as sometimes seems to be the case, as sure proof of a breed's long existence.

Another aspect that should also be considered, when viewing old prints and artifacts, is in respect to mutational forms known to exist many centuries earlier. It cannot be assumed that these cats are related to those breeds showing the mutation today, because such mutations may have appeared at least one or more times in different locations and in different time periods. This means that the lineage of the cats carrying the mutation may be totally unrelated; therefore, care should be exercised so that wrong conclusions are not assumed without other data.

It can indeed be very difficult to establish how old a breed is, other than in the recent breeds, simply because the line between a type and a breed is rarely clear-cut. In the modern sense, one would have to say that a breed is only as old as the oldest recorded standard and known written pedigrees. This is not ideal, but at least it gives a very precise date to the age of purebreeding cats. It can then be assumed that the breed was a number of years older, for it may well have existed in a more or less pure state before it became of interest to cat owners in the Western countries.

BREED DESCRIPTIONS

In the following text, the breed descriptions are not the actual standards as laid down in either the USA, the UK, or Australia, but they are of a general descriptive nature. The full standards are often very repetitious within breeds, as in the Persian colors, for example, where only the color differs within the breed. I have tried to avoid statements that are very subjective; "its eyes convey sweetness, loyalty, and intelligence" or "is suited to home-loving people who will show affection to this breed" are examples of terms that could be applied to just about any pet animal species in the world! Breeds do have different qualities, but they are not as individual as many writers like to imply. All cats, whether pedigreed, hybrid, or alley cats, can be loving, intelligent, playful, and all the other labels one cares to apply to them. To what extent

Siamese Cat, Exotic Shorthair Cat

Abyssinian Cat, Himalayan Cat

Maine Coon Cat, Burmese Cat

American Shorthair Cat, Persian Cat

Siamese Cat, Exotic Shorthair Cat

Abyssinian Cat, Himalayan Cat

Maine Coon Cat, Burmese Cat

American Shorthair Cat, Persian Cat

The popularity of cats as pets continues to grow, as exemplified by this set of United States postal stamps issued in the 1980s.

a cat displays these qualities is influenced by its breed type, but also by the environment it lives in and the way it is reared. These latter factors will actually play a far greater part in determining the characteristics of a cat than will its breed type.

Persians are known as longhairs in the United Kingdom. For years, this has been the most popular breed in the United States.

Breed names: Within the actual breed descriptions, the names used are those by which the breed is known to Americans. However, for British and Australian readers, the name by which a breed is known in their country is indicated in parentheses wherever clarification is thought to be needed.

Colors: Within the breed descriptions, the more popular colors found in the breed are mentioned—in some cases all of the colors. However, in order to avoid undue repetition, especially where the breed's color list is extensive (over 70 variations in some breeds), statements such as "all or most accepted colors" are used. The reader is advised to consult the standard of the association he plans to join, as this will list the colors that are accepted for each breed. In fact, as colors are being added to many breeds each year, no book could be totally up-to-date on this aspect. As color and pattern are so important in the cat fancy a chapter has been devoted to this so that readers can refer to colors independent of reference to them within the breeds. This means there is a degree of duplication in discussion of colors, but the benefits of including a separate chapter on color justified this approach, for it allowed more detailed discussion.

Comparison of Popularity of Cat Breeds
Longhairs: UK Registrations–40.3%; CFA Registrations–78.4%.
Siamese: UK Registrations–24.8%; CFA Registrations–6.1%. (This figure includes the Colorpoint Shorthair registrations, which are regarded as a separate breed in the USA but not in the UK.)
Burmese: UK Registrations–15.5%; CFA Registrations–1.7%.
Other Shorthairs: UK Registrations–19.4%; CFA Registrations–13.4%.

These are given by percentage of total registrations and from these it is clear that the Siamese and Burmese are far more popular in the UK, in relation to all other breeds, including the longhairs (Persians), than they are in the USA—presupposing that the CFA figures are considered a reasonable refection of the American scene as a whole. The other comment that must be made in relation to popularity status is that it reflects the trend in numerical terms compared against its own previous record—and not against all registrations as a whole. A breed may thus be making progress purely in terms of its numbers, but may be losing its overall percentage of all breeds registered.

LONGHAIRED BREEDS

All longhaired cat breeds are, of necessity, mutational breeds since there are no wild species of cat that have long hair. The Chinese desert cat, *Felis bieti*, comes the closest in that its winter coat sports numerous long guard hairs, as does that of the European wild cat, *Felis silvestris*. In these species the genes responsible would be dominant for this feature, but in domestic breeds the gene is recessive in mode of inheritance, as they are in domestic breeds, so that a cat can only exhibit long hair if it is pure for this. However, it can carry the longhaired gene in its make-up. This means that two shorthaired cats can produce longhaired kittens within a litter.

Exactly when and where the longhaired mutation first appeared is not known, but it certainly is old, as longhaired cats are depicted from about the 15th century. As they appear in many different parts of the world, from Europe to China and the Near East to India, it may be that the coat gene has mutated more than once to produce long hair. However, man's travels could easily have transported the original mutation around the world, so we may never know for sure which is the case. The very long and dense coat seen on modern breeds is the result of selection for this feature, and there may be almost no limit to the potential length a coat may become—evidenced in other pets such as the guinea pig, where it has been taken to extremes in the Peruvian variety. It has to be hoped that cat breeders never go to such lengths, for this would surely ruin such cats.

Whilst in the Persians the hair is profuse, in other breeds the length of hair is easily managed—as in the Balinese or the Birman, so there is a nice range to suit all tastes. Any shortcoated breed can be produced with a long coat; it is simply a case of introducing the mutation by crossbreeding and then breeding out the introduced longhaired breed's type in successive generations—it is even possible to have a longhaired rex coat. However, one must remember that, in doing this, one might actually end up with what

is virtually a duplicate of an existing breed, which would seem a somewhat self-defeating objective, with differences reflecting the density of coat, depending on the type of longhaired breed used in the first place.

A dilute calico Persian. Some experts believe that the longhair gene was introduced by the Chinese desert cat, *Felis bieti*.

Longhaired breeds will have exactly the same characteristics as their shorthaired equivalents because the gene for hair length is not known to be in any way linked to other features. However, one must be clear on this point because the characteristics of the Persian are somewhat different from those of, for example, British or

American Shorthairs. This is because the Persians have been subject to very intense breeding for coat quality, and it is this fact, the degree of breeding, that has shaped the nature of these breeds, not the fact that they have long hair.

In deciding to have a longhaired breed, especially one such as the Persian, do give careful thought to the amount of time that must be spent on daily grooming of the coat. This need not be an ordeal but must be attended to regularly, otherwise the coat will soon look a mess—especially if the cat becomes very wet in a downpour of rain. In some longhaired breeds, the coat is of a fine and silky nature; this is easier to cope with than in breeds where it is soft and almost woolen in texture. However, even within the same breed the texture can vary from cat to cat, so seeing the parents of kittens may indicate the likely texture in their offspring's coats. Longhaired cats are available in every possible coat pattern and color shade, so again there is no shortage of choice.

A pair of orange-eyed white Persians. Persians have been selectively bred for coat quality as well as hair length.

BALINESE

Origin: The Balinese is a longhaired Siamese; it was developed from a mutation that first appeared in the USA about the mid 1950s. It was originally called the longhaired Siamese, but traditional breeders objected to this name. As it happened, those specializing in this new mutation were also less than keen on such a name, so it was eventually decided to rename this breed the Balinese. It was thought that the graceful movements of the cat were paralleled by the famous dancers of the tropical isle of Bali, so this seemed an appropriate name to use. It was accepted by most American associations in the early 1970s. Its status in the UK is provisional, but full breed status should follow in due course.

The Balinese should not be confused with the Himalayan, the Birman, or the Ragdoll, to each of which it has a superficial resemblance because of the Siamese gene markings. Confusion can be avoided with the Birman because of the white gloves on the Birman's feet; with the Ragdoll, either on the same grounds or because of its heavy build; and with the Himalayan, which is an altogether stockier cat with a much more profuse coat (the Himalayan is the colorpoint longhair of the UK). On the other hand, the difference between a Balinese and a Javanese is only one of color.

Character: The Balinese has exactly the same characteristics as the Siamese, of which it is simply a longhaired variety. It is thus a very active cat.

Appearance: *Head*—The head is wedge-shaped, the ears are wide at their base and taper to a rounded tip. The nose is straight and of good length. The bite is level. The neck should be proportionate to the cat's size so that it does not look long or short. The eyes should be Oriental in shape and slant towards the nose. Their color should be a clear blue.

Body—The body is of slim build and supported on slender legs, of which the hind ones should be slightly longer than those in the front. The tail should be of good length but, again, in proportionate balance to the rest of the cat.

Coat—The coat should be of medium length and lay flat to the body. Its texture should be fine and silky to the touch. The fur on the tail

A lilac point Balinese kitten. The Balinese is a longhaired Siamese, and the breed was once known by this name.

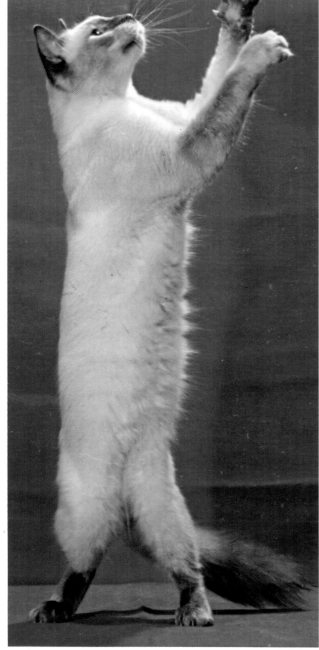

A blue point male Balinese. In the USA, the Balinese is accepted in only the four Siamese colors; in the UK, many other colors are allowed.

is generally longer and gives it a beautiful plumy look when the cat is on the move. The coat lacks a woolly undercoat and thus is easily groomed.

Colors—The Balinese is available in many colors. However, only seal, chocolate, blue, and lilac are permitted as Balinese in the USA, where all other colors are known as Javanese. In the UK, cats of these other colors are allowed to be registered as Balinese. The color of the points (face, ears, feet, and tail) should be clearly defined.

Faults—White toes, kinks in the tail, uneven bite, and tendency to squat.

Comment—This is a most attractive breed that is gaining more followers with each passing year. The long coat, for this author, gives the breed a more beautiful look than that of the Siamese, for it softens the features; however, beauty is in the eye of the beholder. Nonetheless, breeds with long but not dense coats are enjoying great popularity, no doubt because they offer the elegance of a long coat with the practical ease with which they can be kept looking smart.

BIRMAN

Origin: The history of the Birman is lost in the legends of the past. It was believed that in the temples of Burma there lived a race of pure white cats, and that there was a golden goddess who also lived in the temples and was worshiped by the priests. When a priest died his soul returned to earth in the body of a white cat. One day a famous priest was praying, with his favorite cat by his side, when the temple was attacked and the priest killed. At the moment of his death, the cat stood on his body and stared at the goddess. The white changed to a beautiful golden color, darker at the cat's extremities. The eyes became as blue as those of the goddess, but where the cat's paws rested on the priest the fur remained snow white as a mark of purity. The next day all the cats in the temple had also become this same color. The cats became even more sacred in the temples, but as time passed the priests fell from favor and had to flee from Burma into Tibet. They were helped by French and British troops stationed in the area, and as

The Birman breed is known for its white paws, known as gloves or mittens on the front feet and gauntlets on the rear feet.

In France, this breed is known as the Sacred Cat of Burma.

a gesture of appreciation a pair of cats was sent to France to become the foundation of the breed in Europe. Another story says that the cats were sold by disloyal workers in the temple.

It is likely that we will never know the truth, but the fact is that in the first importation, in 1919, there was a pregnant female named Sita; she produced a well-marked female called Poupee. The Birman continued to be developed in France, where it was known as the "Sacred Cat of Burma." The Germans were also very keen on this new breed, and the numbers steadily increased. The breed arrived in the USA from France in 1959, and in the UK about 1965, after which further exports took place from both France and Germany in the following years.

In reality, the genetic base for the Birman's color is that of the Siamese mutation for reduction of pigment at the full color C locus, and the addition of the white paws via a second mutation known as spotting—a variation of that which creates piebald cats. There is then the recessive mutation for long hair, so that the Birman probably arose from either a black or dark brown cat rather than from whites as in the legend. Whether or not Persians were used in the early days of the breed, in order to create the long hair, is a matter of conjecture. Again, whether the Siamese color points were introduced in Burma, and whether the spotting was a subsequent mutation is not known. The Birman is a much more solid cat than the Siamese, but this could have been achieved if the breed was crossed with a Persian; therefore, the markings of this breed provide much source of speculation as to their origins but were probably derived from the Siamese breed.

Character: The Birman is a very affectionate breed that has a quiet nature. However, this does not mean it is not full of life, because when two Birmans start to play, they are as boisterous as any breed. I recall watching a pair owned by friends in Cornwall (England) taking great delight in actually scaling the living room wall, which was clad in jute (Hessian) wallpaper. They perfected this to an art and could run on this vertical surface with great dexterity. Needless to say, our friends did not use this material again when decorating!

Appearance: *Head*—The head is round and the cheeks are full. The nose is straight and of roman type—that is, the tip is turned slightly down. The ears are broad-based, regular, and set well apart. The eyes are not quite round, thus slightly almond shaped. They must be blue, the deeper in color the better.

Body—The body is long and massive, supported on medium length but thick-set legs with neat compact paws. The tail is of medium length.

Coat—The fur of the Birman is medium to long and silky in texture. It should be profuse around the neck so as to form an obvious ruff; it may be slightly curly on the abdomen. On the cheeks it is quite thick but is much shorter on the muzzle.

Colors—The available colors at this time are seal, blue, chocolate, and lilac, but others are likely to be added to the official list, as they are already being bred by those involved with the breed. In each case the paws must be pure white, and are known as gauntlets on the rear feet and gloves or mittens on the front. Those on the front feet should end in an even line across the paw and not pass beyond the ankle. The rear gauntlets must cover the entire foot

The white paws and lacing of the Birman are believed to have been produced by a white spotting, sometimes called piebald, mutation.

and taper up the back of the leg, finishing just below the point of the hock. The tapering of the gauntlets is known as the lacing. Ideally, the white gloving on all feet should be symmetrical, but this can be very difficult to achieve with any consistency.

Faults—Kink in the tail, brown on the gloves, lack of white up the rear legs, white hairs on the chin or chest, and any tendency towards a Siamese type head shape.

Comment—A very appealing breed indeed that combines good looks with a relatively easy to groom coat, but it still requires daily attention. This is one of the breeds that is well domesticated and enjoys lots of human companionship. Quiet voice and gentle disposition.

A red and white Cymric. The Cymric is a longhaired Manx cat; the long hair was not purposely introduced into the Manx but arose from an independent mutation.

CYMRIC

Origin: This breed is a longhaired Manx cat; therefore, the Manx article should be referred to for more details. The long hair was not introduced to the Manx, as in many other cases, but appeared as an independent mutation in North America during the 1960s, as far as we know.

Coat—Coat is of medium length and is quite profuse, as a good undercoat is present. However, this is not as woolly as in the Persian, so it is easier to keep neat than might be thought.

Color— All colors and combinations are permitted except for chocolate, lavender, or the Himalayan pattern.

Faults—Same as for the Manx.

Comment—The Manx has always proven to be an interesting breed with a select band of followers; therefore, the Cymric will probably appeal to those who are partial to the Manx. The Cymric is presently not recognized in the UK.

HIMALAYAN (COLORPOINT LONGHAIR)

Origin: The Himalayan is actually a hybrid between the Persian (longhair) and the Siamese; it is a Persian cat with Siamese colorpoint markings; it is known outside of the USA as the longhaired colorpoint or colorpoint Persian. Even in the USA, some associations regard it as a color variant of the Persian, and this is the overall trend. Up until 1984, the CFA gave the Himalayan separate breed status, but in that year they incorporated it into the Persians as a pointed pattern.

Crosses between black or blue Persians and Siamese are known to have been made as long ago as the 1920s, both in Europe and in the USA. However, it was the British that first started a strong program to produce such a hybrid, but with fixed type. They succeeded, and a number of cats were exported to the USA to add to the gene pool that was already being developed there—it was thus not a wholly British affair. The breed gained UK recognition in 1955 as a Persian variety, any trace of Siamese type having been bred out. In the USA it gained breed status commencing in 1957. The name Himalayan is derived from the many other ani-

A white Cymric kitten.

mals, in particular the rabbit, which carry the darker color points at the body extremities. Only in cats does this trait have an alternative name—Siamese—where it is linked to type as well.

Top: A seven-month-old tortie point Himalayan kitten. **Bottom:** A three-month-old male seal point Himalayan kitten.

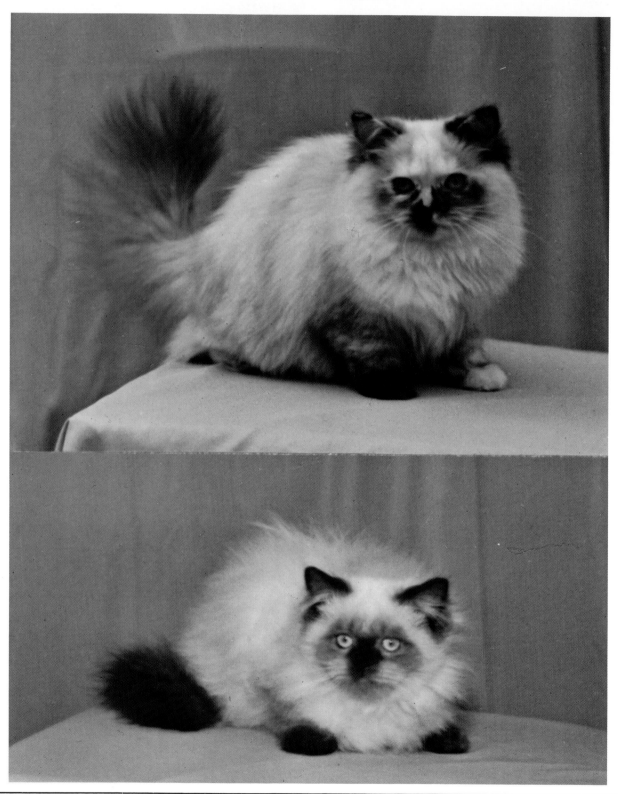

For years the Himalayan was given breed status in several associations. Today, however, most registrations recognize it in the colorpoint division of the Persian breed.

Although it is a hybrid created by crosses to the Siamese, the Himalayan should be Persian in body type.

So established is the Siamese color pattern in the Himmy that there has been no need to cross back to the former breed for many years, but in order to retain good type Himalayans are still mated to quality Persians in the USA.

Character: The Himalayan is very much a family cat, with many generations of domesticity behind it in a purebreeding line, not only as a breed, but also in the inherited qualities of the much longer established Persian bloodlines that predominate its make-up. However, it still retains a touch of the enquiring mind of the Siamese. All cats have a degree of wildness about them, but this is usually much subdued in the longhaired breeds of Persian origin, so this breed will be very happy to stay in or near the home, where it displays a placid temperament, combined with a pleasant and quiet voice.

Appearance: Other than in its color, the Himalayan should conform to the standard of the Persian for its type, and is judged on this basis. The reader should therefore refer to the Persian for description of the body conformation. It should be stressed that a Himalayan is in no way to be confused with the Balinese. The Himalayan is a Persian with Siamese markings; the Balinese is a Siamese with long hair—it is not a hybrid.

Eyes—The eyes should be round, large but not protruding, and as blue as possible.

Coat—The coat is as for the Persian, full and profuse and exhibiting a ruff around the neck.

Color— The Himalayan is accepted in an extensive range of colors in the USA and the UK, and these include the following:

1) Seal point with cream body
2) Blue point with glacial white body
3) Chocolate point with ivory body
4) Lilac point with magnolia body
5) Red point with off-white body
6) Tortie point with cream body
7) Cream
8) Blue cream
9) Lilac
10) Lilac cream
11) Chocolate tortie
12) Tabby point in various colors
13) Lynx point (USA) in various colors
14) Self colors
15) Bicolors

Many people believe that the Himalayan is identical to the Persian in personality; others believe the Himalayan is more inquisitive.

Not all associations recognize all of these combinations. The reader might be wondering at this juncture how one can have a self-blue Himalayan, which seems a contradiction in terms. The answer lies in the fact that if a Himalayan is mated to a blue Persian, then all the offspring will be blue, but they will carry the gene for Himalayan markings. If these cats are then mated to similar hybrids of the same phenotype, then one may produce pure blues, blues split for Himalayan, and pure Himalayan. The visually blue cats could not be shown as Himalayans and, indeed, one-third of the theoretical numbers possible would not even carry the Himalayan gene at all and would be true self-blue Persians. This complex situation is part of the problem seen in this breed, which will no doubt resolve itself one day. Theoretically, one cannot have such a thing as a solid self-colored Himalayan because, to qualify as a self, it must be capable of producing only offspring of its own color—thus it would be a Persian and not a Himalayan. Therefore, casual use of genetic terms can be rather misleading.

Faults—Any similarity to a Siamese in type is a bad fault. Other faults would include lack of distinction between the color points and the body color.

Comment—A very handsome breed for those liking a cobby, thick-set cat with the distinctive markings of the Siamese. Be prepared, however, to devote much time to grooming. When breeding, try to avoid the tendency towards button noses, which have become far more common than they were years ago.

JAVANESE

Origin: Once the Balinese breed had become established, it was not too long before breeders started to introduce new colors by crosses with Colorpoint Shorthairs or Siamese. The Balinese breeders objected to the additional colors, for they felt that the Balinese should be restricted to the four established colors so that it would remain a pure

Above: The Javanese is the name, in several associations, for Balinese cats other than seal, lilac, chocolate, or blue point. **Below:** The Javanese cat should conform to the Siamese standard for type and the Balinese standard for coat.

longhaired Siamese. As the Balinese name itself arose due to Siamese breeders' objections to the term longhaired Siamese, so the breeders of the new colored Balinese decided to call any non-traditionally colored Balinese a Javanese. One could thus say that a Javanese is a Balinese in any color but seal, blue, lilac, or chocolate. Conversely, it could be described as a longhaired Colorpoint Shorthair!

Character: The Javanese will display the same characteristics as detailed for the Siamese.

Appearance: Other than for its colors, the Javanese should conform to the standard of the Balinese for coat and the Siamese for type.

Colors—Any of the colors permitted for the Colorpoint Shorthairs.

Faults—As for the Balinese or Siamese.

Comment—These are very attractive cats, combining the grace and charm of the Siamese with easily managed long hair that is not so profuse that it mats and creates problems. In due course, solid self-colored Javanese will be produced, and it will be interesting to see what name they are given. Whatever their color, these cats make excellent pets.

The Kashmir is basically a self-colored Himalayan, most often seen in chocolate or lilac. The lilac Kashmir is quite similar to this cat.

KASHMIR

The Kashmir is actually a self-colored Himalayan and is not regarded as a separate breed in most parts of the world, or with many American registrations. In reality it is a Persian (longhair) and is normally seen as a chocolate or lilac cat. In my opinion, it is an example of unnecessary splitting of what is a single breed simply in order to create another breed. Nonetheless, whether one calls this color a Persian, a Himalayan, or a Kashmir, it is a most attractive cat with all the characteristics of the Persian. For details of its type, the reader should refer to the description of the Persian.

MAINE COON

Origin: The origins of the Maine Coon are obscure—as they usually are with longstanding breeds. However, it is generally accepted that it is the result of crossings between American Shorthairs of the streets and farms with the Angora, which is thought to have been the first of the longhaired breeds to be taken to the USA (just prior to the turn of this century). The resulting hybrid proved to be a very hardy and attractive cat that became extremely popular—especially in the eastern New England states, one of which for whom it is named.

The origin of the term "coon" is not known but is probably wrapped up in the various local legends that connect it to the raccoon. Whatever the actual history, it was a show-winning cat from the earliest days of cat exhibition in the USA; it then lost favor as more and more exotic breeds were imported. By 1904 it had all but vanished from the show scene, but it managed to survive in the hands

A ten-month-old black Maine Coon female. The Maine Coon continues to grow in popularity with each passing year.

of dedicated followers of the breed. In 1951, a specialty club was formed to cater to the breed, which began to hold its own shows. By 1967, the numbers had grown to the point that a standard was drawn up and accepted by American associations; since that time, the breed has steadily regained its former position as a popular entrant at shows. It is not recognized in the UK, but, as specimens are imported to that country, this situation may soon change.

Character: The Maine Coon is all things to all people, for it may be a very affectionate home-loving cat, or it can equally be a tough individual capable of looking after itself in the wilds of the countryside. Indeed, it is not suited to close confinement, so even in a home it must have a good yard or garden to exercise in. The voice of the Coon is very variable amongst individuals but is usually very pleasant, indeed soft at times.

Appearance: The Maine Coon is a substantial cat that should be well muscled and have good stout legs of medium length.

Head—The head is round and the ears are of medium to large size. The nose is straight and the muzzle is well formed with no tendency towards the dished face of the Persian. The Maine Coon must look very natural with no signs of human "fashioning" to its features.

Eyes—The eyes are large and almost round—they are just slightly almond shaped. The color of the eyes is not related to coat color, though it is always better if it blends with this. The eyes can thus be green, yellowish, copper, or blue—they can be odd-eyed in the white variety.

Coat—The fur of the Coon is long and flowing, and is of a fine silky texture. It is shorter on the shoulders but longer on the chest and sides of the body. A ruff to the front of the neck is desirable, whilst the tail fur should be profuse and plumelike. The muzzle fur is short but lengthens towards the back of the cheeks.

Color—Just about any color is accepted in this breed; its CFA standard cites no less than 23, plus numerous tabby combinations. This gives the interested owner as much choice as in any breed. A good Maine Coon is attractive in any color, but I think that the blotched tabby with white chest and paws is an especially good-looking and very natural combination of colors. Pointed colors are not permitted.

Faults—Poor coat length and lack of good muscle. Any loss of shape to the face.

Comment—This is a really fine breed that has retained a beautiful balance in its overall shape for over a century. It makes a fine pet,

Maine Coons come in many colors and combinations, but those with tabby patterns are the most popular.

but it must be groomed on a regular basis if it is to look its best. It is a breed that matures slowly; therefore, it could take up to four years to be at its very best. Its coat will thin out during the warmer months, but the tail will not.

NORWEGIAN FOREST

This breed is so similar to the Maine Coon that it can be regarded as such from a descriptive viewpoint. However, its origin is quite different but is paralleled by the conditions under which the two breeds developed. Both are breeds which are used to very cold climates; both shed their heavy coats during the warm months but retain the plumelike tail fur. The Norwegian Forest cat is undoubtedly older than the Maine Coon, as reference to its type is found way back in Norse fables. As a breed it was first recognized in Norway about 1930.

Any color is permitted in the breed, thus reflecting the fact that it is very much a "people's" cat developed by non-planned matings, though today selection is made by those who support the breed. It is not recognized in the UK and is seen infrequently outside of its homeland, no doubt because most Western countries have their equivalent of this type of rugged but affectionate cat.

Left: A Maine Coon on a cat castle. All cats love carpeted items like this, which are available at pet shops.

Opposite: Norwegian Forest cats are similar to Maine Coons. Like their American cousins, they have a loyal following.

PERSIAN (LONGHAIR)

Origin: It is believed that the very first longhaired cats to reach Europe arrived via Italy, taken there by the traveller Pietro Valla in the late 1500s. From there the cats were taken to France, and thence into Great Britain, where they were for many years known simply as French cats. The early Persian cats did not exhibit the dense coats of today's breed, but they were still imposing felids and quickly captured the attention of cat lovers. Apart from Persian longhairs, there were also longhairs from Ankara in Turkey; these became known as Angora or Turkish cats, though in the early years of these breeds they were all regarded as Eastern cats, and little distinction was made between them. There was, however, a difference, as the Persian cats had a denser, more woolly coat, whereas those from Turkey were more silky in texture.

Breeders tended to favor the more dense coat of the Persian, and, as the years passed, interbreeding and selection for coat length resulted in the virtual disappearance of the Turkish cats from the scene. (Only in recent years have these beautiful cats started to regain breeders' attention.) In the UK, when cat showing was begun in the late 19th century, the Persian became so popular that the famed British Shorthairs found it difficult to compete; even the arrival of the exotic Siamese onto the scene did not halt the march of the Persians. In the USA, the story was the same, and even today, though no longer the automatic Best in Show winners, the Persians are still the major force in feline competitions.

Over the years, however, the Persians have changed in their conformation, as any reference to very old photographs will illustrate, and one can still see those examples which

Persian kittens. The Persian received immediate attention when it entered the British show scene in the late 1800s.

A blue-cream Persian. Blue-cream Persians result from a dilution of the tortoiseshell gene; therefore, they are almost always female.

In general, the Persian is considered to be one of the more quiet, docile breeds of cat.

have a more pronounced muzzle than others. Coat texture within the breed also varies from the very woolly types to those leaning more towards the Turkish type—though still being extremely profuse, of course. In the UK and mainland Europe, the Persian is known simply as the longhair, and each color is regarded as a separate breed. In the USA, all the colors seen in the Persian are simply varieties of the breed, with the colorpoints (Himalayans) being regarded as a separate breed by some associations but as the Persian by others. The Turkish Van breed of the GCCF and some American registries is not the Persian Van (bicolor or calico) of the CFA.

Character: Having such a long line of selective breeding behind it, the Persian is in many ways the ultimate house cat and is quite happy to spend most of its time in the home—but it still enjoys a walk around the garden. Members of this breed will constantly follow their owners around the home and are happy to be with them for much of the time. However, as with all cats, there are those that will show a more independent nature than others. The voice is generally quiet, and the overall nature is one of docility.

Appearance: The Persian is a cobby cat with a good sized body supported on short thick legs. It is not, however, as heavy as its apparent size might suggest, for much of its bulk is composed of its long, dense fur.

Head—The head should be round and broad, with plenty of space between the ears, which should be small. The nose is short with a definite stop—in many cases one sees indentations rather than stops. (For this author, this ruins the entire face of a Persian, but we all have our little likes and dislikes—and it would be a boring world if we didn't.) The cheeks should be full and the muzzle broad. A strong jaw is desirable, but this should not result in undershot teeth. The eyes should be large, round, and neither pop-eyed nor sunken. The color will range from orange, copper, yellow-green, or blue according the variety (color). The eyes should not slant, as this detracts from the overall expression of the face.

A shaded silver Persian. The head of a Persian is round and broad with plenty of space between the small ears.

Coat—The coat should be long and flowing on the body and exhibit a full frill around the neck; the brush (tail) should be short and broad. The undercoat is woolly and dense. The legs should be well furred. The ears should also be well covered with hair, some being almost tufts from the inner part of the outer ear.

Color—There are many color shades to choose from in the Persian breed, and more are being developed all the time. Some are recognized in the USA but not in Europe.

Tabby Persian kitten. Persian cats are accepted in a vast array of coat colors and patterns.

Blue-cream Persian with deep orange eyes. Deafness in white cats is not confined to animals with blue eyes; a small percentage of orange-eyed whites are known to be deaf.

Here I will restrict descriptions to the more popular colors whilst listing a number of the others available. In broad terms, the colors can be divided into those which are selfs (that is, the same all over), those which combine two colors, the tabbies of various types, and the other colors not covered in the groups named.

White—The oldest self color in Persians is the white with blue eyes, or odd eyes (one blue and one orange), or orange eyes. The white must be pure white with no trace of other colors. The blue-eyed variety is associated with deafness, but this trait is not confined to this color, as orange-eyed whites may also suffer either unilateral or bilateral deafness. Bergsma and Brown reported in 1971 on studies of 185 white cats, and the findings were as follows: 37% blue-eyed and deaf; 31% blue-eyed with normal hearing; 25% yellow-eyed with normal hearing; 7% yellow-eyed and deaf.

Cats which suffer from deafness do not appear to be unduly concerned on this account and adapt to lead quite normal lives, but, obviously, one needs to be aware of the disability and allow for it. When white cats are kittens, they may sometimes exhibit a dark patch of fur, but this color rarely lasts into adulthood.

Black male Persian. Black Persians should be kept out of strong sunlight, as it tends to bleach the coat.

Black—Black Persians were very popular many years ago, but with the greater availability of other colors, and the difficulties in producing jet black Persians, they have lost ground in recent years although outstanding individuals are still to be seen. One problem is that the black color matures late and is adversely affected by strong sunlight, which gives a brown hue to the coat as a result of bleaching. Kittens may sport a few white hairs, but these normally vanish as they mature, often to produce super black cats. To maintain the quality of the color, only dense black adults should be bred from.

Blue—Blue Persians may range from light to dark. They are black Persians carrying the gene for dilution in double, thus purebreeding, quantity. Polygene modifiers control the strength of the blue, so one can selectively breed for light or dark, both being acceptable.

Red—Red Persians are very difficult to produce, as they will invariably carry dark markings which the standard considers a fault. In the USA there is a variety accepted that is known as the peke-faced red, which has a very squashed face, due to a genetic abnormality; this variety is not allowed in the UK because of the negative effect of the flat face on breathing and eating.

Cream—Cream Persians are actually red cats carrying the dilution gene, so, like blues from which the dilution gene came, they can vary between very dark and almost white, depending on the amount of selection that has taken place for the shade over the previous years. Ideally they should be uniform in color, but this is very difficult to achieve, so it is a case of picking the best from given litters.

Blue-cream—This interesting coat color is actually a tortoiseshell dilution, and this means that blue-creams are nearly always females. A blue-cream is produced either by pairing a female of this color to either a blue or a cream male, or by pairing a cream female to a blue male. The differences in the matings will reflect the theoretical expectations based on which pairing is made. For example, if a blue male is mated to a blue-cream female the results will be: 25% blue-cream females; 25% blue females; 25% cream males; and 25% blue males. Both the blue and the cream males and females produced are selfs for their color.

If the male had been cream instead of blue, the expectations would be the same except that cream females would replace the blue ones. The ratios change if a blue male is paired to a cream female, when the expectations will be: 50% blue-cream females and 50% cream males. If matters are reversed and a cream male is paired to a blue female, they will produce: 50% blue-cream females and 50% blue males.

All of these matings follow the rules of inheritance for sex-linked genes; in this case, the cream is the gene concerned, being a dilution of orange (or red, as it is known in cats). In the USA, it is preferable that the blue and cream appear as distinct patches wherever possible, but in the UK the requirement is for the different colored hairs to be evenly intermingled to provide a delicate shade.

Smoke—Smoke Persians have been known for a great many years and were once much more popular than today—these were the dark smokes of black or blue. Sadly, like the blacks, they are subject to the effects of sunshine, and this, together with rain, has the result of changing the true color, and this no doubt accounts for their relative decline. However, new smoke colors have been developed and these are very popular in a limited sort of way.

The smoke coloration is the result of the I inhibitor gene in combination with aa for non-agouti; the result is a restriction on the pigment of the hair so that the undercolor is very light in comparison to the top tipping color. The standard actually calls for white undercolor, but this is all but impossible to produce other than in very light-colored smokes. A black smoke will have a bluish shade of white as an undercolor, whilst a blue will have off-white to blue-gray, depending on the depth of the blue. When at rest, a smoke may appear to be a self color, and only when it moves is the lighter undercolor revealed to create a most attractive pattern.

It is preferred that the tipping be darkest on the back, head, and feet, with contrasting lighter shades on the frill, flanks, and ear tufts—not easy to produce to a high standard. As in blacks, this color is slow to reach its full state. In breeding smokes, it is advisable to breed to the self every few generations in order to retain the best density of the color, be this black, blue, or whichever. Other smoke colors include chocolate, lilac, and tortoiseshell. The red smoke is found in the UK as the cameo breed in varying intensities of shading. The smoke standard requires these cats to have a snub nose.

Chinchilla—This is another old variety that goes back to the 1890s. In the chinchilla Persian the coat is white and tipped with a darker color; this is the reverse of the coat pattern of the actual chinchilla, a rodent from South America. The result is a quite beautiful appearance. There are various shades of chinchilla, and these are either light or dark in appearance, depending on the extent of the tipping. The chinchilla as such carries tipping to the very ends of the hair, but in the shaded chinchilla the tipping extends much further down the hair follicle to give a darker appearance. In the UK, the shaded was

The markings on a Persian cat may be variable in some strains. Obtain a copy of the Persian standard from your registry of choice before purchasing a cat with questionable markings.

withdrawn many years ago because it had become indistinct from the chinchilla, but it is now back again and known as the pewter variety. Chinchillas have green or blue-green eye color. The golden chinchilla has an undercolor of gold with a seal (dark brown) tipping to the hairs and is most attractive. The shaded golden is a darker version of this. In the UK, the golden chinchilla is recognized as the golden Persian, and in this variety the eyes are green or blue-green.

Cameo—Cameo Persians may be regarded as the red series that equates the chinchillas, as the cameos have white undercolor with various degrees of red tipping in different strengths. In the cameos, the lightest colored cats are called shell cameo, then come the shaded cameos, then the red smoke, and finally the tortie cameos. The red smoke has contrasting shades of light and dark on its body. The dilute reds are, of course, the creams, and here one can have shell, shaded, smoke, and blue-cream. The eye color should be deep orange or copper.

It will be appreciated that the smokes, the chinchillas, and the cameos are all variations on a similar theme in which tipping of a white or light-colored coat with darker colors creates a considerable range of shades from almost white to almost a self color, depending on just how much of the hair shaft contains pigment. In all of these varieties, it will be found that the kittens are darker as youngsters, but at this stage only the hair tips will be showing through the skin. As the animal matures, so the extent of tipping and thus the shade will become more apparent. All of the cameo colors are sex-linked, being various intensities of red. Excellent examples of this Persian variety are most impressive, as they have a soft, almost powderpuff, look to them.

Bicolors—Bicolored Persians are cats which carry a single color plus white. There are black, blue, red, chocolate, and cream bicolors—in fact, they are possible in any self color. No more than two-thirds of the coat should be colored, and no more than half should be white; the face should carry both the color and white to form an inverted "V"; white paws are preferred. There should be no white hairs amongst the colored part of the coat.

Show quality Persians with white or light-colored coats must be groomed regularly to prevent staining of the fur.

A chinchilla Persian. Chinchilla Persians have a white coat that is tipped with a darker color; they are known for their green eyes.

Tortoiseshell—These Persians are tricolored cats which combine black, red, and cream in distinct patches of color—each of which should appear on the face. As in nearly all other pets which have this coloration, the tortoiseshell is a rather difficult color because one can never predetermine the way in which the colors will combine; therefore, a well-marked individual may be a once-in-a-blue-moon specimen. This may be because the colors are not wholly genetically controlled; however, if they are, complex modifiers work in such a manner that predicting the amount of color in any given location on the cat is quite impossible. Tortoiseshell is a sex-linked pattern due to the red genes, and this means that a tortie is nearly always a female. Males that are produced can be discounted for all practical purposes, as most are sterile. These factors make the breeding of torties very much a specialty operation which is only for those who are dedicated to the variety and thus familiar with the problems.

Calico (tortie and white)—These Persians are generally more popular than tortoiseshells because the addition of white to the coat makes them very striking cats. In the USA, white should predominate and be interspersed with color, but in the UK the colors are the main feature and are broken up with patches of white. The pattern is again sex-linked, so that torties

Bicolor and tricolor Persians offer the experienced breeder a challenge.

are, of necessity, heterozygotes (non-purebreeding); they are produced by mating tortie females to either a bicolor or a self-colored male. The dilute calico is in fact the blue-cream variety. The eye color should be orange or deep copper. A well-marked calico is a very beautiful feline.

Tabby—Tabby Persians can be found in each of the three tabby patterns: classic, mackerel, or patched. In addition, they come in many colors, including brown, red, blue, silver, and cream. The tabby pattern can also be seen in the Himalayan (colorpoint) and is available in all recognized colors in the UK. Because tabby markings are easier to see in shorthaired cats, they can be found in the American Shorthair description. A nice tabby Persian is a very attractive animal, but, as with tortoiseshells, can be annoyingly difficult to produce—but I guess this is true for any top quality cat of any color.

Faults—Overshot or undershot jaw, kinks in the tail, poor color, and any movement away from the desired type as defined by the appropriate standard.

Comment—The range of color permutations within the Persian (longhair) breed can seem bewildering to the novice. However, one should never forget that type is just as important—even though in most cases the show standards clearly lean towards color in the overall allocation of points. After color—and sometimes ahead of it—the head of a Persian is most important in determining the quality of the cat. A quality Persian is indeed an impressive cat, and there is much scope for those prepared to devote the time to its grooming. The only fear that this author has, where Persians are concerned, is that they have reached such heights of perfection in the density of fur that there may be the danger of taking this to extremes; in addition, the trend towards pushed-in faces does not appeal to me either. Maybe I am old-fashioned where cats are concerned, but for me excess in any one direction always results in a lesser feline.

A cream Persian kitten.

The Ragdoll is a relatively recent arrival on the show scene. Breeders consider good temperament to be a prerequisite for a proper Ragdoll.

RAGDOLL

The Ragdoll was developed during the 1960s in the USA and was first accepted for registration in 1985. It is not recognized elsewhere and is not wholly accepted by all American associations in the same form. The Ragdoll was named for its ability to go limp when handled, but, as all cat owners are aware, this is not an exclusive feature to any breed of cat, as many will do this, depending on their individual natures and the way they are reared.

Character: The Ragdoll should have a very placid temperament, and breeding programs should be geared toward specific selection for this most important aspect of the cat. Therefore, no aggressive individuals, regardless of other virtues, should be used as breeding stock. This is not an easy character to select for, because aggression is as much acquired as it is inherited, so judgments are open to much error in interpretation. As the breed is reputed to have a gentle nature, it is thus suited to people with

Profile of a ruddy Somali.

similar natures who wish to own a quiet and affectionate breed.

Appearance: The Ragdoll is a large cat of good body length and substantial muscle.

Head—The head is round, and the nose is straight and of medium length. The ears are set well apart and are short to medium in size—the inside edge having about a 45° angle towards a pointed tip. The cheeks are well developed. The eyes are almost round and just slightly inclined; they are green in color.

Coat—The fur is medium to long and should form a ruff around the neck. It is not as long as in Persians but is comparable to that seen in Birmans. It is of a silky texture so that grooming is no big chore.

Color—There are three Ragdoll color varieties: those that have mittens of white, those that do not, and those that are bicolors. The first two are, in fact, colorpoints with a variation in that white may appear on the body, especially on the chest. A Ragdoll might be mistaken for a Birman without mitts or for a mismarked Birman that carried white. In fact, the terminology applied to Ragdolls does tend to get a bit confusing, so that a chocolate point bicolor may have a dark tail and ears with the muzzle and chest as white as the paws; this is hardly consistent with the accepted description of a colorpoint. True colorpoints are, however, found in the breed. The accepted colors are seal, chocolate, blue, and lilac.

Comment—An interesting breed of good disposition. Those Ragdolls that show specific coloration (the unmitted seal points or the white-chested colorpoints) are very attractive and offer scope for the future. Other color permutations do tend to look like crossbreeds; therefore, they are unlikely to make great headway. The Ragdoll breed needs time to sort out a unified standard of acceptance in respect to its colors.

SOMALI

Origin: The Somali is to the Abyssinian what the Balinese is to the Siamese—it is simply the longhaired version. The Somali is recognized in the UK and was developed from a mutation appearing in the USA during the 1960s. Like the Balinese in Siamese circles, it created considerable controversy in the Abyssinian breed over the source of the longhaired gene; therefore, the Somali soon took on its own identity. There are those who felt that it was crossed with a Persian to introduce the longhaired gene, but most agree that it was a natural mutation—certainly it is comparable to the Balinese in the effect of the gene, which produces long hair on the tail but much less on the bodily parts. As the gene is recessive, two Somalis mated together will produce only Somalis, but if a Somali is paired to a true breeding Abyssinian, all the offspring will be Abyssinian but split for the Somali gene. Therefore, the gene follows the expectations of normal autosomal recessive inheritance.

Appearance: The Somali looks very much like the Abyssinian, but its features change somewhat as a result of the long hair. The head shows a more round appearance due to the longer fur on the cheeks. The ears may carry tufts of hair. The body fur is only moderately longer than in the Abyssinian; therefore, this breed is very easy to groom and might as easily be termed a medium-coated breed. For all other aspects of the Somali, the reader is referred to the Abyssinian description.

TIFFANY

The Tiffany is the name given to the long-haired Burmese. This is a cat of very pleasing appearance; it is seal brown on the head, back, and feet, with lighter colored hair intermingled with the seal on other parts of the body. It sports a ruff of long fur around the neck and has a plumelike tail. In all other characteristics and features it should be regarded as a Burmese, and the reader is referred to that breed description for such details. There is no doubt that the Tiffany will become very popular, especially if it becomes available in all of the accepted colors once the breed is more firmly established. The fur is long and silky, which indicates that the breed was created by crossing with the Persian rather than arising as an independent mutation within the Burmese.

Although the Somali is a longhaired cat, the fur is not nearly as long as that of the Persian, so it is an easy breed to groom.

The Turkish Angora—called Angora in the UK—is an ancient breed of cat. The Persian cat of today was created with this type of cat.

TURKISH ANGORA (ANGORA)

Origin: The Turkish Angora—or simply Angora as it is known in the UK—is a very old breed indeed, and it is from this breed, and its Persian cousin, that the Persians of today were created. The original Persian cats looked nothing like today's Persians and were more like the Turkish Angora. However, they did have a more woolly undercoat and, as a result, held the potential for considerable development—so much so that in the various crossings between Persians and Turkish Angoras, the latter was to lose its identity by the early years of this century, and virtually vanished from the cat scene as a specific breed.

Angora is the old name for Ankara, the capital of Turkey, and white cats have been associated with this city for many centuries. Even today the Ankara Zoo retains a breeding population of these cats in order to preserve the purity of bloodlines. They keep only pure white cats; any showing auburn markings (Van) are sold or given away as pets. During the 1950s, Turkish cats were imported into the UK; however, these were not the pure whites but a color variant found in eastern Turkey in the Lake Van area, which lies equidistant from the Armenian (Russian) border and that of Iran (formerly Persia). Distinction between the Turkish Angora and the Turkish Van should thus be made, as both have recognition in the UK and USA.

It was during the 1960s that the Angora started to arouse interest in the USA following importations from the Ankara Zoo. Once a nucleus of the breed was established and more imports made, the breed made headway and gained recognition in 1970. Presently, in the UK, it has preliminary status.

Character: The Turkish Angora has a quiet and docile nature, and is graceful in its movements. These cats are very affectionate, and whilst they enjoy playing and are clearly intelligent, they are nowhere near as boisterous as, for example, a Siamese. They are one of the few cat breeds which appear to enjoy water—they are good swimmers.

Appearance: *Head*—The head of an Angora bears no comparison to that of a Persian and should be wedge-shaped, commencing at the nose and going out at an angle in a straight line to form a triangle with the ears. The nose is straight and forms an unbroken line with the forehead. The ears are large and wide at their base but will appear smaller when the cat sports its full winter coat. The eyes are almond shaped and slant very slightly towards the nose. Eyes may be blue, orange, odd, or green. The remarks made in respect to deafness in white Persians also apply to the Angora.

Body—The body is long and elegant and supported by long slim legs, of which the hind are longer than the front. The bone structure is dainty when compared with Persians. The tail is long and thin and should contain no kinks.

The head of the Turkish Angora is distinctly wedge shaped, and the body is long and slim.

Coat—The fur of the Angora is very fine and silky with just a hint of curling on the longer hairs. It should lay flat to the body. There is no woolly undercoat as in Persians, so the hair presents no particular grooming problem, provided it is given regular attention. The fur is of medium length on the body but longer where it forms a ruff around the neck. The tail is bushy and plumelike. During the winter months, the hair becomes much more prolific in its growth and the body fur becomes quite profuse, but this is shed as the warmer months arrive; therefore, the breed can look quite different in its two extreme forms.

Color—The traditional color is, of course, pure white, but other colors can now be seen, according to the association involved. In the UK the breed may have any color that is recognized in foreign shorthairs. The potential color range in the breed is as follows:

1) Black
2) Blue
3) Chocolate
4) Lilac
5) Red
6) Tortie and calico
7) Cream
8) Blue tortie
9) Chocolate tortie
10) Lilac tortie
11) Tabby in all colors
12) Smokes and bicolors

Faults—Kinks in the tail and any tendency towards Persian type are not desirable, nor is any movement away from the dainty bone structure that is so much a part of the breed.

Comment—The Turkish Angora is a most elegant cat, and it represents a very good alternative to the Persian, as it is exotic enough to attract the attention of those not familiar with it. In addition, its more easily groomed coat is an obvious plus. Many Angoras are now being exported from the USA after many years of being overlooked, and it seems that the Angora is here to stay.

The Turkish Van is not nearly as popular in the United States as it is in Great Britain, where breeders have been developing it since the 1950s.

TURKISH VAN

Origin: Whilst the Americans have shown greater interest in the Angora, the British have devoted much time to establishing the Turkish breed, which is also known as the Turkish Van cat. From the imports first made during the 1950s, the breed became established and given breed status during 1969. Many are now exported from Britain to various parts of the world, including the USA. The Turkish goes back for as many centuries as the Angora, and the fact that auburn markings can turn up in litters of Angoras indicates that the two breeds were once probably regional varieties of the same cat.

Character: The Turkish has the same pleasant nature as the Angora, clearly reflecting the fact that it has been domesticated considerably longer than many breeds. Like the Angora, this breed has no fear of water.

Appearance: The Turkish will fit the same basic description as the Angora but has color markings present in its coat.

Head—The head may carry auburn markings, either around the ears or between the ears and the eyes. In the latter case, they usually take the form of elongate patches inclined at an angle just above the eyes. The eye color is amber, but blue-eyed cats are also seen.

Body—The body should be chalk white and free of any color patches, though in an otherwise excellent cat minor body markings may be overlooked. The tail is auburn in color, and it displays rings of lighter and darker coloration along its length; these are less noticeable in young cats and kittens. Though not yet officially accepted, a cream variety is being bred and no doubt will gain acceptance in due course.

Comment—A well-marked Turkish cat is very appealing, especially to those who admire the Turkish Angora but prefer a cat with the distinctive color markings.

A tabby and white shorthaired cat. Shorthairs basically come in two body types—cobby and foreign.

SHORTHAIRED BREEDS

Of the many cat breeds from which one can choose, about two-thirds are shorthaired, and about half of these are of foreign type, by which is meant those with the wedge-shaped face and slim features so characteristic of the Siamese. The remainder are composed of various cobby cats, which most people are familiar with as typical of Western street cats. Of course, these more solidly built cats differ from alley cats in that they have been selectively bred in order to become purebreeding both for their type and color. In the same way, the foreigns are much removed from the street cats of Eastern countries, as careful selection has fixed a visual type that in their native homes was much more variable.

Shorthaired cats have the singular advantage over their longhaired relatives of being easier to groom. Some people may say that they lack the elegance of a longhair, but this is very much a personal view of things and we each have our preferences. If one likes tabby markings, shorthairs are the right choice, for they are seen at their very best in these breeds. A number of the shorthairs have probably retained a greater degree of vigor than any of the longhairs—but, again, this is a subjective view that not all people would agree on. Short hair is the natural hair length of the cat, but even in these breeds there will be small differences in length, as genetic variability is such that the species has the option to increase or decrease hair length according to the environment. Some shorthairs thus have only moderate depth of hair, whilst others will have quite dense coats; some will have very short hairs whilst others will sport longer fur (but this is still short by comparison to the longhaired breeds).

ABYSSINIAN

Origin: The history of the Abyssinian breed, from a recorded standpoint, goes back to the period of the Abyssinian wars, when British officers brought back various things of interest. One of these was the Abyssinian cat, and 1868 is believed to be the year that the first Aby, named

The Abyssinian is an old breed that is reminiscent of the African wild cat, *Felis silvestris*.

Zulu, arrived on British shores. This breed is no doubt considerably older than many, for its type has much in common with the local wild cats of the species *Felis silvestris libyca*, the African wild cat from which it is thought the first domesticated cats of Egypt were bred. An unbroken line of descent from the sacred cats of Egypt is most unlikely, despite such claims; however, in the arid and inhospitable lands of the Sudan and Ethiopia (formerly Abyssinia), it would be quite possible for cat populations to go many years without undue intermingling from outside sources. Thus these cats could have existed in a relatively pure form for centuries, no doubt with gene infusions from wild cats local to their given area.

After the first import, others soon followed, and by 1882 the breed had gained recognition; however, its name was dropped and it was called the British ticked. The reason for this lies in the fact that similar looking cats appeared in litters born to street cats; this, in turn, provides ammunition for those who feel that the breed is not a natural one but is the result of careful selection from early British cats. Theoretically, one cannot deny this possibility, but the weight of logic falls heavily against such beliefs. The overall structure of the Abyssinian is such that it is highly unlikely that anyone would have contrived, years ago, to produce such a breed, and there are no records that would support such a theory. The mere fact that similar cats could appear from street cat matings simply illustrates the heterogenic make-up of such mongrels, which would no doubt have genes for just about every possible permutation. Indeed, it is quite feasible, given the many years of British involvement in the Near East, that Abyssinians, or similar cats, had been introduced at a much earlier date but went unnoticed at the time; these cats would have spread their genes amongst local cat populations in the UK.

We can therefore assume that the breed is a true representative of the type still found in much of Africa to this day. The name Abyssinian was reintroduced following the formation of the Abyssinian Cat Club in 1919; this club remains active to this day. The first imports of the breed to the USA were made about 1907, from England, and in the following years many more were to follow as the breed gained in popularity. However, it was not until 1935 that the Aby was actually bred on American soil, but once this happened the breed truly came of age—without ever competing in the popularity stakes with breeds such as the Persians and Siamese, which were, of course, the glamour cats of the period. Today, the Abyssinian retains a great number of faithful devotees.

Character: The Abyssinian is a very intelligent cat; this fact means that it can be either a superb pet or an antisocial animal, depending on how much time the owner is prepared to devote to it. This, of course, applies to all cats, but this is one of the few breeds in which this aspect stands out. I have seen the breed described as mistrustful, but such a choice of word is unfortunate, as no cat can ever be mistrustful, though one can understand its implication. Essentially, any intelligent animal that becomes bored becomes less predictable in its nature, but this merely underlines the fact that the animal is given insufficient attention. Abys can be ex-

The wild Abyssinian is a cat that is in the process of being developed. Note the distinct lines on this cat.

The eyes of the Abyssinian are almond in shape and their color is green. The head shape is somewhat foreign but is not as extreme as that of the Siamese.

tremely affectionate cats if their owners have enough time for them. They are very playful and enjoy the freedom to explore, and many Abyssinians quickly learn simple tricks that appeal to them. Aby owners tend to be very loyal to the breed once they have had their first one.

Appearance: The Abyssinian is a breed that will appeal to those who like a cat that is very natural looking. It is a cat that has a very regal bearing when it sits alert.

Head—The shape of the face is neither round nor of the sharp Siamese wedge. Overall, it has a look of the foreign about it, so the wedge shape is there but is not over-exaggerated. The ears are large and broad at their base and gently curve to a rounded tip. The muzzle is clearly defined but never pointed. The eyes are almond shaped and inclined in the Oriental manner. Their color is amber, hazel, or green.

Body—The body is fairly long, lithe, and muscular. The hindlegs are longer than the front, whilst the tail is long, straight, and wide at its root, tapering to a rounded tip.

Coat—The coat is uniformly short, the long-haired variety being regarded as a separate breed (the Somali). The texture of the fur is smooth and silky. It is of the agouti pattern, by which is meant that each hair should be ticked with two or, preferably, three bands of color in different intensities.

Color—In the USA just three colors are recognized: ruddy, red, and blue. In the UK, the ruddy is termed "usual" whilst the red is the sorrel. Britain also accepts the blue, the chocolate, the lilac, the fawn, the silver, the sorrel silver, and the blue silver. Other colors, including tortoiseshell, cream, and cameo, are being produced and will no doubt gain recognition in due course. It should be mentioned that the use of the term red in the USA is not without its problems, because that color is seen as a true red, which is sex-linked, and cinnamon, which is inherited as a normal recessive gene. The dilution of the genetically red gene will produce a cream, whereas the dilution of the cinnamon will be a fawn. From the true reds one can produce a tortoiseshell—but not from a cinnamon red. The silver Abyssinian is an unusual variety; it is created by the dark ticking being present but the ruddy being inhibited to produce a chinchilla ef-

The Abyssinian has a long, lithe, muscular body characterized by hindlegs that are longer than the forelegs.

fect. The future holds much promise for color development within this breed, though the natural colors, hopefully, will still remain the overall favored choice.

Faults—Kink in the tail, lack of muscle, lack of dark fur up the rear legs, and lack of dark markings around the eyes.

Comment—A very nice choice for those wishing to own a very individual breed which they have the time to devote to, and the space in their home or garden to see the cat at its best.

AMERICAN SHORTHAIR

Origin: The American Shorthair is a breed as old as the American nation itself—if this is viewed in terms of its settlement by Europeans. When colonization of North America began in earnest during the 1600s, the British took their cats with them, both to protect the ship cargoes

A shaded silver American Shorthair kitten with green eyes.

predictable group. Wisely, American breeders decided that type was to remain the major consideration—a good American Shorthair can never be a bad color.

The first registered shorthairs were British imports during the early 1900s—they were cats of obvious similarity to the American cats, for at this time selective breeding had not really taken place on any sort of scale. The name Buster Brown is of importance in this breed, for he was the first all-American to be registered, this taking place in 1904; he was of unknown parentage from American street cats.

The American Shorthair is judged by its own standard and is now every bit as much a pedigreed breed as any others, but in some registries it is still possible to register a cat of unknown pedigree providing it meets the standard for the breed. This has the advantage of ensuring that the breed stays natural, and, of course, it brings infusions of genes into the breed to retain the wild vigor that is always found in cats of town and country. It is a people's cat, one that everyone can relate to. The show cat can look just like the one at home on the hearth to a non-exhibitor visiting a cat show. Herein lies its great appeal. If the day should come when the purebred American Shorthair starts to look different than your regular cat about town, then it will have strayed from the concept of retaining the breed's true identity.

Character: The American Shorthair has all the attributes of its species. If treated with care and affection, it will repay its owner by only showing the pleasant characteristics of feline nature—it will be playful, intelligent, curious, and loving. American Shorthairs are excellent mousers and intrepid hunters of any small critters that fall within their natural prey species. American Shorthairs vary in their independence. Some are happy to stay around the home; others, however, wish to be out and about, searching, hunting, and becoming familiar with all of their territory, still controlled by the primeval call of the wild, which remains in all breeds but which is especially strong in these natural cats.

Appearance: The American Shorthair is everyone's idea of the average cat—it is a breed with no exaggeration of any of its bodily parts.

from mice and, after arrival, to protect the grain and homes from these same rodents. These were tough, hardy cats that interbred with the cats brought from Germany, France, Holland, Norway, and elsewhere. One could say that they changed from being simply cats of the British colonies to American Shorthairs on July 4, 1776!

As the cat fancy became more and more organized, the American Shorthair stayed very much in the wings. After all, everyone was familiar with this very ordinary cat that was owned and loved by millions of people; the Persian, the Siamese, and other foreign breeds were far more exotic and desirable for exhibition purposes. However, very slowly people began to realize that in the ordinary street cat lay the potential of a fine felid, if selective breeding was to be done to separate its genes for color into a

Head—The head is round, but in some examples the very full cheeks may give the cat the appearance of having a greater width to the face than the height from crown to lower chin. A good average for height to width ratio would be five to four. The neck is short and thick. The nose is straight and formed from a gentle slope from the forehead. The ears are small to medium in size and are set well apart. The eyes should be large and round, and their color may vary from blue to green to gold, according to the color of the cat.

A classic red tabby American Shorthair. American Shorthairs have round heads with very full cheeks.

The tabby American Shorthair is probably the best known member of this breed.

Body—The body is longer than it is tall and should be neither too cobby nor lithe. It is a well-muscled cat with good strength of shoulders. The body is supported on medium length legs. The tail should be thick at its root and taper very gently to a rounded tip.

Coat—The fur of the American Shorthair is sleek, glossy and short. It should be dense, but this will vary both from cat to cat and season to season—obviously, it is thicker in the colder months than during the summer. Cats living in perpetually warm areas will have less dense fur than those from colder regions.

Color—The beauty of the American Shorthair is that it can be seen in every possible color and combination of colors, other than chocolate and lilac, so it is not necessary to list these all here. Most will be found under the colors of the Persian. Here we will look carefully at the tabby pattern, as this is seen at its very best in this breed. Tabbies may be one of four basic types, but one of these is very special and is seen in the Abyssinian so it need not be considered in respect to American Shorthairs. This leaves the three well-known patterns, which are: classic tabby (also known as blotched); mackerel tabby; and spotted tabby.

Tabbies may be seen in many colors, including silver, red, brown, blue, chocolate, cinnamon, or cream; however, they are not all accepted by the various registration bodies. The silver tabby, in which the ground color is a silver-gray and the bands are dense black, has always been a particular favorite with people and is most striking in the spotted tabbies.

Mackerel tabby—This pattern is comprised of narrow stripes of dark fur contrasting with lighter bands of ground color which, genetically, are referred to as agouti. The mackerel tabby is known as the wild type—it is the one seen in wild cats. On the forehead there should be a letter "M" created by the dark hairs, which gives the cat a frowning look. From the outer corners of the eye, a stripe should run towards the neck, and below this should be a series of thinner lines. The neck should carry a series of unbroken darker necklaces—the more the better. An unbroken dark band should run down the spine, and on either side of this should be a narrower line from which the thin mackerel type lines run

A black American Shorthair kitten.

down the sides of the body—the more of these there are the better. The tail should carry numerous broken or unbroken rings, and the tip of the tail should be the same color as the darker body markings. The legs also should be ringed with a series of even bracelets, giving way to spots on the paws. The abdominal region will also be spotted. A final consideration is that both sides of the cat should be marked identically. It will be realized that ideally marked cats are exceedingly rare, so it is a case of getting as close to the ideal as possible. The mackerel tabby gene is T and it is dominant to that of the classic or blotched tabby.

Classic tabby—In the head, tail, and leg mark-

The American Shorthair comes in a variety of solid colors. However, chocolate and lilac are not permitted, as they suggest Siamese influence.

ings, the classic tabby is similar to the mackerel; the differences are thus seen on the body. In the classic, the shoulder markings, seen from above, form the outline of a butterfly, with both pairs of wings visible—the centers being of the ground color. In the center of the butterfly, a line of dark fur extends down the spine to the tail; again there are lines on either side of this, but from these, whorls of darker fur radiate around the sides of the body. At the center of the whorls, there should be a patch of fur in the shape of an oyster. Again, finding a well-marked individual is not easy, as the whorls often merge. As in the mackerel, the underbelly is spotted, and the body markings should be identical on either side of the cat. The gene for classic tabby is t^b and it is recessive to mackerel in mode of transmission.

Spotted tabby—A good example of the spotted tabby is a very imposing cat that will always attract attention. The spotting should ideally be round, oval, or rosette. From a purely genetic standpoint, the spotted tabby is regarded as being a modified mackerel tabby, as the presence of a separate gene for this feature has not been established. It is not known whether the spotting is inherited as a mutation in its own right, which has then been selectively bred for, or whether it is simply the result of selection from broken-lined mackerel or classic tabbies. It is accepted practice to assume that selection from the established variety is the case in the absence of evidence to support the view of a separate mutation.

Faults—Any movement towards a foreign type of head or body or any exaggeration of any bodily parts. Poor markings in tabby patterns, kinks in the tail, and lack of overall balance in one part of the cat to all others.

Comment—If you are the sort who likes a cat that is as close to natural as one can get, then the American Shorthair may be the breed for you. This is a beautifully proportioned animal that has retained all the characteristics of its wild cousins, yet has become quiet and friendly in the years of association with humans. American Shorthairs are tough, hardy cats that are able to cope with most temperatures, are reliable breeders, and, all in all, are very difficult to fault either as pets or as exhibition cats.

A pair of red tabby American Shorthair kittens.

The American Wirehair was created by a mutation that appeared in a litter of farm cats. It is characterized by coarse, hooked fur.

AMERICAN WIREHAIR

The American Wirehair first came about when a cat with a sparsely furred, abnormal coat was born in a litter of farm cats in Verona, New York. Instead of the smooth, sleek coat of a shorthair it had coarse, hooked fur, and was clearly a mutational form. This happened in 1966, and when this cat (named Council Rock Farmhouse Adam of Hi-Fi) was mated to his litter sister, two of the four kittens produced also carried the gene for wire hair—and a new breed came into being.

A carefully planned breeding program established the mutation in numerous parts of the USA and Canada, and examples were also exported to Europe. It was first recognized in 1978, for exhibition purposes, by the Cat Fanciers' Association, and since its early days the density of coat has been improved so that it is now like coarse sheep wool. In terms of its character and overall conformation, the American Wirehair may be regarded as an American Shorthair, and it is found in the same range of colors as that breed. The gene causing the change in the hair is symbolized by *Wh* and is transmitted as a normal autosomal dominant. The breed is not recognized in Great Britain.

The Bombay is a hybrid breed created by crossing a black American Shorthair with a sable Burmese.

BOMBAY

Origin: The Bombay is a hybrid breed that was created in the USA during the early 1970s by crossing a black American Shorthair with a Burmese. The result is a very attractive pure black cat that combines the features of the two breeds that go into its make-up. It was so named because it was thought to resemble the melanistic leopard of India, and it was accepted as a breed in 1976 in the USA. It is not recognized in the UK.

Character: The Bombay inherits the virtues from both of its originators, so it may exhibit the full spectrum of characteristics, ranging from being the same as an American Shorthair to being just like a Burmese or a mixture of both. This means it will be playful, very intelligent, always curious and wanting to be involved in whatever is going on in the home—often when help is not wanted! Always affectionate, Bombays will be happier with company than without it. They will vary in their desire to wander around their territory—assuming they have a garden to exercise in; some will stay very close to the home at all times, but others will want to be off exploring for hours at a time.

Appearance: There are two striking features to the Bombay, its beautiful glossy black coat and its large round eyes.

Head—The head is basically round but with a foreign look to it, which is created by the short muzzle, large eyes, and medium sized ears; but these may appear to be bigger in some individuals than in others, for it must be remembered that this is a hybrid, not a breed of fixed type. The eyes are large, round, and yellow or copper in color, the latter being preferred. They should appear well spaced apart.

Body—The body is on the lithe side but should not be thin; it must be well proportioned and muscled. The legs are medium in length and the tail is likewise.

Coat—The fur is short and very glossy—this is most important in this breed.

Color—The only color accepted is black, and this should be as dense as possible. In order to produce Bombays, any of the following matings are acceptable: American Shorthair (black) × Burmese (sable); Bombay × Bombay; Bombay × American Shorthair (black); and Bombay × Burmese (sable). The particular cross used will determine the ratios of Bombay in the litters produced. It must be remembered that, being a hybrid, the Bombay cannot breed true in early crossings; for example, a Bombay × Bombay mating will produce 25% purebred black American Shorthairs, 50% Bombay, and 25% pure-breeding sable Burmese. This comment applies to the color of the offspring and not to the phenotype in bodily terms.

It is sometimes stated that black is a dominant color, but the reader should understand the genetic inaccuracy of this statement. Black will mask albino, to which it acts as a dominant, but it is itself a recessive color in cats, created as the allele to agouti. Both the American Shorthair (black) and the Burmese are non-agouti *aa*. However, at the albino locus, the American Shorthair is *CC* for full color expression, which in this case is black. At the same locus the Burmese is $c^b c^b$. Crossing these produces Cc^b, which is black split for Burmese, which is , of course, Bombay. If two Bombays are paired, their genes will segregate in the ratio of 1:2:1. Only by selection of the all-black cats will one eventually produce purebreeding Bombay kittens. The conformation of the early crosses may well appear Bombay, but here we are looking at the color possibilities based on their genetic state.

In the UK, the Bombay could be produced by crossings with the British Shorthair (black) and the Burmese. If Bombay kittens are carefully examined in the right sort of illumination, they will be found to carry tabby markings. Thus confirming the basis of their black coloration as being non-agouti *aa*.

Faults—Lack of density in the black color; any patches of non-black in the fur; kinks in the tail, poor quality coat.

Comment—A very attractive cat of good character that presents interesting breeding possibilities if selection for type is undertaken.

BRITISH SHORTHAIR

Origin: The British Shorthair is the result of selection from the best street cats, and its origins are rooted as far back as the first cats taken to the UK by the Romans. The man who is regarded as the father of the cat fancy, Harrison

A tortoiseshell British Shorthair. The British Shorthair comes in many colors, but the British blue is probably the most famous member of this breed.

Weir, was passionately fond of the shorthaired cats of Britain, and these figured very strongly in all of the early British exhibitions. However, they declined as more breeders became besotted with exotic foreign breeds. Following World War II, the British Shorthair steadily regained the attention of British breeders and today it is very popular in all of its many colors—each regarded as a breed in the UK. In the USA, only the British blue was accepted initially, then the black, and then more and more colors, so that today most of the colors are accepted in the USA, but still not as many as in Britain. In the USA they are judged by a standard comparable to that used in the UK, but the allocation of points differs.

Character: The British Shorthair is to the UK what the American Shorthair is to the USA.

It is a people's cat developed from tough street cats, therefore a very hardy breed with no exaggeration of features. It enjoys human company but can get along quite well without it if necessary, as it is still an independent and spirited breed. It is a quiet cat not prone to over-use of its voice, so is very much in the British tradition of conservatism. Like its American cousin, it is what its owner makes of it.

Appearance: The British Shorthair is obviously very similar to many American Shorthairs, but is possibly more consistent in its facial type. The head is nicely rounded when viewed from any direction and does not show quite the width seen in some American Shorthairs. From a general descriptive viewpoint, the reader is referred to that of the American Shorthair, as, in this sense, the two breeds may be considered the same. Only if the two were placed side by side would the subtle differences be seen—and these are by no means so clear-cut that the two could not be confused.

Coat and color—The British Shorthair is accepted in all the colors listed for the American Shorthair. In the UK it is also available in chocolate, lilac, red, blue classic tabby, chocolate tortoiseshell, lilac tortie, blue tortie and white, and shorthair colorpoint, but these colors presently have only preliminary recognition. The faults are as for the American Shorthair.

Comment—A superb all-around cat with lots of character, this breed is not too demanding of its owner's time. The choice of colors in the breed is vast, and the time spent on grooming is minimal. Although described as a people's cat, a top British Shorthair is a very refined animal that can no longer be mistaken for being anything other than a pedigreed cat. However, its features remain unaltered, as it has been bred to perfection.

BURMESE

Origin: The Burmese is one of numerous foreign types indigenous to Asia, and attention to it was first brought about by Dr. Joseph Thompson. He returned to the USA with a brown Oriental type cat named Wong Mau. When she was mated to a very good Siamese, the resulting litter looked liked poorly colored Siamese—or poor Burmese, whichever view one wished to hold. If one of the litter was mated back to the Burmese, the color was improved, though poorly colored Burmese and Siamese would still have resulted. By continual selection for the rich brown, the Burmese eventually became purebreeding for both its type and color. The breed gained recognition in 1936 and is recognized throughout the world. It has been responsible for producing other breeds as well.

The Burmese is a mutational breed, for its color would originally have been black or tabby, the latter being the oldest original color of the breed. When black is reduced in strength, it becomes dark brown—known as sable in the USA and seal in the UK. This happens because the normal gene for full color mutates. If the gene mutates again at the same locus, then this increases the potential varieties by one—full color, mutation one, and mutation two. In genetics these are not numbered but are given letters. A full color cat will be CC, a Burmese $c^b c^b$, and a Siamese $c^s c^s$. Therefore, the Burmese is just one shade down from full color. If the gene mutates again so that more brown is taken from the fur, but with the points remaining brown, the famous Siamese color is created. In point of fact, numerous mutations have appeared at this gene position; the bottom gene is the pink-eyed white cat, which is devoid of any color pigment at all. For this reason the gene location is also known as the albino locus. The original wild gene C is completely dominant to the other mutations, which can all be arranged into a series based on their visual expression. Each of these is incompletely dominant to the one immediately below it but totally dominant to the gene two places below it.

The original Burmese imported to the USA would have been $c^b c^b$, and when mated to the Siamese it produced kittens which were all $c^b c^s$, as the Burmese gene is not fully dominant to the Siamese gene; an apparent halfway stage, or blending, would take place. Breeding kittens back to the parent Burmese would produce mostly Burmese in type but in color they would vary from pure Burmese through "poor" Burmese to pure Siamese. Continual selection for the darkest offspring slowly eliminated the occurrence of the c^s gene to create the purebreeding

Burmese, both for type and color. Once this had been achieved, it was then possible to introduce other mutations to the breed in order to create the many colors that can be found today in Burmese (though not all are accepted in the USA and certain of them are sometimes given a different breed name).

Character: The Burmese is a breed full of character and intelligence. These cats are also very vocal, with the complete range of sounds associated with the Siamese and all Oriental breeds of cat. Burmese have no difficulty in getting themselves into all sorts of trouble in the home, for they are full of natural curiosity. Their minds are capable of working out how to do little things—such as opening refrigerator doors when they feel like a late night snack! They will literally sit and watch you do things until they get the general idea.

If they have any drawback at all, it is that they do need a lot of attention; if this is given to them, they will make superb pets, as they have many endearing habits that are more often associated with dogs than with cats. The Burmese is one of the breeds that can be trained to a lead if this is considered necessary. They are always happy to be carried about and will wrap themselves around their owners' necks—but they do have very sharp claws, which they sometimes unknowingly use in an affectionate, overzealous fashion.

The Burmese is best known in its sable form. It was this coat color that the breed was selectively bred for at its inception.

Appearance: There is variation within the head and body shape of any breed of cat, but this is more marked in the Burmese than in many other breeds, and more so in respect to the Burmese of different countries. In the USA a "fuller" cat is preferred, whereas in the UK a Burmese displaying a more foreign type is considered the ideal.

The light phase Burmese are available in blue, platinum (lilac in the UK), and champagne (chocolate in the UK).

The head of the Burmese should be slightly rounded with good width between the ears. The Burmese face in the USA is more round than it is in Britain, where it has a slight wedge.

Head—The head should be slightly rounded, and there should be good width between the ears. In the USA, the shape of the face is rounded, but in the UK a slight wedge should be seen to impart the foreign origin of the breed. The eyes should be nicely rounded in the USA; in the UK, the top line of the eye should be slanting in the Oriental manner, but the lower line should be rounded. The ears are described as medium in size, but in many Burmese these will look more large than small, in comparison to the shape of the face. Again, this is more obvious in British Burmese than in American; in the latter, the fuller cheeks give the illusion of reduced ear size. The eye color can be any shade of yellow from chartreuse to amber, with golden yellow preferred. Green eyes are a fault in this breed.

Body—The body must be muscular; this is evident when the cat is picked up, for Burmese are heavier than their appearance might suggest. In the USA, a more compact cat is considered the ideal, but in the UK the body will be a bit more lithe, indicating the foreign type. The tail is medium in length and is not thick at its base, and it shows only a moderate taper along its length. It should be straight and show no signs of any kinks.

Coat—The fur of the Burmese should be short and satinlike, and it must lay close to the body. The sheen is most important; it is the result of both genetic and nutritional influences.

Color—In all cases, the underparts of the cat will be lighter shades of their color than the sides and back. The darkest fur will always be found on the head, legs and tail. In the USA, only certain colors are accepted as Burmese, and these vary between the different registries; therefore, we must distinguish between basically three situations:

1) Sable brown was the original Burmese color and is still the only color accepted as a Burmese in some associations.

2) Where a Burmese has been bred in the following colors, those associations that insist that only sable is acceptable as a Burmese regard these colors as belonging to the breed known as Malayan: champagne (chocolate in the UK), platinum (lilac in the UK), and blue. However, the CFA and the ACA are amongst those that accept all of the four colors as Burmese; CFA dropped the Malayan breed status in 1984.

3) In the UK, the Burmese may be each of the four accepted American colors, but the following are also recognized: red, brown tortie, cream, blue tortie, chocolate tortie, and lilac tortie. The term sable is not used in the UK, where this is known simply as brown and described as seal brown. The red, thus cream and tortie, are sex-linked colors.

The basic genetics of the Burmese has already been discussed with respect to the major gene mutation that creates a Burmese, and the other colors can be bred by consideration of how they are genetically created.

The sable (brown) Burmese is simply a black cat, $aaBB$, in which the mutation at the C locus has reduced the effect of full color expression to that of a dark brown, which is just slightly "pointed" as in the Siamese. If, at the D locus, a mutation appears that will reduce the density of color, it then becomes a d dilution gene. In double quantity, dd, the black will be reduced to blue; therefore, with the c^b gene action on this, we have the blue Burmese, $aaBBc^bc^bdd$. If the black gene mutates to brown at the B locus, the champagne (chocolate) Burmese is created, which is $aabbc^bc^b$; if this then carries the dilution gene in double quantity, it produces the platinum (lilac), which, from a genetic standpoint, is a very light shade of brown. The formula for lilac will be $aabbc^bc^bdd$.

The red Burmese has the simple formula of c^bc^bO (female OO); this is because the orange, o, gene will totally mask any other colors carried. The cream Burmese will simply have the addition of dd to the formula, as this reduces the strength of the red to cream. The tortie Burmese female will be aac^bc^bOo, where o represents non-orange or, put another way, any other color but orange, which could thus be sable (brown), champagne (chocolate), plati-

The body of the Burmese must be muscular; American breeders prefer a compact cat, while those in the UK strive for a lithe, foreign body type.

The eye color of the Burmese ranges from chartreuse to gold, with any shade of yellow in between. In the USA, the eyes should be round; in Great Britain, the top line should have an Oriental slant while the bottom is rounded.

num (lilac), or blue. If the tortie carries the double quantity of dilution genes, *dd*, then the black is thus reduced to blue and the red to cream, thus producing the blue-cream tortie, or simply blue tortie; likewise, the platinum (lilac) tortie is the champagne (chocolate) tortie which carries the paired dilution genes, *dd*, to reduce the strength of the color.

Within each color there is still quite a high degree of variation because, although a major gene controls the basic change of a color (black to brown or black to blue, for example), many other genes can affect the shade in very small amounts; however, collectively they can change its intensity towards the dark or the light end of the potential spectrum of that color. This means that the distinction between major gene action and modifiers is not always clear-cut. The dark end of the champagne (chocolate) spectrum (a mutation on the black color gene) may be indistinguishable from a light phase sable (brown) where the black gene has not mutated.

The Burmese was originally crossed with the Siamese and then refined into a pure breed, and history is also repeating itself within these same two breeds, for this same cross has resulted in the Tonkinese. Interestingly, in the UK, the light phase Burmese was often referred to as Tonkinese in the days when such cats were not used for exhibition— before the other colors gained acceptance.

Faults—The Burmese should be of a very distinctive type, and any tendency towards too Siamese or cobby in type is considered a bad fault.

Comment—This is a most likable breed of cat with much character, a great deal of charm, and an attractive short coat. If you like a cat that talks to you a lot, then you will find the Burmese the ideal feline for your family. Be prepared for a bit of mischief, because these cats do like to amuse themselves and their idea of fun may not always be the same as yours—like clambering up the curtains! They will annoy you at times, but their cheeky natures always gain forgiveness with a smile from you.

A Burmese mother with a rather large litter. Burmese kittens are especially well known for being active and inquisitive, and, like most other Oriental breeds, are rather vocal.

Most breeders now believe that the Chartreux is a French breed that was helped, after World War II, by crosses to the British blue.

CHARTREUX

Origin: The Chartreux is a breed that has been at the center of many a debate between its followers and officialdom. The crux of the argument is in respect to its origins. Devotees insist that it is an old natural breed from France, while others believe it is actually a hybrid resulting from French street cats and the famous British blue. In North America, some classes for the breed are called "British Blue Chartreux," while in others the breed is listed as an Exotic Shorthair! A number of registries are now accepting it as a breed unto itself, and these include CFA, ACA, and TICA. It is not recognized in the UK.

The probability is that the Chartreux is a truly French breed, as reference to the color was made by such people as Linnaeus, Buffon, and Lesson—all famous naturalists of the 1700s. Their works, mostly in French, would seem to support the view that such cats were not uncommon in France at that time. In Britain, the blue was a bit of a sensation when it was first exhibited in 1883, which indicates that it was not a common color in the UK at that time. However, the British developed the color with great skill, and by the turn of the century it was very much an established color; even to this day the British probably lead the world in the breeding of blue cats.

Herein lies the connection with the Chartreux.

The first cat to be shown under the name of Chartreux did not appear until 1931, by which time the British blue was world famous. In addition, the events of World War II all but decimated the population of French blues; therefore, British blues were incorporated into the bloodlines, as were Persians. The oldest longhaired breed club in the world just happens to be the Blue Persian Society of Great Britain; therefore, all roads point to the probability that the UK revived the color in France. However, this does not mean that the breed did not exist in France before this British connection. In point of fact, the blue mutation (created by the dilution gene on black) was known in Russia, so it is not impossible that both the British and French blues (Chartreux) are Russian in origin, having reached that country possibly from Persia, where such cats were also known to exist. As the color is also known in Malta and Spain, one can see its spread both north and west from Asia Minor.

The Chartreux was first imported into the USA during 1970, and since then it has been developed on purely French bloodlines, with great efforts being made to stick to this policy.

The Chartreux has a round face with full cheeks and medium sized ears. Its eyes are copper or gold and its nose is blue.

A blue lynx point Colorpoint Shorthair. In some associations, the Colorpoint Shorthairs are given acceptance as Siamese cats, not as a separate breed.

Character: The Chartreux is a quiet and gentle breed that is not disposed to overzealous use of its claws; it is also a happy and playful breed. The voice is soft, but these cats possess a deep, quite audible purr. They are hardy cats that enjoy companionship, but they also find pleasure in exploring their territory and should be given access to a garden for this purpose.

Appearance: The Chartreux is a typical European cat in its type, so it is well muscled.

Head—The Chartreux has a pleasing round face with full cheeks and medium sized ears. The eyes are round and large and may be copper, orange, or deep gold. The nose is blue.

Body—The body is cobby and supported by medium to short stout legs. The foot pads are blue in color.

Coat—The fur is short and plush, being very dense and displaying a good gloss.

Color—The preferred color is a light gray-blue, but the intensity of the color is quite variable due to the polygene modifiers, which can be selectively bred for to lighten or darken the shade. The color should be even from tip to root of the hair, and the skin should likewise be gray-blue.

Faults—Silver tipping to the coat or any suggestion of uneven coloration or incorrect eye color. Any conformational faults, such as kinks in the tail, poor bone structure, etc.

Comment—A good example of the Chartreux always commands attention because the color is most attractive. In addition, the breed has a very nice temperament and is well suited to those who prefer quiet, gentle cats. No one would ever mistake a good blue shorthair for anything other than a pedigreed cat.

COLORPOINT SHORTHAIR (SIAMESE)

Origin: The Colorpoint Shorthair is to the Siamese what the Himalayan is to the Persian. The original Siamese cats were pointed (face, feet, and tail) in dark brown and, once established, mutations appeared in the form of dilutions and resulted in the additional colors of chocolate, blue, and lilac. These colors all appeared spontaneously within the breed and were not introduced, but when other colors were required, such as red, tortie, and cream, these were produced by crossbreeding the Siamese to other cats such as the Abyssinian and short-haired domestic breeds. In addition, it is known that although blues resulted from mutations within the Siamese, they were improved by crossbreeding with the Russian Blue, though the incidence of this was low.

Such matings outraged the breed purists, who did not wish such hybrids to be accepted as Siamese. However, once the fresh colors were transferred to the breed, it was not necessary to mate beyond Siamese to Siamese, so that any impure "type" that had resulted from such crossings was quickly removed in successive generations; therefore, the influence of these other breeds was small enough to be of no account. In the UK, these additional colors were accepted as Siamese in 1966, but in the USA the arguments continue to create divisions, both by breeders and by the associations that represent them. Some registries accept them as Siamese, but others do not; therefore, whether or not a Colorpoint Shorthair is a Siamese or a separate breed depends on where you live and in which association you choose to register your cats.

Character and appearance: The Colorpoint Shorthair, other than in its color, should be regarded as a Siamese; therefore, the reader is referred to this description for details. As the British accept a wide range of colors for the Siamese, these are also listed in that discussion.

CORNISH REX

Origin: The rex mutation, which reduces the guard hairs and produces a wavy coat, was named for a similar mutation that has existed for many years in the rabbit (where it has been developed to quite magnificent standards of excellence). The first rex in the cat fancy caused quite a sensation when it appeared, in 1950, in a cat of domestic type from Cornwall (England). Ten years later, in the neighboring county of Devon, a second rex cat was born; this one, however, was created by a mutation at a different gene location. Both rex mutations are trans-

The Cornish Rex arose from a mutation found in a litter of cats in Cornwall. The rex mutation reduces the guard hairs and produces a wavy coat.

The eyes of the Cornish Rex should complement the color of the cat's coat, and they should be oval with a slight Oriental slant.

mitted as simple autosomal recessives to the normal cat coat. As the two rex types are separate mutations, each is accorded breed status.

The Cornish and Devon types of rex are not the only ones to appear in cats; a third rex appeared in a litter of kittens in Oregon (USA), and in East Germany a rex at the same locus as that of the Cornish has been found. In the USA, the rex of Cornwall has been crossed with the one from Germany but is still known as the Cornish Rex; some lines are still pure for the latter.

In the Cornish, German, and Oregon Rexes, the guard hairs are believed to be missing, or are reduced to such an extent that they cannot be distinguished as such (other than by microscopic study). In these cats, the awn and down hairs are reduced and are curly, creating wavy patterns in the fur. The Oregon Rex is the more profusely coated animal, and careful study reveals that its awn hairs project just above the down hairs, as they are less wavy. The German Rex is next in coat density, as it has a more wavy pattern. The Cornish Rex is the most sparsely coated of these three rexes and has the most crimped coat.

The rex mutation is not at the same locus as that which creates a normal coat, so it was possible to produce a longhaired rex—a double recessive. However, this cat was not especially striking and does not appear to have been developed further.

Character: All of the rexes have wonderful personalities, and the Cornish is no exception. The Cornish Rexes are exceptionally good jumpers.

Appearance: The Cornish Rex has an Oriental appearance; in the UK it is found in the foreign shorthair section of the GCCF official breed standards.

There are actually four types of rex cats. Three (Cornish, German, and Oregon) are similar and are registered together. The fourth (Devon) is now classified as a separate breed by most associations.

Head—The Cornish Rex has a medium wedge-shaped head, the length of which should be about one-third greater than the maximum width. The forehead runs in a straight line to the tip of the nose. The ears are large with a wide base, and they taper to a rounded tip. The eyes should be oval, with a slight Oriental slant to them. In color, they should blend with the color of the coat, but in the case of the Si-Rex they must be chartreuse, green, or yellow in the UK.

Body—The body is slender and supported on long legs, which give the breed a somewhat rounded or arched look. The legs are narrow and dainty. The tail is long and thin and should be well covered with curly fur.

Coat—The fur should be short, curly, wavy, or rippled. Generally, the fur of the Cornish Rex is more profuse than that of the Devon, but it will vary in individual cats due to different genetical backgrounds. As polygenes influence coat quality, this factor should be selected for by breeders.

Color—Most feline colors are accepted in this breed, but white markings on the Siamese coat pattern are disqualifying faults. Cats with the Siamese pattern (colorpoints) are known as Si-Rexes.

Faults—A coat that is too shaggy or too short, bare patches, small ears, cobby body, short or bare tail, and kinks in the tail.

Comment—All the rexes are very interesting cats whose looks will intrigue some fanciers. They have lively personalities, yet their voices are soft.

DEVON REX

Origin: In 1960, the second of the rex mutations appeared, this time in Devon (England). It was quickly discovered that the Cornish and Devon mutations were not of the same gene location, because when the two were crossbred, normal-coated kittens were the result.

The Devon Rex contains all three types of hair found in a cat's coat—namely guard, awn, and down—but they are very sparse and somewhat coarse, possibly due to the fact that the guard hairs are fragile and break easily, such as when the cat grooms itself. In addition, a num-

The head of the Devon Rex is somewhat more wedge shaped than that of the Cornish Rex—it has larger ears and a more pointed muzzle.

The Devon Rex comes in many colors and patterns, including bicolor and tortoiseshell.

ber of whiskers are often missing in the Devon.

Presently, Devon Rex cats are still permitted to be outcrossed with several other breeds until 1993, due to the limited gene pool. These outcross breeds include British and American Shorthairs, European Shorthairs, Burmese, Bombay, Siamese, and the Sphynx.

Character: The Devon Rex is a lively cat with a charming personality. It is an excellent sprinter, and it makes a wonderful pet.

Appearance: The Devon Rex, like the Cornish Rex, has an Oriental appearance. In the UK, it is found in the foreign shorthair section of the GCCF official breed standards.

Head—The face of the Devon Rex is more wedge shaped than that of the Cornish Rex. It has a pixie look about it, which is created by the large ears and more pointed muzzle. The eyes should be oval and slightly slanted. Eye color should blend with fur color; however, the eyes of the Si-Rex must be green, chartreuse, or yellow in the UK.

Body—The body of the Devon Rex is similar to that of the Cornish Rex but has a more racy appearance, due to the longer hindlegs.

Coat—The fur should be fine, wavy, and soft. The thickness of the coat varies due to the genetic backgrounds of the individual cats; therefore, breeders should selectively breed for coat quality.

Color—Most colors are allowed in the breed, but in the UK any white markings on the Siamese coat pattern disqualify the cat. A cat with the Siamese pattern is known as a Si-Rex. Bicolors are not accepted in the UK but are allowed in the USA.

Faults—Too shaggy or too short a coat, bare patches, small ears, cobby body, short or bare tail, kinks in the tail, any white markings other than in the tortoiseshell and white variety.

Comment—The Devon Rex is an unusual and lovely breed, with an interesting personality and a soft voice.

EGYPTIAN MAU

Origin: The Egyptian Mau is a relatively recent breed that was developed in the USA during the 1950s from cats originally imported, via Italy, from Cairo. Those in the breed like to think that it is a direct descendant of the sacred Egyptian cats, but, as impressive as this may seem, the reality is that it has no more claim to direct lineage from such cats than other breeds. In fact, one could put forward a theory that suggests that this breed has less direct descent from such cats and is more likely to be related to the wild African cat.

Whatever its origin, the Egyptian Mau was imported into the USA in 1956 and gained recognition with various associations beginning in 1968, as far as championship status was concerned. The breed is accepted in certain European countries, but not in the UK.

The most outstanding feature of the Mau (which means cat in Egyptian) is its spotted coat, which has been improved by selective breeding for this feature. A well-marked individual is an impressive cat—as are any of the breeds which display spotting. However, it also has a very distinctive overall shape which is clearly similar to that of the cat commonly found throughout Africa.

Character: The Egyptian Mau is an intelligent cat that is somewhat shy but, according to owners, very affectionate. These cats quickly learn from observation and are said to be excellent hunters, which would be in keeping with a breed that has, in its recent past, probably more than a few wild ancestors in its make-up.

Appearance: The Egyptian Mau is a most striking breed of cat.

Head—The head is slightly wedge shaped, and the ears are an obvious feature, being large, wide at the base, and rounded at their tip. The nose forms a continuous line with the forehead. This breed should have large, almost round eyes which are just slightly inclined towards the ears. The upper eyelid line is almond shaped, whilst the lower forms a neat half circle. Eye color may be green or amber, but the latter is not permissible until the cat is mature.

Body—The body is lithe and Oriental but has somewhat more muscle to it; it is supported on longish legs which are narrow and elegant, end-

The Egyptian Mau is a relatively new breed of cat that is quickly winning the hearts of fanciers on both sides of the Atlantic.

The body of the Egyptian Mau is lithe and Oriental yet quite muscular. Owners say that members of this breed are excellent hunters.

ing in compact paws. The tail is of medium length and is nicely rounded at its tip.

Coat—The fur is short and silky in texture and should exhibit a good glossy shine. The pattern is as described for mackerel tabby (see American Shorthair), except that the stripes are, of course, broken to form spots or ovals. Some cats are well marked, but others are less so and their pattern may lack impact. Constant attention needs to be paid to the selection of suitably spotted mates in order to increase the number of polygene modifiers that are presently thought to control the regularity of the spots.

Color—There are four colors accepted in this breed: silver, bronze, smoke and pewter. Others, such as cinnamon, blue, and lilac will no doubt gain acceptance in due course.

The silver variety has a very light gray ground color on which black markings are superimposed; these may appear dark gray on some cats. The bronze is genetically a chocolate tabby, having a honey-yellow ground color with brown spotting; this is created by the replacement of the gene for black pigmentation by the mutant gene *b*, which results in brown pigment. The smoke has a white ground color which is tipped with dark gray, with the spots being dense black. This color is similar to that found in the wild species *Felis libyca libyca* (the nominate race of the species and one of 19 subspecies), which is indigenous to Morocco and Egypt and is commonly known as the African wild cat. The pewter has fawn ground color and gray or brown markings. The dilution gene will reduce the black pigment to blue and the brown of the bronze to lilac.

Faults—Any kinks in the tail, loss of clearly defined spotting and any loss to the overall head or body shape, which must be neither too cobby nor too Siamese in type.

Comment—The Egyptian Mau is an attractive addition to the cat fancy and has all the attributes to make it a very popular breed in the coming years. It offers plenty of scope and challenge to breeders of both pattern and color. As a pet the Egyptian Mau has much to offer; it has a sweet, almost chirplike sound coupled with an affectionate nature—if the owner has the time to devote to the cat. Its name is a surefire conversation starter when friends pay a visit, so owners should brush up on their Egyptian history.

The head of the Egyptian Mau is slightly wedge shaped and the ears are large with a wide base.

The Exotic Shorthair is a hybrid that was created by crossing a Persian with an American Shorthair.

EXOTIC SHORTHAIR

Origin: The Exotic Shorthair has its roots in the days when the Persian breed was sweeping all before it in the show ring. Breeders of American Shorthairs hit upon the idea of crossing their breed with Persians, to improve the quality of coat and to give it a more Persian look. Quite naturally, the diehards wanted nothing to do with such efforts for, win or lose, they wanted to keep the American Shorthair an all-American breed with, maybe, just a dash of British Shorthair in there somewhere. Something similar had occurred in the UK some years earlier and, like the Americans, many British breeders wanted nothing to do with this new half-way type of cat. In the UK, nothing more came of these matters, and any Persian in the breed disappeared in the following years. In the USA, however, some of the breeders of this new hybrid liked what they saw and decided to concentrate their efforts on creating a fixed type which was actually a short-haired Persian. In some American Shorthairs one can still see the influence of the Persian genes in the shape of the cat's face, but it has all but been bred out in most strains.

Because of the objections to the hybrids being called American Shorthairs, it was decided to rename them. The Exotic Shorthair came into being and was accepted in the early 1970s as a separate breed. For a while other breeds were introduced to programs, one of which was the Burmese, but it was soon determined that these were not of benefit; therefore, fixed crosses were agreed upon and these were: Exotic × Exotic; American Shorthair × Exotic; American Shorthair × Persian; Persian × Exotic.

It was once believed that the best cross was Exotic to Persian, but there is no reason to believe that this will ensure better cats than any of the other crosses, as it all comes back to how good the parental generation is for its quality. Using simple genetic theory, it is easy to calcu-

The Exotic Shorthair is judged against the Persian standard for body type, and it is accepted in all American Shorthair and Persian colors.

A copper-eyed black Exotic Shorthair.

late likely expectations from the various crosses—at least in respect to the ratios of long-haired and shorthaired cats and to the proportions of heterozygous and homozygous cats. The gene for long hair is transmitted as a simple autosomal recessive to the dominant short hair gene.

Character: When two breeds are crossed, it should not be assumed that the character of the offspring will be a nice blend between the two parent breeds. The classic example of this is when Poodles were crossed with wolves in Germany. Often, the hybrids that looked more like the wolf had the character of the Poodle, and vice versa, thus proving that external appearance and other characteristics are not necessarily inherited together but may cross—or not—at random. Of course, the differences between two cats are hardly comparable with those of the example given, for with cats we are talking about matings between two domesticated varieties, so differences in character are much more subtle. Therefore, an Exotic Shorthair may look like a shorthaired Persian and have the same independent spirit that its American heritage would suggest, but it could also have the very docile and friendly disposition of the best of Persian cats. All in all, one can say that the Exotics will have very pleasing characters, some being far more home-loving than others.

Appearance: In appearance, the Exotic Shorthair is judged against the Persian standard for excellence of type, though it will only achieve comparable quality in this respect after many years of careful breeding.

Color—The Exotic may be seen in all colors accepted for either the American Shorthair or the Persian—this means virtually every color known to exist in cats—quite a good choice!

Comment—This is a variable breed determined by the random segregation of the genes of its parent breeds. Some will look more Persian than others, but all should show nice dense fur. Some will tend to be more woolly than others, as this will reflect the type of fur of the Persian. If one breeds Exotic to Exotic, a number of longhaired cats will be produced. Only selection for shorthairs at every generation will reduce the incidence of long hair genes, but in the process Persian type might suffer; the breeding of any

hybrid is not without its problems. These problems aside, the Exotic is an excellent breed and makes a delightful pet.

HAVANA BROWN
Origin: The Havana Brown, known in the UK simply as the Havana, was first developed in Britain. Although self-brown cats were known in England as early as the 1880s, these were not taken seriously; therefore, a specific breeding opportunity was missed. It was not until the 1950s that the color was selected for on a deliberate basis.

The first Havana Browns were produced by crossing a black shorthair with a seal point Siamese; concurrent to this, another breeder paired a Russian Blue with a Siamese, so it is not surprising that the breed is very much of the Siamese type—at least in the UK. Although the first Havana Browns in the USA were British imports, the respective breeding policies on either side of the Atlantic have been such that the two breeds are no longer comparable in their appearance, except in color. The American breeders quickly discontinued crossing back to the Siamese, and, as a result, the Siamese influence, in terms of type, receded. In the UK, mat-

The Havana Brown is an active, vocal cat that thrives on attention from its owner.

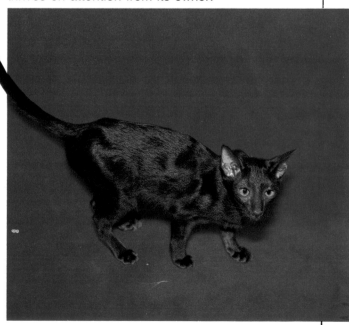

In the UK, the Havana Brown is the equivalent of the chestnut Oriental Shorthair in the USA.

ing back to the Siamese continued in order to stamp type into the Havana, but this no longer takes place and the breed is produced by Havana to Havana matings. In the USA, the breed that is most closely equated to the British Havana is the Oriental Shorthair, which is a self-colored Siamese. The Havana Brown of America is a somewhat more cobby cat that possibly has more in common with the Russian Blue, in conformation, than with the Siamese.

The Havana Brown was accepted as a breed in the USA in 1959; in the UK, it gained breed status a year earlier, having appeared at shows from 1953 onwards.

Character: The Havana Brown still shows many characteristics of the Siamese, so it is an alert, intelligent, and very affectionate cat that thrives on companionship. Its voice is softer than that of the Siamese and it tends to be less vocal than that breed, but is more vocal than the average cat.

Appearance: The Havana Brown of the USA is a somewhat shorter and more cobby cat than the Havana of the UK.

Head—The head is basically a wedge shape, but this is more obvious in British Havanas, which are very much of the Siamese type. Those of the USA are somewhat more rounded in the face but are still clearly of foreign type. The ears are wide at their base and taper to a rounded tip. The nose is straight; in the USA, it has a slight stop at the eyes, but no stop should be present in a British Havana. The eyes are almond shaped and have a typical Oriental slant which, again, is more obvious in British examples than in those of the USA. Eye color is green.

Body—The tail is long and tapering and the legs are long and slim.

Coat—The fur is short and extremely glossy with a satiny texture.

Color—The preferred color is a rich chestnut brown (the breed was called by this name in the UK a number of years ago). However, there will always be variation in the depth of the shade, because two mutations at the black gene loci are known. These are b, which produces the darker shade of brown, whilst b^1 produces a lighter color. Both are also subject to polygene modifiers; therefore, quite a range of shades, from one extreme to the other, is possible. In the UK, the breed known as the foreign lilac is judged to the standard of the Havana, which it resembles in all features other than in color. This is the lavender cat of the early Havana days of development and is the result of the dilution gene reducing the intensity of the brown; it was probably introduced into the breed from the Russian Blue.

Faults—Kinks in the tail, any white appearing on the body, and a tendency to have an uneven color.

Comment—The Havana Brown will appeal to those who like a dark chocolate colored cat that is lively and affectionate in its nature.

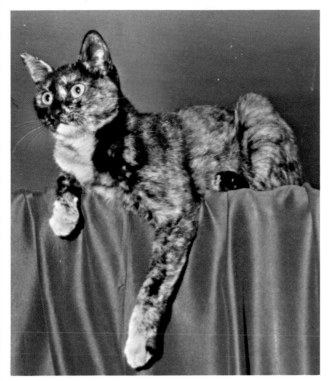

Tortoiseshell Japanese Bobtail.

JAPANESE BOBTAIL

Origin: Although now known as the Japanese Bobtail, this breed of short-tailed cat exists in various parts of the Far East. It is named for Japan because the first examples to reach the USA came from that country. It was first imported to the USA in 1908 for breeding purposes, though examples were known in the USA prior to this, as servicemen brought individuals back as pets. It was accepted for registration in 1971 and gained championship status soon afterwards. It is not recognized in the UK and is not a common breed even in the USA.

Unlike the Manx cat of Great Britain, the Japanese Bobtail's tail is not known to be linked to any genetic abnormality. It is, of course, a mutational breed for its tail, which is inherited as a simple recessive gene. This means that a Bobtail mated to a Bobtail will produce 100% Bobtail kittens. If it is mated to a normal-tailed cat, then all the kittens will have normal length tails, but all will carry the gene for the short tail.

Character: The Japanese Bobtail has the personality of all Oriental cats; it is lively, intelligent, friendly, and curious—ready to explore everything.

Appearance: Of the examples I have seen, there did appear to be quite some variation in the shape of the head and in the overall structure of the cats, and there is no doubt that a number of Bobtails have been crossbred with American Shorthairs at some point in the development of various strains—possibly due to a shortage of mates at the time.

Head—The shape of the head is that of a triangle which is formed by imaginary lines drawn from the nose outwards to the tips of the ears. There is a slight curve down where the forehead goes into the nose so that, whilst the Bobtail is clearly foreign in type, it does not resemble the Siamese. The ears are set wide apart and are broad at the base and rounded at the tips. The eyes should be large and nicely rounded, with only the slightest Oriental slant. The eye color should blend with the particular coat color.

Body—The body is muscular without being too cobby, and the legs are long and of medium thickness. The obvious feature of the breed is its short tail, which ranges from very short to somewhat long, maybe attaining up to 12.5 cm (5 in) in some examples; however, the CFA stan-

The Japanese Bobtail type is muscular yet not too cobby.

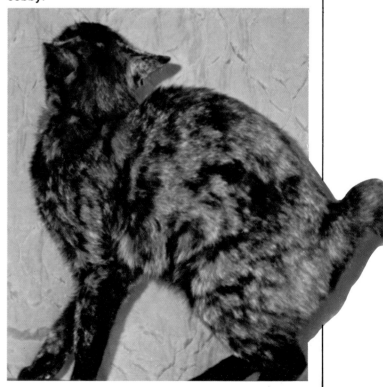

Left: The fur on the Japanese Bobtail's tail is longer than that on the rest of its body. Below: The head of the Japanese Bobtail is triangular in shape.

dard restricts bone length to 7.6 cm (3 in). The tail should feel like a single bone rather than a collection of bones. The tail fur is longer than that on the body and may appear like a small pompon at the tip. The tail is normally carried in a gay, upward manner.

Coat—The fur is again somewhat variable in individuals but is essentially short, with a minimum of undercoat. It has a glossy look.

Color—A number of colors are accepted, but the tabby, colorpoint, or Abyssinian patterns are not preferred, and attempts have been made to restrict color bicolored or tricolored (Mi-ke) cats. Black, red, and white in well-marked patches are highly favored, as are tortoiseshells. In due course, I feel quite sure that we will see all known cat colors appearing in the breed, as this is the normal trend with any breed. However, certain colors may well be given a different breed name, depending on the general feelings on this aspect within the breed fancy at the time.

Faults—Any movement away from the present body type—which should neither be too Siamese nor too cobby.

Comment—This is a pleasant, fuss-free breed that makes a nice pet. It offers plenty of scope for those interested in developing color varieties, and a longhaired variety will be produced in due course.

KORAT

Origin: The Korat is named for the area of Thailand (formerly Siam) known as Cao Nguyen Khorat, which lies in the east-central part of the country. It is thought to be a quite old breed and is mentioned in various Thai texts which date back two or three centuries. The Korat is a natural breed, but the color is mutational, being a dilution of the black pigment to blue. It is the least known of the four major blue breeds (British blue, Chartreux, Russian Blue, and Korat); of these, the Russian Blue is visually the most similar to the Korat.

In Thailand, the breed is not common, so it is highly prized and may be given as a gift of esteem to another person. It is believed that the Korat was seen in England as long ago as 1896, but the cat judges of the day insisted it was a blue Siamese, whereas the owner claimed that it was a true separate breed of Siam. Nothing came of the Korat until 1959, when it was imported for breeding purposes into the USA. It was recognized by the different associations during the period of 1965-69 and in 1969 in Australia, but it had to wait until 1975 to gain recognition in the UK. It still remains a somewhat rare breed, but this pleases the breeders, as it ensures that the standards remain at a good level. In Thailand, the breed is known as the Si-Sawat. In order to retain purity of bloodlines, the major breed societies for the Korat insist that a cat is only a Korat if it can trace its ancestry back to Thailand.

The Korat is known for its heart-shaped face and green eyes, but its most striking feature is the beautiful silver-blue coat.

The body of the Korat is cobby with legs of medium length.

Character: The Korat is an intelligent and affectionate breed which is also of a mild disposition. It is not an especially vocal breed, which is somewhat unusual for cats from this area of the world, but their voice is pleasant.

Appearance: The Korat, like all blue shorthairs, is an attractive, striking cat.

Head—The head when viewed from the front is described as being heart shaped; this shape is formed by the well-developed cheeks and the nicely rounded ear tips. The bite is level. The shape of the eye, when fully opened, is round, but this becomes slightly Oriental when partially closed. The color should be green, though an amber cast is acceptable. The full eye color does not show until the cat is adult, at about two years of age.

Body—The body is semi-cobby and muscular, and the cat is of medium size, the body supported on medium length legs. The tail is of moderate size and is quite thick at its root.

Coat—The fur is short and plush; it lays close to the body and should exhibit a nice sheen.

Color—The color should be a silver-blue. It is produced by the blue hair being tipped with silver, the more tipping the better. Si-Sawat means silver or a green-blue in the Thai language. The blue color is the result of the dilution gene which reduces the intensity of black pigment. This is the major gene, but polygenes clearly control the tint of blue seen. Therefore, when breeding, continual selection for the shade desired will increase the number of genes for a given shade.

Faults—Poor face shape, poor color, and any visible kinks in the tail. Lack of prominent eyes.

Comment—The Korat is an impressive cat that makes a delightful pet. It is not commonly seen, so a potential owner might have to search around a while to find a kitten. However, making contact with the nearest registry association will no doubt result in a list of breeders in your area, or you could contact one of the Korat specialty clubs.

MALAYAN

The Malayan is actually a Burmese cat of a color that is not accepted by certain associations as a Burmese color; therefore, it is one of many instances where disagreement between various factions results in unaccepted color variants being given separate breed status. This happens more often in the USA than in Europe or England, where breeders tend to be more patient and are prepared to wait for their ruling bodies to accept additional colors.

In the UK, Burmese are accepted in a number of colors, but in the USA, certain registries only regard the brown cat as a Burmese. This means that blue, together with the light phase browns known in the USA as champagne and platinum, have gained acceptance under the name of Malayan. This is a recent development which dates back to 1980. Readers are referred to the Burmese for details of this breed.

MANX

Origin: The origin of the Manx mutation that produces this tailless cat is not known, but various stories exist about it. Some say it came from the Far East via trading vessels, and others say it arrived on the Isle of Man when a shipwrecked galleon from the defeated Spanish Armada sank near the island. Whatever the truth may be, the fact is that the Manx became well established on this small island just off the English coast and has become world famous. The Manx government retains a breeding population of the cats so that they are always available; in addition, the breed is featured on Manx coins and on two Manx stamps, as the islanders are proud of this unusual cat.

However, were this breed to be found as a mutation today, it would certainly receive no

The Malayan is a Burmese cat with a coat color other than sable. Most registries now accept these cats as Burmese rather than giving them separate status.

recognition in the UK. Britain has strict policies against the breeding of genetic abnormalities that are linked to structural defects, prenatal deaths, and numerous other problems—all of which are exhibited by the Manx.

The longhaired Manx is known as the Cymric in the USA and Canada, but has no connection with Wales. Some say that the mutation for long hair arose within the Manx breed and was not introduced via any other breed, but, given the

Black and white bicolor Manx.

the ears medium to long. The eyes are large and round, and their color should blend with the color of the fur.

Body—The body is solid, compact and ends in a rounded rump. The legs are short and strong at the front, whilst the hindlimbs are longer in order to give the rear end extra height.

Coat—The fur is double, with a short undercoat and slightly longer guard hairs. The quality of this coat is more important than its color or pattern.

Color—The Manx may be of any color or pattern other than that of Siamese (Himalayan). In some American associations, chocolate and lavender (lilac) are not accepted.

Taillessness—Absolute lack of tail is essential in the exhibition Manx cat. Other Manx with tails of varying lengths are known and are as follows:

1) Rumpy-riser—A few vertebrates can be seen or felt as an upright projection.
2) Stumpy—Here the tail is longer and often kinked or otherwise deformed.
3) Longie—This tail is shorter than full length but longer than the other forms.

Faults—Any visible tail vertebrae, or any such vertebrae that can be felt. Lack of level bite. Any other visible deformity.

The quality of the Manx coat is more important than color or pattern.

heterozygous genotype of the Manx, this would be difficult to substantiate and is not a matter of great importance, as the end result is a long-haired Manx. In this variety, the coat length is not restricted to certain areas, as in the Balinese, for example, but is more general over the whole cat.

Character: The Manx is an obligate heterozygote, by which is meant that it is not a pure-breeding breed. Manx are produced by mating Manx to normal-tailed cats, which ensures that the offspring will, in the main, be viable. As a result, the Manx has a variable personality which reflects the tailed cat that has gone into its make-up. Provided that they are of a really healthy type, then Manx make nice, intelligent, and affectionate pets.

Appearance: The overall appearance of the Manx is that of the British Shorthair but with a more raised rear end. Of course, it has no tail at all or one of only rudimentary length.

Head—The head is fairly round and the cheeks are well developed. The bite is level and

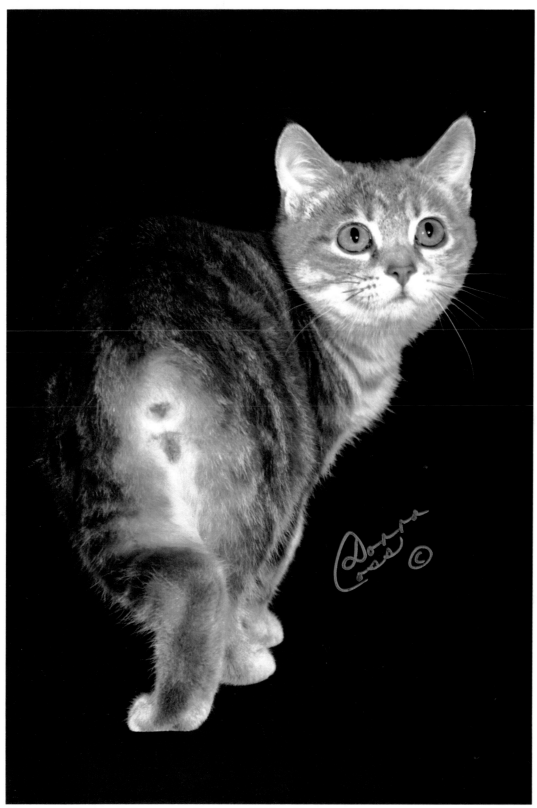

Absolute taillessness is a must for the exhibition Manx.

The Manx is often seen with a tabby coat pattern.

A red tabby Manx.

Comment—The Manx will no doubt always have its followers, as a strong, healthy Manx is a fine animal. However, the possibility of problems occurring within given litters does exist and even cats that survive to maturity may well still develop problems of the intestinal tract and other physical disabilities, including the "bunny-hop" gait. Those who do decide to own and breed the Manx should be prepared for problems and must cull any kittens that show signs of deformity.

For those interested in the genetic state of the Manx, the gene for lack of a tail is created by the dominant gene M, which is lethal, or mostly so, in its homozygous state. If two rumpies are mated, a percentage of the offspring will either be stillborn or resorbed. At present, it is not possible to identify the percentages of rumpy-risers, stumpies, or longies that will turn up at random in litters. There is no connection between the Manx and the Japanese Bobtail, the latter of which is created by a simple recessive gene which has no negative genetic implications.

OCICAT

Origin: This is a hybrid breed that bears a superficial resemblance to the Egyptian Mau. However, its head shape is not quite as distinctive in the sense that it is less foreign, though this is changing with increased crossing to the Abyssinian.

The Ocicat is recognized by the CFA (1987) and by TICA, and it will no doubt gain further recognition as the breed becomes more established. The breed is named for the ocelot, the beautiful wild South American cat. The Ocicat was produced by crossing Abyssinians with American Shorthairs and Siamese; however, today the only permissible outcross is to an Abyssinian, and this only until January 1, 1995, by which time enough generations should have been produced to ensure a good gene pool of pure descent.

Appearance: The Ocicat is a quite large and very well-muscled cat which, in terms of a general description, is not unlike the Egyptian Mau, but it has a somewhat less·wedge-shaped head. Its eyes are large and almond shaped with a very slight Oriental slant. The distance between the eyes must be more than the length of an eye. Any color is permitted except for blue.

Coat—The fur is short and sleek—but must be long enough to allow for the agouti banding of hairs that creates the colors of the breed.

A blue-gray Oriental Shorthair, called foreign blue in the United Kingdom.

Color—The recognized colors at this time are as follows:

1) Tawny (brown spotted tabby)
2) Chocolate
3) Cinnamon
4) Blue
5) Lavender (lilac)
6) Fawn
7) Silver
8) Chocolate silver
9) Cinnamon silver
10) Blue silver
11) Lavender silver
12) Fawn silver

Comment: This is a more substantial breed than the Egyptian Mau and will obviously be a rival to it. When breeding, only the best spotted cats should be used; otherwise, there will be a tendency for the spots to form blotches, as in the classic tabby pattern, from which the spotting is believed to have originated. This is an active breed not suited to confined living space.

ORIENTAL SHORTHAIR

Origin: The Oriental Shorthair, in the USA, embraces all colors of the Siamese breed that are not accepted as either Siamese or as Colorpoint Shorthairs. Thus the self-colored Siamese are Orientals, as are the shaded colors, the smokes, the tabbies, and the particolors. In the UK and mainland Europe, the situation is somewhat different because the self-colored Siamese are known as foreigns, with each color creating an individual breed, such as foreign red or foreign black and so on. The tabbies, torties, and spotted tabbies of the UK are known as Orientals.

The first Orientals appeared as mutations within the Siamese when British breeders were attempting to create the Havana (Havana Brown) during the 1950s. They were exported to the USA and gained recognition, together with other mutational colors, during the 1970s; since then they have enjoyed increasing popularity as even more colors are added to the already extensive list. The Oriental Shorthair breed is thus a mixture, both of colors that may have arisen spontaneously within the Siamese and those which have been introduced by hybridization to other breeds. The latter were then bred out in terms of type to produce what are essentially true-breeding Siamese of the new colors.

Character: The Oriental Shorthair may be regarded in terms of its personality as a Siamese, and the reader is therefore referred to that breed for further details.

The eyes of the Ocicat may be any color other than blue.

The first Oriental Shorthairs appeared during the 1950s when breeders in Great Britain were trying to develop the Havana.

Appearance: The Oriental (foreign) Shorthair is to be regarded as a Siamese in its basic anatomy; therefore, the reader should refer to that breed for a detailed description.

Color—There are many colors available in this breed in the USA, the UK, and elsewhere. Whilst Americans group these together under the single heading of Orientals, the situation is more complex in Great Britain, where each color is a breed. Further, whilst many of these are termed foreign, still others are called Oriental.

Solid colors—In addition to the following colors, the UK also accepts the foreign caramel, which is a bluish fawn.

1) White—Must be even in color down to the hair roots. Eyes blue, green, or yellow, but not odd-eyed. Called the foreign white in the UK; eyes must be blue.

2) Ebony—Coal black to the roots. Green eyes preferred but yellow accepted. Called the foreign black in the UK; eyes must be green.

3) Blue—Blue-gray, the lighter the better. Called the foreign blue in the UK; eye color is green.

4) Chestnut—Medium brown, including whiskers and pads. Called the Havana in the UK (in the USA, the Havana Brown is a separate breed).

5) Lavender—An even pinkish gray created by the action of the dilution gene *d* acting on the chestnut color. Called the foreign lilac in the UK; eye color green; the shade of body color should not be too blue or too fawn.

6) Cinnamon—The mutational gene *b* pro-

The Oriental Shorthair is basically a Siamese cat—it is Siamese in type and personality.

duces the chestnut color, but a second mutation at this locus has resulted in the b^1 gene, which lightens the shade to create the cinnamon. Called the foreign cinnamon in the UK.

7) Red—Should be bright red and even throughout the coat. This is a sex-linked color with the gene being known genetically as orange, OO (female) and OY (male). Called the foreign red in the UK.

8) Cream—a buff-cream is desired, the lighter the better; the nose and pads are pink. Cream is created by dilution of the red gene, symbolized as $OOdd$ or $OYdd$, according to sex. Called the foreign cream in the UK, where it is described as being "a cool-toned cream"; it should be as free of tabby markings as possible.

Shaded colors—The shaded shorthairs are created by the cat's light undercolor, which is tipped with a darker shade. Ideally, the undercolor should be white or as near to this as possible; in red or cream cats, however, a cream undercolor is preferred. Any color accepted for Oriental (foreign breeds) in the UK may be seen in a shaded form. In the USA, the cameos should be red or cream with a white undercolor. The eye color should be green in all but the red, cream, or tortie, where it can be any shade of copper through green, with the latter preferred. In the USA there is somewhat more latitude in eye color.

Smoke colors—As with the shadeds, the smokes may be any color accepted for Oriental. The color is created by the coat being tipped in a color over a white undercolor. The tipping is more extensive, so the cat appears to be a self color until it moves, when the undercoat shows its white (or as close to white as possible) undercolor.

Tabby pattern—The Oriental Shorthair is accepted in all of the tabby patterns, including spotted, and these are found in any color accepted for the Oriental breed.

Comment—In order to try and remove any confusion in the reader's mind about the status of the Oriental Shorthair, it can be summarized as follows:

1) In the USA, any self-colored Siamese is an Oriental Shorthair.

Ebony Oriental Shorthair. The various solid colored Orientals are considered separate breeds in the UK.

White Oriental Shorthair. The white Oriental may not be odd-eyed; in the UK, its eyes must be blue.

2) In the USA, any tortoiseshell, shaded, smoke, or tabby Siamese is an Oriental Shorthair.
3) In the UK, any self-colored Siamese is a foreign shorthair.
4) In the UK, any tortoiseshell, shaded, smoke, or tabby Siamese is an Oriental Shorthair.
5) In the UK, the breed known as the Havana is a foreign shorthair.
6) In the USA, the breed equating to the Havana of the UK is the Oriental chestnut. The Havana Brown of the USA is a separate breed.

Russian Blue.

RUSSIAN BLUE

Origin: No one knows for sure how long the Russian Blue has been known, but it is thought to be a few centuries old. It was first imported into the UK during the 1880s and was exhibited at the early shows, although there was much confusion in those days as to breeds and cats were often referred to under different names. The Russian Blues were called Archangel cats for the port in Russia that they were generally imported from. Type had not been established, so no doubt Russian Blues and British blues were mated for some time after the British blue had become a separate breed (it was possibly developed from the Russian Blue).

In the USA, the Russian Blue is thought to have arrived from England as early as the 1880s, but early records are not clear on whether they were Russian Blues or just blue shorthairs. However, they were certainly known as Russian by the turn of the century, when imports from the UK were increasing. Subsequently, many of these cats came from Sweden, so today's American Russian Blues are a combination of Anglo-Swedish lines. However, as in a number of breeds, type started to change from one side of the Atlantic to the other. In the UK, the breed was perfected as a foreign and has remained such, but in the USA the breed has tended to become wider in the face and more like the domestic shorthaired blues in a number of lines.

The blue color is created by the dilution gene d acting upon black pigment, which is reduced in density. Being a recessive gene, the blue is only visible if both genes carry the mutation, that is, if the cats are therefore purebreeding for their color.

Character: The Russian Blue is a placid breed which is both affectionate and hardy. These cats make excellent pets and have quiet voices.

Appearance: As with many breeds, the differences between the British Russian Blues and those of the USA are more readily appreciated if one sees good examples of each; they are not so easily clarified in a general description. However, in the USA the ears are more inclined at an angle than in the UK, where

The Russian Blue is an elegant breed of cat with long legs and a long, tapering tail.

these should rise vertically when seen from the front. Likewise, the Americans prefer a less foreign type face and body than do the British, whose breed is more elegant in its proportions. Nonetheless, one cannot mistake a Russian Blue for any other breed, on whichever side of the Atlantic one lives.

The Russian Blue should never be cobby; the body is supported on long legs which are never stocky—they are slimmer in the UK than in the USA. The tail is long and tapering. The eyes should be almond in shape and set well apart. The eye color must be green, the more vivid the better.

Coat—The fur is a most important feature of this breed; it should be very dense, though short. The guard hairs are tipped with silver, giving the coat a glossy sheen. The fur should stand up from the body to feel soft and plush to the touch.

Color—The preferred color is a light blue in the USA, medium blue in the UK. In the UK, both the Russian Black and the Russian White are recognized breeds; they should have pure white or dense black coats with no traces of any other color. In all Russian Blues,

Above: The eyes of the Russian Blue must be green, the deeper the better. **Right:** The Russian Blue's coat must be short yet very dense.

the color should be even and show no trace of tabby markings, though these may be seen whilst the cat is a kitten.

It is perhaps worth reminding the reader that black is not dominant to blue, as one often hears stated, nor is it a dominant color in cats, as it is the recessive mutation of the agouti dominant A. The recessive gene a results in the wild type agouti patterning being masked so that the coat appears black. However, faint tabby markings can still be seen under certain light conditions, and this is why many standards require minimal tabby markings. The gene for full density of color, D, is dominant to the dilution mutant, d, and this is the reason that black is confusingly regarded as being a dominant color. If pure tabbies are mated to pure blacks, all the offspring will be tabby, thus proving the recessive state of the black.

Faults—Kink in the tail. Any white hairs appearing in the coat (other than in the Russian White!).

Comment—The Russian Blue, whether English or American, is a beautiful cat that is sure to please those who acquire the breed. It is elegant yet very hardy and makes a fine pet and a super exhibition animal that always commands attention.

Russian Blue.

Brown tabby Scottish Fold.

SCOTTISH FOLD

Origin: The Scottish Fold is a breed developed from a genetic abnormality that appeared in a kitten born to farm cats in Perthshire during 1961. The mutant gene results in flopped ears that give the cat a comical and attractive appearance. The breed was exported to the USA, Australia, and elsewhere and gained full recognition. It should be remembered, however, that this breed resulted from a genetic abnormality.

The Scottish Fold is very similar in type to the American Shorthair and is accepted in the same coat colors.

Cream tabby Scottish Fold.

Tricolor Scottish Fold.

The gene responsible for the folded ear is also associated with more sinister conditions such as dysplasia, in which the feet swell, the tail becomes short and thick, and in some litters the animals will walk with difficulty or not at all. Such conditions are seen only in the homozygous (pure) state, and breeders in the USA are recommended by their breed associations to mate only to healthy normal-eared cats, either American or British Shorthairs. The gene for this mutation has been symbolized by the letters Fd, so that most folds will be $Fdfd$. It is the $FdFd$ cats that pose the real problem. The mutation is incompletely dominant to normal ear carriage, which means it varies in its expression. It is possible that the full internal implications of the mutation have not yet been investigated, which is why any person who contemplates keeping or, especially, breeding these cats should be aware of what he is dealing with.

Character: The Scottish Fold has an excellent personality, as one would expect from a cat that is basically a British or American Shorthair.

Appearance: The reader is referred to the American Shorthair section for a description of the Scottish Fold. However, the ear carriage is, of course, of the fold type and it is preferred that the ears be as small as possible. The tail is rarely full size, and often the legs will appear short and thick. The Scottish Fold is accepted in all colors found in the American Shorthair, so the list is extensive.

SIAMESE

Origin: The Siamese cat is so well known that it needs little description, as most people are aware of this breed which has been popular for about 100 years in the Western world. Its origin is Thailand (Siam), and it is associated with the royalty of that country, who, it is thought, jealously guarded this breed and allowed only noblemen and temple priests to own them. Cats of the Siamese type are quite common in the whole area that surrounds Thailand, so it is not surprising that many present-day foreign breeds have their roots in Asia.

Present-day Siamese are not, of course, the same cats that they were 100 years ago, as they have been much refined, first in England, and then throughout the world as their popularity grew. The original Siamese were not as svelte and were rounder in the face. The breed owes its fame to its unique markings, which were created by a mutation that reduced the intensity of color on the body so that the face, lower legs, ears, and tail appear darker in color. Such a mutation is popular in rabbits, guinea pigs, mice, and other small pets, where it is more commonly referred to as Himalayan. This term is retained in cats only for the breed of that name in the USA (the Himalayan in the UK being known as the colorpoint longhair).

The first Siamese that can be traced with certainty in the UK were two exhibited in the first-ever cat show, which took place in July 1871 at the famed Crystal Palace. A sketch of these appeared in the *Graphic* on July 2, which de-

The Siamese cat is probably the best known cat breed in the world. The distinct body type and characteristic colorpoints set this breed apart from all others.

scribed them as "fawn-colored creatures with jet black legs, an unnatural nightmare kind of cat." They were also described as being elegant by another writer, having faces like black pug dogs and blue eyes with red pupils. Of course, they did not actually have jet black legs, as we know now that the color must have been an extremely dark brown, for the Siamese mutation is actually a reduction of black to brown, with a pale cream body, thus producing the classic or royal seal point Siamese. The breed proved extremely popular in the following years and is thought to have appeared in the USA by the late 1880s. Gifts from the king of Siam to both British and American friends are thought to have introduced better quality to the Siamese of the day, which may not have been of the best lines: indeed, it is quite possible that early examples of the breed may well have been the result of crossings with other breeds, including domestic shorthairs, thus producing the more cobby cat known in the early days of the breed's development in Western countries.

(The author notes that Spanish Siamese cats are still very similar to the early types and have shorter, more cobby bodies. Most British or American owners of this breed would regard them with horror, yet they are most attractice. Additionally, many Spanish Siamese have short to medium length tails, but I have been unable to ascertain whether this is a mutation from within the breed or one introduced from without.)

Although the blue point Siamese is said to have been seen in 1896, its owner disputed the name of Siamese, insisting that it was a different purebreeding type from Siam—possibly a Korat. It was some years before the blue was accepted as a color, and it is thought that it may have been crossed with the Russian Blue to help matters along—even if spontaneous mutation in the Siamese for dilution occurred as well. The chocolate point Siamese was first thought to be a poor seal color, but it was eventually realized that it was an independent mutation and became accepted, as did its diluted form, lilac. In the USA, only these four colors are regarded as the Siamese breed, but in the UK many more colors are also accepted.

The Siamese colorpoints are found on the ears, muzzle, tail, and paws.

Character: The Siamese is a highly individualistic breed in its personality; it is very intelligent, very playful, and very vocal. Siamese cats enjoy company, and they are confiding pets with their owners. They can be extremely mischievous as well, for they can only be happy when they are fully at peace with their environment, so they want to know what is behind every door or cupboard and will ponder just how they can satisfy this curiosity. If the owner hears a sudden crash of pots and pans, it is probably the cat going where it shouldn't!

Appearance: The Siamese, together with its many color forms that are known under different breed names, is an easily recognized breed.

Head—The head is wedge shaped and carried on an elegant neck. The ears are wide at their base; they are set well apart and taper to a rounded tip. When viewed from the front, the head should create a perfect triangle from the outwardly inclined ears to the fine muzzle. The nose is long and straight and should merge into the forehead without any distinct break. The bite is level. The eyes are almond shaped and slightly inclined in the Oriental manner. They must be blue in color, the density varying depending on the body color.

Body—The body is long and svelte. The legs are slim, with the hindlegs longer than those in the front. The tail is long, slim, and straight, with no kinks at all along its length. The paws are small and oval.

Coat—The fur is short and fine in texture. It must be very glossy and lay flat to the body.

Color—The Siamese is recognized in the USA in only four color forms. In the UK, the following are also accepted: tabby point; tortie tabby point; red point; seal tortie point; blue tortie point; chocolate tortie point; lilac tortie point; and cream point. The Colorpoint Shorthair of the USA encompasses those colors not accepted as Siamese. Self-colored Siamese are the Oriental Shorthairs of the USA and the foreign shorthairs of the UK. However, in the UK, other breeds, such as the Russian Blue and the Korat, are also found under the foreign shorthair designation, so all "foreigns" in the UK are not necessarily Siamese in other colors.

Siamese varieties—The reader is reminded that the following breeds are Siamese type cats regis-

Seal is probably the Siamese point color most people are familiar with.

The Siamese cat loves attention and will certainly voice its approval upon receiving it.

tered under various breed names: Balinese, Javanese, and Tonkinese.

Points—The face mask, ears, feet, and tail should be of a dense and well-defined color, which should be the same shade on all points. There must be a clear distinction between the colorpoints and the body color. The color on the mask should cover the complete face and should be connected to the ears by tracings. The color on the feet will rise up the legs to about the level of the elbows, and the color for all points will be at its darkest at the bodily extremities. The color in the Siamese is thermosensitive, which means it will be darker in cold climates than in warm ones. However, even in warm countries there will be variation in the depth of color, as this is controlled by polygenes and is subject to breeder selection. Bleaching by sunlight is, of course, another factor that will lighten the color of the points in hot climates; this can make color judgment for breeding purposes difficult under such conditions.

Genetic state—The Siamese mutation is created by reduction of color on the body but not on the points. It is symbolized by the formula $c^s c^s$, being one down from Burmese at the C or full color (albino) locus. At the same gene locus can be found the so-called albino Siamese, which is symbolized as c^a. In this color the cat is pure white but the eye color is a very pale blue-pink; this indicates that it is not a true albino, which would have to be red or pink eyed. A true albino would be c for color. Although such a color is well established in most pet animals, it is disliked in both dogs and cats. Unlike pure white (with colored eyes), albinism is not associated with loss of hearing.

Faults—Any visible kink in the tail; uneven bite, permanent squint in one or both eyes (defined as being placed as to look permanently at the nose); a complete hood of color on the head; eyes tinted with green; odd-sized eyes; and lack of contrast between points and body color.

Comment—The Siamese is a breed that will appeal to those who like very slim cats which have a very vocal voice. Because the Siamese proved so popular years ago it was bred almost on a commercial scale, with little regard to health and quality. This is always an unfortunate penalty of popularity, as it brings into such breeds a number of people whose sole object is to make money. The legacy they leave behind them when they move on to another up-and-coming breed is one of bad type and a high incidence of loss of vigor, resulting in all manner of health problems.

The Siamese cat often becomes very attached to its owner.

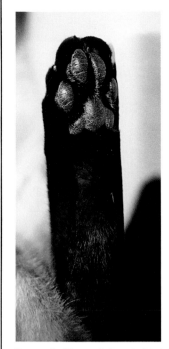

Rear (left) and front (right) paws of a cat. Before purchasing any purebred cat, be sure that each paw has the proper number of toes.

Conscientious breeders must strive to combat such effects on the breed, as they take many years to overcome. In addition, a newcomer to Siamese should pay particular attention to the quality of any Siamese cat purchased. A talk with the local veterinarian may result in advice about any lines known to be poor in health and vigor. It pays to be prudent when purchasing any very popular breed of cat. For those contemplating breeding Siamese, health and breeding vigor should always outweigh any other considerations—but this applies equally to any breed of cat or animal species.

The Siamese makes a truly delightful pet and will continue to be a very popular choice in the foreseeable future. Many specialty breed clubs can be found in all countries, so there are lots of activities available to Siamese owners.

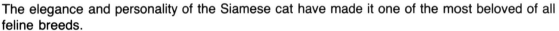

The elegance and personality of the Siamese cat have made it one of the most beloved of all feline breeds.

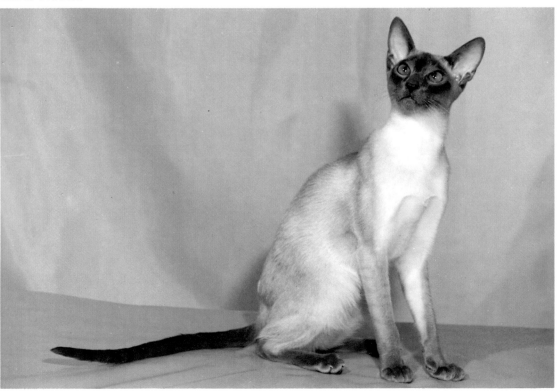

Profile of a Singapura. This breed is now accepted by several cat registering organizations.

SINGAPURA

Origin: The Singapura is a very recent breed that has been imported to the USA from Singapore, where it is a common street cat. It is said that Singaporeans do not like cats and that is why the Singapura is a shy breed that is not used to people. This is an unfair remark, as the people of Singapore are no less cat lovers than many nations. The Singapura is presently only accepted in one color—brownish with certain ticking in the fur—but in Singapore itself one can see just about all colors in the local street cats. These colors will no doubt appear in this new breed which, presently, has little recognition in either the USA or elsewhere. The CFA recognized the breed in 1988, as did TICA.

Appearance: The Singapura is a medium to small sized cat with a lithe body and a foreign type head. The ears are large and inclined, creating a triangle toward the muzzle. The eyes are large and just slightly almond shaped, and their color is chartreuse which varies according to fur color.

Coat—The coat is short and sleek and should exhibit a fine sheen. It lays close to the body.

Color—The present available color is a sandy brown flecked with dark brown or black tipping of the agouti pattern. The chest and underbelly are a pale cream. The tail is dark, almost black, on its upper surface but is agouti patterned as it progresses to the sides and underparts. The breed could be mistaken for an Abyssinian based on the examples I have seen—though not on the street cats I have seen in Singapore itself, which are very variable in their type, as one would expect of local cat populations that are all but feral.

Comment—This is a pleasant cat that will make a good pet. It is clean of line, has an easily managed coat and a quiet and friendly disposition. How well it will succeed in the fancy remains to be seen, as it has a great deal of competition from established shorthaired breeds.

SNOWSHOE

This is another quite recent hybrid that is presently seen in a variety of types. It has no official recognition other than that of a developing

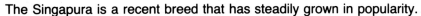

The Singapura is a recent breed that has steadily grown in popularity.

The Snowshoe is a hybrid of the Siamese and bicolor American Shorthair.

breed and no standard of excellence, so it is really a breed in the making. The basic feature of the breed is the possession of white paws or mittens (as in the Birman), a short coat, and colorpoints on the remaining bodily extremities. Type seems to vary considerably at this time. The Snowshoe is produced by crossing a Siamese with a bicolored American Shorthair. The first generation will not carry the colorpoints, so one must pair offspring back to the Siamese or to another hybrid of similar genotype in order to produce the double c^s recessive state of the Siamese. Type will vary between those looking very foreign and those that more closely resemble the American Shorthair.

The Snowshoe's mittens are believed to be created by the spotting gene S, which is present in the bicolored shorthair. However, it is very variable in its expression, so it will take a very well-planned breeding program to establish well-marked individuals of a fixed type. The Snowshoe would appear to be very similar in many respects to the Ragdoll, the difference being one of hair length; in character, however, the Snowshoe is probably the more outgoing, due to its Siamese heritage.

SPHYNX

Origin: The Sphynx is unique in cats at this time because it is the only breed which carries the genes for hairlessness. This condition has appeared before in cats—as it has in many other animal species—but such abnormals were usually destroyed at birth as freaks. The Sphynx, however, has attracted a few devotees who are trying to establish the mutation. At this time the breed is not recognized, nor is it likely to be, in the UK; it is not recognized by the majority of American registries. The present hairless breed appeared as a mutation in a litter of cats born in Canada during 1966. It was perpetuated to the degree that it was originally accepted by the Canadian registry as a breed, but this status was later revoked.

Hairlessness is symbolized as *hr* in the Sphynx in order to distinguish it from the earlier form found in France, which was designated *h*. In the Sphynx this gene is carried as a recessive; this holds considerable problems for the cat fancy at large, because it means that this trait can spread unseen into numerous breeds.

Not all Sphynx are totally hairless—in fact, none are—but the coat, where it does appear, is

The Sphynx is a mutational breed that first appeared in 1966.

so short that for practical purposes it is not apparent. As the cat ages, whatever hair it has is lost and the skin becomes wrinkled.

Appearance: The Sphynx is, to say the least, a strange-looking cat. It is of foreign type, partly because the mutation appears to change the visual type (as is the case in the rex breeds), and partly because Siamese were used in numerous early crosses. The skin is warm to the touch. This hairless mutation appears to have no especially harmful effects other than the state of hairlessness. This, however, is sufficient to give the breed major problems in any but mild climates. It is unable to cope with any extremes of temperature; therefore, it will be as badly affected by strong sunlight as it will be by winter temperatures, and must always be protected from both.

The Sphynx can be produced in any coat color because, as stated, a very short coat is grown and pigment remains in the cells of the skin. In terms of its personality, it is similar to any other cat—playful, intelligent, and affectionate.

Comment: The fact that hairlessness is inherited in the recessive manner means that hairless cats mated to normally haired cats will produce normally furred offspring which are split for hairlessness. Some fanciers fear that such cats may unintentionally spread the gene to other cats. The other problem, breeders feel, is that it may take some time for these genes to show themselves, as they can only do so when there are two of them, but by such a time it is possible that the genes have reached high numbers in a given population. Therefore, those who advocate the establishment of the Sphynx should be aware of the potential problems of hairlessness.

Other fanciers, however, see no danger in breeding for hairlessness, as the feel that any such undertaking will be done responsibly. Additionally, some see no danger in hairlessness at all. All of this, however, is subject to opinion.

Due to its hairlessness, the Sphynx must be protected from strong sunlight, as sunburn is a concern with this breed.

The Sphynx is very similar to the Devon Rex in body and head type.

TONKINESE

Origin: The Tonkinese is a hybrid produced by pairing a Siamese with a Burmese, and the result is a cat which is visibly somewhere between the two breeds. In the UK this is less obvious, as the differences between the two parent breeds are not as great as in the USA. The breed was developed in the USA during the 1960s and has received recognition in Canada and in a number of American associations; it is not recognized in the UK.

Character: The Tonkinese is a lively, intelligent, and affectionate breed that is equally comparable to both of its progenitors.

Appearance: The Tonkinese, like all breeds based on the Siamese, is an attractive foreign type cat.

Head—The head is a medium wedge but it lacks the straight lines of the Siamese. In addition, its cheeks are more full and rounded. The ears are wide at their base, rounded at their tips, and are inclined at a slight angle away from the forehead. The nose is straight and has a slight

stop where it joins the forehead. The upper eye is almond in shape, while the lower part is round; the color of the eyes is blue-green in various tones.

Body—The body is lithe and muscular and is of a heavier build than that of the Siamese. The tail is long and slender. The legs are medium to long, and the hindlegs are longer than the front legs.

Coat—The fur is short, lies close to the body, and should exhibit a good gloss; its texture is silky.

Color—Five colors are presently accepted, and they are as follows:

Natural mink—This is a brown shade in which the points are a dark brown.

Honey mink—This is a ruddy brown tone with points in chocolate.

Champagne—This is a beige color with pale brown points.

Blue mink—This is a blue-gray color with slate points.

Platinum—This is pale gray with darker gray

Natural mink Tonkinese.

points.

Although the colors in this breed are given their own names, they do, in fact, equate to the colors found in the Siamese and Burmese. When breeding Tonkinese, the usual procedure is to mate Tonkinese to Tonkinese once the first cross between the two parent breeds has been made. This is to establish type rather than color, which is inherited independently. Genetically the Tonkinese is symbolized by the formula $c^b c^s$, which means it is a dark Siamese or a light Burmese, whichever view one wishes to take (Burmese is incompletely dominant to Siamese). The actual shade of a color can be lightened or darkened by polygene modifiers, which can be selectively bred for. The base color of blue mink is simply the brown Burmese carrying the dilution gene, d, and should not be considered a genetically different color from the blue of its parent breed—in the same way the platinum is the lilac of the UK and is created by the dilution gene acting upon the champagne (chocolate in the UK) color.

Once a distinct type has been established in the Tonkinese, it will no doubt be available in all colors and coat patterns, if the breeders accept them. If not, they will arrive anyway, and those carrying the unaccepted colors will probably be given a different breed name.

Faults—The Tonkinese should not have the very svelte appearance of the Siamese, nor the rounded and heavier build of the Burmese. No kink should be found in the tail, and, presently, only the stated colors are acceptable.

Comment—This is a very nice-looking cat with a good personality which, therefore, makes a fine pet. In the UK, the light phase Burmese is called a Tonkinese, but this is simply a Burmese of lighter colors, not a hybrid with the Siamese. The Tonkinese as a breed is not recognized in the UK.

NEW BREEDS

At this point, mention can be made of some of the very latest breed which presently have experimental status on many registers. They are all American in origin and only time will tell if they prove to be popular enough to become established breeds that are recognized by all associations and which may be exported to other countries.

Registration bodies receive a steady flow of applications for registration of new breeds, but often, after initial enthusiasm to establish them, the breeds drift into obscurity as they do not have that extra special quality that is needed to gain wide popularity—especially with so many beautiful breeds already in existence.

Within any country there are always variants on a similar theme and this makes popularity on an international basis more difficult to obtain. For example, the well-known Manx either has no tail or a short one. The Japanese Bobtail has a short tail, whilst this author recently acquired an example of what he calls the Spanish Bobtail (acquired through sympathy rather than desire!). Daphne Negus advised me that she saw bobtail Abyssinian types in Thailand. Each of these are probably separate mutations, so each could give rise to individual breeds. However, the more of them that there are, the less chance the later ones have to gain acceptance simply because there is sufficient market for only a limited number of owners for such breeds. If a variant is unusual in a country it may possibly

The body of the Tonkinese is somewhat heavier than that of the Siamese.

become popular, but elsewhere that same variant may be quite common in street cats (such as bobtails in Spain) and will be of little interest to people.

Any person contemplating the establishment of a new cat breed, even mutational forms, should make enquiries to find out if a very similar breed is already known elsewhere (in another country), for such a variant may be superior to that on hand.

AMERICAN CURL

The most well established of these breeds is the American Curl which is available as either a long or shorthaired cat. The uniqueness of the breed lies in the way the ears curl away from the head at their outer edges. The breed first appeared in 1981, and TICA gave the breed recognition in 1985, with CFA giving it miscellaneous class status in 1986. The mutation is a simple dominant, which means that only one parent needs a single curl gene in order to pass on a theoretical 50% curl offspring potential. These

will be single gene youngsters. If two of these are mated, then 75% of their offspring will be curls, of which one-third will be purebreeding—that is, 25% of all kittens (but remember this is in theory). Any normal kittens from curl litters have no curl potential from a breeding viewpoint—they are just like any other cat. The breed is semi-foreign in type, not cobby, and the longhaired variant should have minimal undercoat. Presently, breeders are still experimenting with outcrosses in order to widen the genetic pool. There is no link with the Scottish Fold, and I have received no information that would indicate the mutation is linked to adverse abnormalities. Even so, in my opinion curl to curl matings as a continuum are not advised until the mutation is much more fully established, thus giving plenty of time to see if any problems do appear. The breed is full of charm and appeal, and registrations are progressing at a very healthy rate. A specialty has been formed for the breed; contact your registration authority for details.

The American Curl is one of the more popular breeds in the making.

In addition to its typical shorthaired form, a longhaired American Curl has been produced.

CALIFORNIA SPANGLED

A breed that caused quite a bit of rumpus in American cat circles is the California Spangled, which was a breed visualized and bred by Paul Casey in California. The idea was to produce a spotted cat that was wild looking yet very domestic. The breeding program included the introduction of African and Malayan cats together with domestics, including the Abyssinian. By the 11th generation, the Spangle became a reality. Kittens were sold through a well-known mail catalog at $1,400 in a his and hers X–mas surprise present package that caused an uproar from numerous bodies of people.

The cat itself is very attractive, and the colors available are silver, bronze, black, charcoal, gold, red, blue, and brown. The snow leopard variety is white as a kitten but develops dark spotting as it matures. In all cases, the color is not fully developed until the age of one to two years. It is shorthaired. The breed was first marketed in 1985 and gained recognition from TICA, though it is not yet of championship status, being on the TICA experimental category V list. Whether the breed will prove different enough to become popular in the face of other established and excellent spotted breeds such as the Ocicat and the Egyptian Mau of the USA and the various spotted cats of the UK and elsewhere, we will know as the 1990s unfurl.

OTHER NEW BREEDS

Another breed that has been in the wings for some years is the Chinese Harlequin, which is a shorthaired black and white cat. The tail is black and the head carries black whilst patches are found on the body. The author owns a cat of foreign type that corresponds to this breed, which is attractive but has never really made much progress. It is recognized in category V of the TICA listings. On the same listing is the Nebelung, which is a longhair Russian Blue. I have never seen example but would imagine it to be an attractive feline.

Other breeds that I have noted as experimental are the Bristol, the Bengal, and the Safari.

The creation and perfection of new breeds provides a constant challenge for cat breeders.

The popularity of the Abyssinian cat has spawned many new breeds, such as the Bengal, that feature the agouti or wild coat coloration.

COAT COLOR IN CATS

Before discussing the various colors and coat patterns that are seen in cats, it is worthwhile to consider how the agouti pattern in mammals is created, because this is fundamental to the understanding of how all other colors and their combinations are possible.

Hair color is produced by the effect of light on the pigments within the cells of the hair shaft. The pigments are phaeomelanin, which is yellow or reddish (orange), and eumelanin, which is brown or black. These melanistic pigments are contained in the cells, which are interspersed with air sacs. Melanin is formed from the amino acid tyrosine, which is found in various foodstuffs, and enzyme action on this creates melanin of the two types mentioned. The enzyme is known as tyrosinase, and if it is absent or present only in small quantities, the skin and hair will produce no color or only color that is much diluted.

It has been found that visible color is the result of the way in which the cells of the hair are shaped or positioned; therefore, anything that affects the cell shape will obviously modify the color. Clearly, anything that affects the actual pigments will likewise change the colors, and if the pigments are diluted or missing, this will also modify what we perceive as color. There are thus many factors that control color, rather than just simple gene action for a given color, which, of necessity, is often implied in basic texts. Beyond the mutation of genes, the many metabolic chemical reactions will all play their role in modifying the full expression of a gene; indeed, it

The genetics of coat color in cats is a fascinating subject that is well worth further study.

may well be that certain mutations may be induced by chemicals within foodstuffs, but this aspect of genetic make-up is still poorly understood.

The environment also plays its part in affecting color. This is most readily seen in the Himalayan (Siamese) pattern, which is sensitive to changes in the atmospheric temperature and shows this in those bodily parts which are the furthest from the heart and the least covered with fat layers.

The agouti pattern consists of a mixture of two hair types. First, the shorter undercoat contains hairs in which the base is black, giving way to a band of brown which is variably tipped with yellow (red). The longer guard hairs are much darker. The two types create the familiar pattern of a basically brown or gray color tipped with black. In cats, a second factor is seen, in which the areas of black are much more extensive and contrast quite sharply with the agouti areas; this creates the tabby pattern effect. It is generally believed that the spots of breeds such as the Egyptian Mau are created by a break-up of the wild type mackerel tabby pattern; however, it is quite possible that tabby itself was originally created by spots which fused and spread in various patterns to form the stripes and patterns seen in the numerous wild species. The potential number of colors in combination is greater in cats (wild) than in any other carnivorous family.

The agouti locus can be considered the all-important locus as far as color in cats is concerned, because what happens at this locus determines all other potential color combinations. The many other gene loci will modify the agouti color pattern, or they will act on the only other alternative to agouti, which is non-agouti, or black, in domestic cats.

Cameo Maine Coon. Terms for the various coat colors sometimes vary from one country to the next and from registry to registry.

THE COLORS

In domestic cat breeds, there are about 25 different color terms used, but from a genetic standpoint these comprise just 14 types. In many cases a given color name is used within many breeds, so that chocolate, for example, will be found in numerous breed standards. In other cases a color name will be restricted to a single breed; for example, sable is presently only used in relation to the Burmese, whereas its equivalent color, seal, is applied to many breeds of Siamese origin. Some colors are not at all what the beginner might visualize from their description—lilac and lavender are not the purple colors that most would think of, but are pinkish gray-browns derived from the dilution of the brown color.

Most color terms are global in their application, but there are some differences in names, which depend on whether one lives in a country influenced by British standards, such as Australia, or by American standards, such as Japan. Generally, Americans will use more color names than will the British, so that the term chocolate is also called champagne in the USA, depending on the breed in question; its dilution, lilac, is also known as platinum in certain breeds in the USA, but is called lilac in others. The first color discussed, sable, is known simply as brown in the Burmese of the UK, and is then described as a seal brown within the actual text of the standard.

The potential exhibitor or breeder should become familiar with the names applied to colors in his chosen breed and in his home country. All of the colors discussed in the following text can be incorporated within the vast majority of breeds, less so of course in the UK, where the color itself may have breed status. Likewise, the colors can be incorporated within the various patterns seen in cats, so that one can have a black, blue, or white American Shorthair, and one can have a brown or a blue tabby or a seal or chocolate colorpoint, and so on. The fact that a given color is not recognized in a breed does not mean that the breed cannot carry that color, but simply that breeders have not yet developed it in that breed to the satisfaction of the registration body, which usually requires a number of generations of the color to be established before full recognition is achieved.

SOURCES OF REFERENCE

There are a great many cat registration bodies in the world, and each defines colors in a slightly different manner. In order to keep the chapter as simple as possible, it was decided to refer to the standards of just two ruling bodies. For the UK this was the Governing Council of the Cat Fancy, the sole registration body for Great Britain. The USA has several associations, of which the largest is the Cat Fanciers' Association, Inc.; it was felt that their standards have great application in North America. Between the two sources it can be assumed that the chapter reflects a reasonable guide to the color of cats as they exist around the world at this time. Differences between the American view of color and that of the British are indicated so that the text is applicable to each side of the Atlantic.

In the following text, a number is repeated if the genetic base of the color is exactly the same as one that is simply known under a different name. It must always be remembered that a color can vary in its shade, so that in some cases it can be difficult to correctly apply a name; in other words, two contrasting color names could be applied to the same cat, it being purely a matter of opinion as to which is correct. This variation means that one cannot always judge the genetic state purely from the visible color, as an apparently very light-colored cat may not be carrying the dilution genes but may simply represent the extreme of breeder selection for lightness within a given color's range. The genetic make-up of the color is stated in parentheses.

NON-DILUTED COLORS

1) Black (*aa*): This is produced by the mutation for non-agouti which effectively replaces most of the yellow pigment with black or very dark brown. Ideally, black areas on cats should be dense black down to the roots and should show no movement towards brown. This can be very difficult to achieve in longhaired breeds.

1) Ebony (*aa*): This is simply another name

Tricolor kittens.

applied to black and is used in the Oriental Shorthair breed.

2) Sable ($c^b c^b$): This color is produced by a mutation that reduces the amount of black pigment so that it appears brown, not an even color all over but darker on the extremities of the body. In the USA, it is described as being a rich, warm, sable brown. In the UK, it is referred to as being a rich, warm, seal brown.

2) Seal ($c^s c^s$): This is the same brown as is seen in the Burmese, but in the Siamese mutation the color on the body is greatly reduced in strength to create the pattern for which the breed is associated.

3) Brown (*aabb*): The brown mutation results in a decrease in the black pigment and a corresponding increase in the amount of brown pigment at the *B* locus. It is very variable in its expression and ranges from dark red-brown, seen in the Havana breed and in the Oriental Shorthair, to the golden-browns and honey-beiges of the Burmese, through to the milk chocolate of the Siamese and numerous other breeds. This variation is possible because of breeder selection for the influencing polygenes, which can lighten or darken a color. (The brown used in connection with the tabby, that is, brown tabby, does not refer to the mutated brown gene but refers to the normal wild type brown found in the agouti pattern. This remark also applies to the tawny used in the description of colors for the Ocicat.)

3) Chocolate (*aabb*): This is the milk chocolate color common to many breed standards. In the Burmese of the USA it is called champagne.

3) Champagne (*aabb*): This is the chocolate of the UK; it is used in the USA for describing the color found in light-colored Burmese and in the related Tonkinese breed. In all other breeds, the term chocolate is used to describe this shade of brown.

3) Chestnut (*aabb*): This term is used to describe the red-brown found in the Havana Brown and in the Oriental Shorthair. In the latter breed it is also used to describe the tabby of comparable color.

4) Bronze (*A-bb*): This is the term used to describe the brown markings of the Egyptian Mau, so it is the mutated gene allele of the normal black spotting. Black spotted tabbies are known in the fancy as brown tabby; therefore, one should not confuse the genetic state of a cat with the terms used by breeders. Genetically, the bronze Mau is the true genetic brown and refers to the spotting color and not to the ground color, which in this case is a much lighter shade of brown.

5) **Cinnamon** (aab^1b^1): This color is the result of a second mutation at the B black locus and expresses itself as light brown, which is termed cinnamon in the cat fancy. It is also known, somewhat misleadingly, as red in the Abyssinian. This color is best described as being a light chestnut. In the UK, cinnamon is used to describe the foreign breed of that name. In the Abyssinian breed in the UK, the same color is termed sorrel.

5) **Sorrel** (aab^1b^1) This term is used only in the Abyssinian breed of the UK. It is the same as cinnamon, which has more general application in various cat breeds.

5) **Red** (aab^1b^1): This description is used in the USA in respect to the Abyssinian. It is misleading because it refers to the non sex-linked

The Abyssinian coat typifies the agouti coat pattern in cats.

cinnamon color and not to the sex-linked red which is found in most cat breeds. As more sex-linked reds are bred in the Abyssinian, breed distinction will have to be made between the two genetic types, and one would assume that the recessive red will be renamed cinnamon or something similar. The use of cream to describe the dilute form will likewise need to be dropped in favor of fawn, cream being the dilute form of the sex-linked red. The recessive red has been developed by careful selection from those individuals who exhibit rufism, a tendency to produce red-brown in the hair cells.

6) Red (*O* male, *OO* female): This is the only known sex-linked color in cats. The effect of the red (more correctly orange) gene is to remove all black pigment from the coat. The *O* gene is epistatic to other colors but not to white; this means that, regardless of what other colors a male may be carrying in his genetic make-up, the presence of the *O* gene will make him a ginger tom. He can still be tabby, but the tabby pattern will be in orange. A female may be all red (*OO*), or she may be tortoiseshell (*Oo*). In the latter case, the *o* (for non-orange) gene will allow the colors on the chromosome to show themselves regardless of whether they are dominant or recessive.

WHITE

The white seen in cats is not a simple variation on a single mutation as in brown, but may be the result of totally different gene loci.

7) Dominant white (*WW* or *Ww*): In the pure white cats, such as the Persian, the white must be glistening white without a shade or marking of any kind. The nose leather and paw pads should be pink; the only indication that the cat is not an albino will be the eye color, which will be either in blue, orange (copper), or odd. Dominant white is epistatic to all other colors, including orange, which accounts for the black, blue, or other colored kittens that can be produced when two cats split for non-dominant white are paired together. Two albinos paired would only produce more albinos.

8) White spotting (*SS* or *Ss*): White spotting in cats can vary from just a few solitary hairs to an almost completely white cat, and the common observation of piebald in cats and in other mammals (as well as pied in birds) is that it is subject to considerable variation; therefore, it is all but impossible to selectively breed for the extent of white spotting. Two low grades of spotting can produce a high grade of spotting.

Spotting is a feature of numerous varieties such as bicolors and tricolors, and when it is more fully understood it may well result in a number of new breeds based on the placement of white areas. Although it is regarded as being the result of the dominant or semi-dominant gene *S*, it is quite probable that at least one other gene may influence the extent of spotting. Normally, spotting starts on the underbelly and then progresses up the front legs and chest to the head, continuing along the flanks and rear legs until only the tail and a head patch remain the ground color. However, this is not always the case, as I have seen street cats in Spain that were all tabby except for a complete band of white encircling the midriff. In the USA, Judith Lindley does excellent work in gathering information on tortoiseshell cats via the Calico Registry International, and a similar project devoted to spotting in cats would be most useful for any person or group inclined to study this perplexing aspect of feline coloration.

It was thought that the gloves on Birman cats were the result of low grade spotting, but more recent studies would suggest that this is not the case; likewise, the Turkish Van is believed to be the result of the opposite, that is, *SS*, but this seems to be a convenient simplification. Clearly, more factors are at work than we are presently aware of.

9) White Siamese (*cᵃcᵃ*): This color is just one stage up from the true albino; it is all white but has a pale blue-pink eye color. In the USA, this color is seen as the white Oriental Shorthair, whilst in the UK it is the foreign white. Poor specimens are likely to exhibit a trace of yellow in the hair where a bit of pigment was formed. The advantage of the white Siamese is that the color is not associated with deafness as in the case of the dominant white. It would be possible to produce a really pure white foreign type cat with vivid blue eyes by introducing the white dominant gene to the white Siamese; both body and eye color would be improved, but the

White coat color in cats should not be confused with albinism. White cats are usually the product of the dominant white gene. Albinism, rarely seen in felines, is due to recessive genes and would, in theory, produce cats with pink eyes.

White Siamese kittens have blue-pink eyes. They are not true albinos, but are one step up.

W would also introduce the incidence of deafness and the probability of copper eye color. The latter, however, could be reduced by continual selection of only blue-eyed specimens.

10) Albino (*cc*): The true albino is totally devoid of any pigment in body and eyes, which are pink or red due to the reflection of hemoglobin in the blood vessels of the eye. This "color" is very popular in many bird species (budgerigar, cockatiel, and zebra finch) as well as in mammals such as mice, rats, hamsters, rabbits, and guinea pigs. It is rarely seen in dogs, as it is not encouraged, and it is virtually never seen in domestic cats. In my opinion there is no reason why true albinos should not become established, as they are not associated with any particular defect except for loss of vigor after generations of breeding albino to albino. This loss of vigor holds true for many types of matings, in which occasional outcrosses are recommended. However, the contrary can also be argued.

DILUTED COLORS

The following colors are all produced as a direct result of the mutation that reduces the intensity of the given color. In order for the dilution effect to become visible, both genes of a pair must carry the dilution gene *d*; if not, the cat will show the darker color but will still be capable of passing on the dilution gene to its offspring

11) Blue (*aadd*): When black is diluted it becomes blue, and this blue is a very popular color in cats. It is known under no other name, though in the Tonkinese breed of the USA the term mink is added to it. It is the sole color of the Korat, Chartreux, and Russian Blue—though the Russian is now seen in other self colors in the UK. The British blue is not a breed in itself in the USA but a color variety of the British Shorthair. The blue color is very variable in its expression, so it can be seen as almost black through to very light gray-blue, and it is the latter, with the requisite silver tipping, that is preferred in the three all-blue breeds. All other blues, including the British blue, should show no tipping or indication of white whatsoever, and must be an even shade down to the roots.

12) Lilac (*aabbdd*): This color is described as either frost gray, warm lavender with a pinkish tone, or pinkish dove gray; it is the dilution of the chocolate color. All standards require the color to be even down to the roots.

12) Lavender (*aabbdd*): This is an alternative name for lilac that is used in some American standards, but not in those of the UK.

12) Platinum (*aabbdd*): This is a further alternative name for lilac or for the brown dilution. It is described as a pale silver-gray in the standards of the Burmese and Tonkinese in the USA but is not used in the British standard for the Burmese, where lilac is preferred.

12) Frost (*aabbdd*): This term is used in the standards of the pointed breeds in the American Cat Fanciers' Association (ACFA); it is the same as lilac. It is also used by this association to describe the mitted feet of the Birman breed.

13) Cream (*OOdd* female, *Odd* male): This is the dilution of the red color and should be buff cream to light pink cream or a cool-toned cream, depending on the standard under consideration. The color should be free of white hairs and as free of tabby markings as possible; as a result, the lighter shade of cream is always the more desirable, as this reduces the effect of tabby.

A brown tabby longhaired Scottish Fold.

14) Fawn (*aab¹b¹dd*): This is the dilution of the cinnamon color and is described as being a warm fawn, a pale pinkish fawn, or a light lavender with pale cocoa overtones, depending on the standard under consideration. It appears in the USA within the Devon Rex, the Ocicat and the Oriental Shorthair, but in the UK is applied only to the Abyssinian at this time. The dark fawn seen in the Egyptian Mau is probably of the genotype *aabbdd*; therefore, it is lilac and the dilution of the bronze of that breed.

14) Caramel: This color name is used, for the first time, in the UK in relation to the foreign caramel, which presently has preliminary status. It is described as a cool-toned bluish fawn. I was unable to ascertain its genotype.

14) Honey mink: This color appears solely in the standard (American) for the Tonkinese, where it is described as light to medium ruddy brown. Its genotype may well be that of either the fawn or the cinnamon, the latter being the more likely.

A black and white longhair. Black and white cats were often called magpies in years past.

BICOLORS

Bicolor, or two-colored, cats have always been popular as pets, but it is only in relatively recent years that they have come to be appreciated from an exhibition viewpoint. The term bicolor is applied to cats that exhibit colors that are marked with white. (Years ago, black and whites were the most common bicolors and were called magpies.) The colors must form solid patches; therefore, smokes, silvers, and similar cats that are also two-colored are not bicolors in the cat fancy, as their color appears on the same hair as the white, in the form of tipping. Likewise, the Turkish breed of the UK is not a bicolor even though its colors are in patches. The various definitions of a bicolor should clarify the meaning of the term in respect to the breed and to which side of the Atlantic Ocean.

In comparing British and the American attitudes, it is clear that in the UK, bicolors are quite simply a solid color and white; no other definition is accepted. In the USA, three types of bicolors are recognized: a solid color and white, where the color should predominate; a solid color and white where white must predominate (van bicolor); and patterned and white, where the pattern may actually consist of two or three colors as in tortie or tabby.

Calculating the genotype is quite straightforward, as one need only add *Ss* or *SS* to the genotype of the color in question. A black and white bicolor would thus be *aaS-* (*S-* meaning it can be *Ss* or *SS*), whilst a blue bicolor would be *aaddS-*. If one had a longhaired bicolor, then *ll* for long hair would need to be added. American cat owners with patterned bicolors would need to add the coat pattern to the genotype, so that a tabby bicolor would be *A-S-tᵇtᵇ* or whatever tabby type or pattern of the cat.

USA BICOLORS

American Shorthair: White with unbrindled patches of black, blue, red, or cream. Eye color gold. The van bicolor is black, blue, red, or cream, each with white. The color is confined to the extremities; head, tail, and legs, but one or two small patches of color on the body are allowed.

Bicolored cats are produced by the action of the white spotting gene on the coat color.

Cornish Rex: Solid color, smoke, or tabby, etc., each with white. Cats with no more white than a locket and/or button do not qualify as bicolors, and the white will not be penalized in the appropriate color class that they enter.

Cymric: White with unbrindled patches of black, blue, red, or cream. Comments regarding locket and/or button as in the Cornish Rex also apply.

Devon Rex: Solid color and white, tabby and white, tortoiseshell and white. To include the torties with bicolors does seem rather strange and inconsistent with the general concept of a bicolor.

Exotic Shorthair: Black, blue, red, or cream, each with white. As a preferred minimum, the cat should have white feet, legs, undersides, chest, and muzzle. Less white than this to be penalized proportionately. Inverted "V" on face desirable. Eye color brilliant copper. Van bicolor as for American Shorthair.

Japanese Bobtail: The standard does not define bicolor but accepts any, with black and white or red and white being singled out and specifically named.

Maine Coon: A combination of a solid color with white. The colored areas predominate, with the white portions being located on the face, chest, belly, legs, and feet. Colors accepted are red, black, blue, or cream. The Maine Coon also has a tabby and white class, which includes tabby and patched tabby and white. Here the colors accepted are silver, red, brown, blue, or cream. White on one-third of the body is desirable, and it must appear on the bib, belly, and on all four paws.

Manx: White with unbrindled patches of black, blue, red, or cream. Comments regarding locket and/or button in the Cornish Rex also apply.

Persian: Black, blue, red, or cream, each with white. As a preferred minimum, the cat should have white feet, legs, undersides, chest, and muzzle. Less white than this to be penalized proportionately. Inverted "V" on face desirable. Van bicolor as for the American Shorthair. Tabby and whites are considered a separate entity but should be as described for the white areas.

Scottish Fold: White with unbrindled pat-ches of black, blue, red, or cream. Eye color gold. Van bicolor as for the American Shorthair.

BRITISH BICOLORS

Longhaired bicolor: Any solid color and white, the patches of color to be clear, even, and well distributed. Not more than two-thirds of the cat's coat to be colored and not more than half to be white. Face to be patched with color and white. Eye color deep orange or copper.

Shorthaired bicolor: Patches of white and any self color accepted in the recognized British breeds. Preferably one-third and not more than half to be white. Symmetry of design is desirable, preferably with patches of color on top of the head, ears, cheeks, back, tail, legs, and flanks. Eye color copper, orange, or deep gold.

Cornish Rex: Bicolor is not specifically referred to in the standard, which states that all coat colors are allowed. It does, however, state that asymmetrical white markings are allowed.

Devon Rex: The standard specifically states that bicolors are not accepted and that white, other than in the tortie and white, shall be considered a fault.

Manx: The standard does not specifically refer to bicolors, but these are accepted in the breed.

TIPPED HAIR

There are six color varieties of tipped hair to be seen in cats. Each of these, from a genetic viewpoint, is a variation on the expression of the inhibitor gene I, which restricts the amount of pigment that is formed in the hair. The result is that the hair varies between two extremes; it may be just tipped with a pigment or it may have pigment from the tip to well down the hair shaft. The extent of tipping determines the name applied to it. Genotype: simply add I- to the color or pattern.

Smoke: The undercolor is white and the tipping is well down the hair so that, when at rest, the cat appears to be a solid color; when it moves, the hairs part and the white undercolor is seen. The face, feet, and back are more heavily tipped, so the white undercolor is only seen when the hair is parted. The frill and flanks are

The definition of bicolor differs in Britain and the USA. In Great Britain, a bicolor has solid color and white. In the USA, the amount of white in the coat determines what type of bicolor the cat is.

Black and white Manx kitten. Bicolored cats must show clear patches of the colors in the coat. Individual hairs that contain two colors do not qualify a cat as a bicolor.

the least tipped areas so that the overall effect is one of smoke with contrasts of light and dark. Smokes are normally seen as smoke (black), blue, red (cameo), cream, or blue-cream, but it is possible to have any color such as chocolate, lilac, fawn, cinnamon, and so on. Likewise, any pattern is possible with a smoke equivalent, so it is a case of checking with the standards of your registration body for those that are accepted for exhibition purposes.

Cameo: The cameo is the smoke in red colors, so there is the red, the cream, the tortie, and the tabby. These are further divided, on the basis of the extent of tipping, as follows:

1) Shell—Sparkling silver appearance, lightly dusted with rose-pink. In the USA, the shell cameo is also known as the red chinchilla.
2) Shaded—White evenly shaded with red, giving the overall effect of a red mantle. In the USA, the shaded cameo is also the red shaded.
3) Cameo smoke—This is the red smoke of the UK. Body red, shading to white on the sides and flank. Mask and feet red. In the USA, they may have a narrow band of white at the roots, but in the UK they must be red with no markings.

In each of the above cases, the cream series is described in the same manner. The tortie cameo of the UK becomes the smoke tortoiseshell of the USA and is simply the tortie pattern with a white undercolor.

Chinchilla: The chinchilla is described as having a pure white undercoat on the back, flanks, head, ears, and tail; it is tipped with black, the tipping to be evenly distributed, thus giving the characteristic sparkling silver appearance. The legs may be slightly tipped, but the chin, ear tufts, stomach, and chest must be pure white. The eye color is green or blue-green. When the color was being developed in Britain at the turn of the century, there were both light and dark chinchillas; the latter became known as shaded silver. The two became hard to distinguish, even though a standard was available. When a cat went on to win prizes as both, during a 1902 show, the British dropped the shaded standard. However, it remains in the USA, Australia, and

elsewhere; the shaded silver is a chinchilla with a much darker overall effect. In the UK, shaded silver has now returned to the show scene under the name of pewter.

In the USA, there is a chinchilla golden and a shaded golden, which are both described as having black tipping on a cream undercoat. In the UK, the equivalent to this is the golden Persian, which has an apricot to gold undercolor. It is tipped with seal brown or black; it is more akin to the shaded golden than to the chinchilla. It should be mentioned that the choice of the word "cream" in the American standard is perhaps unfortunate, as it might lead some people to assume it is the sex-linked dilution of red rather than a separate mutation. Presently, its genetic state is not known.

British Tipped: This is the shorthair equivalent to the longhaired chinchilla, being very finely tipped in any color accepted within the British breeds. In the USA, it is the chinchilla American Shorthair, but presently the American standard does not accept colors other than black for the tipping. Eye color copper, orange, or gold; black tipped cats should have green eyes.

TORTOISESHELL (TRICOLOR)

The tortie should ideally have distinct and well-broken patches of black, red, and cream; the colors should be very rich. A blaze of red and cream is desirable on the face. This definition of the tortoiseshell is seen in the American Shorthairs and the British longhair, but another description is seen in the British Shorthair, which states that the pattern is a mixture of black, rich red, and pale red evenly intermingled, with the colors clearly defined over the whole animal but without any obvious patches of any color, with the exception of a short narrow blaze on the face, which is permissible. Any white appearing on a tortoiseshell is a bad fault and can result in disqualification. Eye color brilliant gold or copper. Breeding tortoiseshell cats is very difficult, and they will almost always be females; males are possible but are so rare that their availability can be dismissed. Torties may be black, chocolate, or lilac, each color being patched with red and cream. The blue tortie is known as the blue-cream, and in the UK it is preferred that the colors are intermingled, whereas in the USA distinct patches are the favored choice. The lilac tortie will, of course, be the lilac-cream, so no red will appear in the coat due to the action of the dilution genes.

CALICO AND TORTIE AND WHITE

If you add white spotting to a tortoiseshell cat, you then have the tortie and white—a calico. The latter term is used in the USA and is derived from the printed cotton of three colors. The term is not used just in cats, for, in the USA, goldfish of three colors are also called calicos. In the UK, there is some misunderstanding over the term, where most cat owners think that it is simply used on all tricolored cats in the USA, but this is not always the case. Some registries only recognize calicos, but others also recognize tortie and whites, so a definition of each should clarify the position.

Calico: White with unbrindled patches of black and red. As a preferred minimum, the cat should have white feet, legs, undersides, chest, and muzzle. Less white than this minimum should be penalized proportionately. Inverted "V" blaze on face desirable. The key word here is minimum, which means that the preference will be for cats with plenty of white.

Tortoiseshell and white: At least one-third and not more than one-half of the coat to be white, with patches of color on the top of the head, ears, cheeks, back, tail, legs, and flanks. A blaze is desirable. From these definitions it can be seen that many calicos would not be eligible for tortie and white classes in the USA, were these scheduled. Likewise, a good tortie and white with well-marked color on the legs would not qualify as a calico. Once a cat has more than half of its total body in white, then it is a calico. Below this amount it could qualify as either, depending on the placement of the color. Once the amount of white is less than one-third of the body, it has little chance, if any, of winning at exhibitions. As with tortoiseshells, it is possible to combine the normal black and red with the dilution genes to produce blue-cream and lilac-cream, as well as having a chocolate tortie and white. Again, good tortie and whites are very

difficult to produce, due to the fact that most cats exhibiting this pattern are females. The additional problem of the variability of the white spotting merely makes it even more difficult to produce good exhibition stock, so these cats are always somewhat unique because no two are ever quite the same.

The tortie or tortie and white pattern can be transferred to other patterns, such as the Siamese or tabbies. The actual genetics of the tortoiseshells are very complex but interesting to those who enjoy the subject. (Anyone who simply likes the tortie in all its variation, whether up to show standard or not, will gain from joining the Calico International Registry, which specializes in the tricolored cat and gathers information on it from all sources possible.) In simple terms, the tortoiseshell has the genotype of Oo, whilst the tortie and white will be $OoSs$ or $OoSS$, the latter more likely in the calico. The basis of the genetics is that the orange O gene prevents the formation of any black or brown pigment, so these appear as shades of red and cream. The o for non-orange, which is present on the other X chromosome of the female, allows whatever color is there to show itself. This means that a recessive, even though it is in single dose, will be visible, thus one can get a blue or a lilac. As these two genes act independently of each other, one gets both appearing in the same animal, and the tortie is the result. The male has only one X chromosome, so it must be either for O, a red cat (or Odd, a cream), or it is o for non-orange, in which case it can be any other color but orange (red). The rare tortie male will have the genotype of XXY, but is usually sterile.

To produce the best chances of breeding tortie and/or whites, a red male should be paired to a black female or to a black and white bicolored female; this will give the theoretical expectation of 50% black or bicolored males and 50% tortie females.

POINTED CATS

There are now a large number of choices open to anyone wishing to own a colorpointed cat, and these choices are not restricted to the colors, for there are a number of pointed breeds, both

A tortie and white household pet.

A colorpoint Persian (Himalayan).

shorthaired and longhaired. These include the Siamese, Oriental Shorthair, the Cornish and Devon Rexes, Persians, Balinese, Javanese, Birman, and others. In fact, the genes that create pointed colors can be transferred to most breeds that lack them. The most popular pointed cats are those in which there is a simple combination, such as the chocolate point or blue point; in these, the dark extremities contrast with a lighter body shade. The actual genes concerned are those for Siamese, $c^s c^s$, which restrict the development of the full color that the cat carries. This is a mild form of albinism, which is unusual in that the eye retains some pigment and is blue, rather than pink or red.

There is no restriction on what the genes for pointed pattern can combine with, so one can have a lynx point, tortie point, red point, or a blue-cream point. The tabby point of the UK is the lynx point of the USA, whilst the red point of the UK is also known as the flame point in the USA. The tortie points will, of course, be females, as will blue-creams.

If one introduced the genes for pointed into a breed that did not already have them, none of the first generation would carry the pointed pattern but all of them would be split for it. If these are then paired to similar split cats, 25% of the offspring would be visibly colorpointed, whilst 50% would carry the colorpoint gene. The breed used to introduce the colorpoint gene is not important, but one would most likely use a Siamese for shorthair, or a Persian for longhairs, as these would ensure that purity of coat length was maintained.

In crossmatings between existing colorpoints, when calculating expectations, the c^s genes need not be tabulated as, obviously, they would be present in all permutations. One aspect of color breeding that often gives the beginner a problem is in relation to mating two recessives and pondering what the offspring will be like. Let us assume that one wanted to pair a blue colorpoint with a lilac colorpoint: what will the offspring be in terms of color? The answer is blue—all of them. Blue has the genotype of $BBdd$ whilst lilac is $bbdd$; the only gametes these can produce are Bd and bd which, when combined, would give $Bbdd$, which is diluted black—blue. Such blue points will, of course, all carry the gene for

brown, and this must be considered in future matings. This again underlines the importance to color breeders of both understanding the basics of heredity and, of course, of knowing the genotype of the breeding stock; failure in these aspects could result in wasted efforts, additional cost, and more than a little frustration.

A final comment in respect to colorpoints is that where lynx points (tabby) are concerned, it would be all but impossible to say which tabby pattern is being seen. This is not so important in view of the very limited expression of the pattern in colorpoints but, this stated, if one had a choice, the mackerel type is the better option simply because it will show less tracings in the coat than would the blotched (classic) type.

TABBIES

Although the wild type tabby pattern is of the mackerel kind, it is the recessive classic (blotched) type that is the more common in domestic cats. The Abyssinian tabby is not used in many breeds because it is so faint, whilst the spotted tabby is restricted to just a few breeds. Tabbies can be seen in just about every possible color, so that there are brown, chocolate, blue, lilac, cinnamon, red, cream, and silver. One can also have tortoiseshell tabbies, which are known as patched; these too can be found in the full range of colors, which include the blue tortie or blue-cream. Most of these varieties are already accepted on both sides of the Atlantic and in Australia and elsewhere, either having championship status or preliminary recognition.

The tabby cat is made up of two components, agouti and dense black pigment. In an all-agouti cat, a second set of genes is able to impose itself on the agouti and create the tabby. The agouti hairs are banded in yellow, brown, and black, whilst the tabby areas contain only densely pigmented black hairs; their arrangement in the fur creates the different tabby patterns. All cats, regardless of their visible color, are tabbies, as it is a case of the non-agouti gene a masking the tabby pattern in the non-tabby colors and patterns.

The wild type tabby is black, but in the cat fancy it is referred to as being brown, which is perhaps rather misleading, as a good brown tabby should have dense black patterning set on a coppery brown ground color. The latter is much improved over the wild type, due to careful selection and the build-up of what are known as rufus genes. These give the yellow and brown areas of the agouti fur a more reddish appearance.

If the tabby carries the dilution genes, the black areas will be reduced to blue. At the same time, the ground color will be changed to a bluish gray of a lighter hue, due to the action of the genes on the black and brown banding of the hairs. The silver tabby is the result of the inhibitor gene I, which prevents the formation of pigment in the hairs. It is most effective on the less densely pigmented areas, thus it reduces the yellow to white and the black and brown of agouti to a light gray. Its effect on the dense tabby markings is minimal, so the result is a quite striking contrast that produces a most attractive tabby.

The introduction of the brown mutation produces the true, genetically brown tabby—the chocolate—where the tabby markings are a rich chestnut brown against a lighter ground agouti. The cinnamon tabby is somewhat lighter in shade, and its dilution produces the fawn tabby with a corresponding lightening of the agouti. The lilac or lavender is the dilution of the chocolate, so it is a pinkish gray on an even lighter ground color. Clearly the diluted tabbies are far less striking, as tabbies go, because there is a tendency for the agouti ground color to merge in with the tabby pattern. However, this is a fact with all tabbies; therefore, only the best marked tabby cats should be mated.

The red tabby is quite different from the run of the mill ginger tabby because of the continual selection of only the best reds, so in exhibition cats it is a deep orange-red. It will appear more so in the blotched tabby because there are more black fur areas for the orange gene to work on. The red is, of course, sex-linked, which will tend to produce more red tabby males than females. This is because a number of the females will carry the non-orange gene and will be tortoiseshell or patched tabbies. The dilution gene will produce the cream tabby as well as the blue-cream.

SPOTTED CATS

It is not known whether the spotting in cats is the result of a break-up of the mackerel tabby pattern into streaks, which are then selectively bred for until they are reduced to ovals or spots, or whether a separate mutation is involved. Whichever is the case, the fact is that spotted cats must be paired to the best spotted partners possible. The earliest cats of this type were exhibited in England and were of a very high standard—and the spotted British Shorthair of good exhibition quality is still a most impressive animal indeed. The head markings are exactly the same as for mackerel or classic tabby, and the available colors are the same, too.

The other spotted cat breeds are the Egyptian Mau and the Ocicat, and in both cases the present number of available colors is restricted to those stated in the breed section. However, it is quite possible for all the tabby colors mentioned to appear in these breeds, and no doubt they will do so as the breeds themselves become more popular, which I feel sure they will.

THE FUTURE

The interesting thing about mutations is that one cannot predict when they will occur and in what way they will affect the cat. Some, of course, will be totally undesirable, so it is hoped that with a better understanding of genetics, such abnormals will not be perpetuated. Some mutations will carry no health risks with them, so they will add interest to cat breeding. If one looks at other mammalian pets, one can see certain possibilities. For example, in coat patterns, one might produce half-siders, where the cat is black down one side of its body and white on the other, with the colors reversed on the head. Similar to this is, of course, the Dutch pattern seen in rabbits, guinea pigs, and other pets (the actual half-sider is already a reality in budgerigars). Banding is an obvious possibility that is already popular in hamsters. Each of these would create tremendous interest in the cat fancy. The satin mutation in hamsters and guinea pigs produces a quite exquisite silky fur. A rosette crest on the head of guinea pigs is also now quite popular; this is well established in canaries, though, sadly, is lethal in double dose, so

A pair of brown tabby longhaired kittens. Although the tabby pattern is more easily recognized in short-haired cats, many people find the longhaired tabbies equally attractive.

Brown mackerel tabby Manx.

it is a risky mutation. There is no reason to suppose that these mutations will not happen in the cat in the coming years, but often they are not always recognized at first because in their basic form they may not look like anything special. Only careful breeding for the best examples establishes unusual mutations, and many are lost because they are not recognized as being different.

Where color is concerned, there is perhaps less scope, because there is clearly a limitation on how many colors one can produce from black, brown, and orange. Possibly, a passable yellow could be produced, but a true red is unlikely. Likewise, a really striking blue seems most unlikely, unless a mutation arose that changed the reflective nature of the cells to create a different optical illusion. More likely to arrive will be albinos and pink-eyed dilutions, as both have appeared in the past but never became established; I have never liked red-eyed animals but, as stated earlier, they are well-established in many pets, so, obviously, many other people do find them appealing.

The negative side to such possibilities is that it has taken over 120 years of breeding many millions of cats for exhibition to produce the small handful of mutations presently seen in cats, so it could take as long for a few more to appear. In the meantime, there is more than a sufficient number of colors, body types, and coat patterns to keep even the most ambitious breeder satisfied for quite some years to come.

CAT REGISTRATION BODIES

The object of registration bodies is to compile various lists of cats based on their known heritage and to grade these according to the degree of purebreeding. Such bodies or associations also prepare a show standard for each recognized breed and a set of rules which determines how exhibitions will be run and officiated. If a cat club is formed within a given area in North America it will normally be affiliated with one of the major registries, which includes one in Canada. In Australia, one registration authority is found in each state. In the UK, the whole cat fancy is run under the auspices of a single authority, whilst in continental Europe there are numerous associations, with one large one that exercises control over many countries.

All of these various organizations are run independently of each other, and membership in one gives no privileges in the other, nor are awards from one organization carried over to another. Considerations are, however, made in respect to actual registration particulars from one registry to the other, insomuch as proof of ancestry from one association is usually accepted by another if one wishes to register with another association.

The status of a cat within an association will determine whether or not it can compete in championship classes. For example, if you have an Ocicat, it cannot become a champion in the American Cat Association at this time, as this association does not recognize it; the Cat Fanciers' Association does, however. Likewise, the Norwegian Forest cat is accepted by the American Cat Fanciers' Association but not by the Cat Fanciers' Association. Neither of these breeds has recognition in the UK. It is usually the newer or more unusual breeds that have variable acceptance. All the really popular breeds will be accepted by all associations.

REGISTERS

Each association will normally maintain a number of separate registers, and a breed will be eligible to go in one or the other. At one end of the spectrum will be the full or stud book register, whilst at the other will be the household pet register. Full registration is restricted to cats which have purebreeding ancestry for at least three generations, where all cats on both sides of the pedigree are of the same breed as that being registered. In the UK, a supplementary register accommodates cats that have been bred from two different breed sections within the last three generations. Once progeny of supplementary cats have three generations of single breeding behind them, they are automatically entitled to be placed on the full register.

There are experimental registers which house developing breeds and the household pet registers for cats of totally unknown ancestry. The various associations may apply different titles to registers, such as the Book of Registry, Provisional Register, and so on, but they all perform the same function of placing a cat into a suitable register based on its state of purity as a breed, as a hybrid, or as a cat of mixed breeding. One could thus start off with a mixed breed and, over the years, develop a cat of fixed type, so that one could trace its ancestry through the different registers as it progressed towards breed recognition. When a new color is introduced to a breed, the offspring will change from the full register and go down one step, as it were, until three generations of the color are purebreeding; at this point, the color would normally again qualify as a pure breed.

Each association applies codes to the breeds and to the colors within a breed, and it may also indicate on the registration how many generations of pure breeding the cat comes from (up to seven generations are indicated). If a cat is exported from one country to another, the new association usually requires proof of registration in the previous country, in the form of registration papers and a pedigree showing at least four generations of registered ancestors with the previous registration authority.

REGISTRATION ASSOCIATIONS
United Kingdom

Governing Council of the Cat Fancy (*GCCF*)—The address is: 4-6 Penel Orlieu, Bridgwater, Somerset, England TA6 3PG. Telephone: (0278) 427575, GB. The GCCF was founded in 1910 from the National Cat Club (which was formed in 1887) and numerous other clubs with the objective of uniting all clubs under a common banner. Presently, there are 99 other specialty and all-breed cat clubs affiliated to the GCCF.

USA and Canada

In North America there are six registration authorities at this time plus one which is highly specialized.

Cat Fanciers' Association (*CFA*)—This is the largest American registry. The address is: Cat Fanciers' Association, Inc., 1309 Allaire Avenue, Ocean, New Jersey 07712. Telephone: (201) 531-2390. The CFA was founded in 1906, when it held its first shows in Buffalo and Detroit. Its oldest member club is the Empire Cat Club, which was formed in 1913. The CFA presently has 572 affiliate clubs in the USA, Canada, and Japan which run over 300 shows a year. It offers an impressive range of publications and services, and responds promptly to all inquiries.

American Cat Association (*ACA*)—This is the oldest American registry. ACA was founded in 1897, a fact that its members are very proud of. ACA offers a range of services and responds promptly to all inquiries. The address is: 8101 Katherine Avenue, Panorama City, California 91402.

The International Cat Association (*TICA*)—The address is: PO Box 2684, Harlingen, Texas 78551. TICA offers a range of services and publications and responds very promptly to inquiries. TICA also recognizes a very extensive list of breeds.

American Cat Fanciers' Association, Inc. (*ACFA*)—The address is: PO Box 203, Point Lookout, Missouri 65726. Telephone: (417) 334-5430. The ACFA was founded in 1955 with the object of introducing a greater willingness to accept new ideas. They were the first association to accept wins from other associations, the first to grant championship status to altered cats, and the first to introduce new concepts in terms of multi-ring judging. They provide a range of services, publications and respond to all queries.

Cat Fanciers' Federation (*CFF*)—The address is 9509 Montgomery Road, Cincinnati, Ohio 45242. The CFF was founded in 1919, and the Atlantic Cat Club held the first CFF show in New York CIty. The Federation currently has 98 affiliated clubs (1988) in the US and Canada. Thirty-one breeds are recognized for championship status and five for experimental status. CFF provides a full range of services.

Canadian Cat Association (*CCA*)—The address is: 52 Dean Street, Brampton, Ontario, Canada L6W 1M6. The CCA offers a wide range of services, and it publishes an excellent quarterly magazine in both English and French.

Calico Cat Registry International (*CCRI*)—The address is: PO Box 944, Morongo Valley, California 92256. Telephone: (619) 363-6511. The CCRI was founded, and continues to be run, by Judith Lindley in 1978. It is a specialized registry that is based on color rather than on bodily form; thus it registers only tortoiseshell and tricolored cats, tortie and whites and calicos, together with their dilutions. Its object is to impart information on these most unusual felines. Registration is open to any cat, purebred or mixed origin, of this color.

Opposite: Cream tabby kitten and a blue-cream tortie kitten. Many clubs and organizations are organized due to interest in a particular coat color or pattern. To obtain a list of member clubs, contact one of the major feline registration bodies.

Opposite: Somali kitten. Each cat registry has its own specific rules, such as the age at which a kitten may be shown, whether a specific breed is accepted, etc. A complete set of rules is available from each registering body.

The movement of any animal from one country to another is strictly controlled. This is especially true of wild animals, such as this leopard cat, *Felis bengalensis*, which would prove dangerous in the hands of anyone but an expert.

EXPORTING CATS

The movement of cats from one country to another is usually strictly controlled by the government of each country in order to minimize the spread of infectious disease. In particular, rabies-free countries, such as the United Kingdom, Australia, and New Zealand, apply very stringent quarantine regulations; failure to observe these can result in very heavy fines, re-export of the cat, or even its destruction. Therefore, it goes without saying that any attempt to smuggle a cat into a country in contradiction of its regulations is a most irresponsible act. There are two ways one can go about exporting a cat.

1) Engage the services of a company specializing in this. Such companies are numerous and handle all types of pets. Your vet will usually be able to advise you of such a company; alternatively, the airline you plan to use will often be able to suggest some such agencies.

2) Attend to the required paperwork and export of the cat yourself. This will be less expensive but maybe less convenient in some cases.

THE FIRST STEP

If you plan to live abroad and take your cats with you, be sure to give yourself ample time to attend to the documentation required, allowing for postal delays and the normal passage of the documents through the appropriate ministry. First, make contact with the ministry that issues export certificates; your veterinarian will advise you about the proper ministry to contact. Next, contact the consulate of the country to which you plan to export the cats, in order to verify their exact requirements. Your own ministry will advise you of these requirements, but will not accept any responsibility in the event that this information is not wholly complete, so it pays to double check on this matter.

Arrangements will need to be made with your veterinarian so that he or she can examine your cat just prior to its departure, and also to give the cat anti-rabies injections if necessary (as in most cases). In the UK, veterinarians are not allowed to keep such vaccinations, so they must be ordered for each individual cat—another reason why you should discuss matters with your vet well in advance of the proposed departure date.

THE TRANSPORTATION

The vast majority of cats will be exported by air. If so, you must contact the appropriate airline to request details of their particular requirements and charges. Some make greater reductions than others if you are travelling on the same flight as your cats. All airlines require the cat to be placed in the regulation sized container; as this is subject to change, one is always advised to contact the cargo department of the airline in question for exact dimensions (including the placement of airholes in the box). It is always simpler, from the documentation viewpoint, if you can use a direct flight to the country of import.

There is also the possibility of transporting cats on a boat. In such cases, contact the ferry company to see what the requirements are. Normally, they require the cats to be kept in a suitable box, but no specific dimensions are quoted. The cat must remain in the box during transit, and there is normally no charge made for the cats if kept in such a box and accompanied by the owners. Upon docking, customs officials will inspect your paperwork on the ferry and apply the necessary stamp, assuming that the papers are in order. Again, for those who might be travelling by boat, the paperwork is simpler if a direct ferry is taken.

REQUIREMENTS FOR MAINLAND EUROPE

The normal minimum requirements for cats entering European countries, other than the United Kingdom and Ireland, are as follows.

Health certificate: This must be issued not more than 48 hours prior to exportation of the cat. It will be obtained from a veterinarian and must state that the veterinarian is an approved agent of the ministry responsible for the issue of export certificates. It will state that the cat is free of any sign of infectious or contagious disease and that the cat showed no sign of rabies.

Rabies vaccination certificate: Animals native to Great Britain and which are domestic pets under the age of two months do not require rabies certificates. All other cats will require a valid vaccination certificate which was issued not less than one month, and not more than 12 months, before importation into the country concerned. It can be mentioned that this certificate may not be required when a cat is imported from a country which has been free of rabies for six months prior to importation (e.g., the United Kingdom, Ireland, or Australia). However, one is still strongly recommended to attend to this, both in the interests of the cat and in order to ensure that there are no problems on this account with the customs of the country of destination.

Export certificate: A valid export certificate is required from the appropriate ministry of the country of residence of the cat. This will state that the cat has resided at an address which has not been infected, within the previous two years, by any disease for that species which is, by law, notifiable to the appropriate ministry or department of the country in question. This certificate will be signed and dated by your ministry or department and is the certificate that will be stamped with approval, all else being in order, on arrival in the new country of residence.

IMPORTATION INTO THE UK AND IRELAND

Cats, without exception, are required to complete a period of six months quarantine at an approved station. If they have not already been vaccinated against rabies, then this is obligatory and will be attended to on arrival at the quarantine station. All cats exported to the UK and Ireland must have applied for an importation certificate in advance. This is obtained from the Ministry of Agriculture; this ministry will provide a list of approved stations. British expatriates are advised that no matter how short a time a cat has been out of the United Kingdom, it must still go through the required quarantine period and will be subject to any other requirements that may be in force at that time.

IMPORTATION INTO AUSTRALIA

All cats entering Australia are subject to quarantine regulations, and prior permission to export to Australia is required. This can be obtained from the Commonwealth Department of Primary Industry, or from any of the quarantine officers in each state or territory. The current regulations state that, with the exception of cats from New Zealand and the Cocos Islands, all cats will be required to complete the following quarantine periods: two months from the UK or Republic of Ireland; four months from Norway, Sweden, or Hawaii; and nine months from any other approved country. Cats from non-approved areas are required to complete a period of 30 days residency in an approved country, usually the United Kingdom or Hawaii, and comply with the requirements for importation from the listed countries. Other approved areas include various Pacific islands such as Tahiti, Fiji, the Solomons, etc.

IMPORTATION INTO THE USA AND CANADA

Cats entering North America will require similar documentation to that required for mainland Europe, plus bills of lading and a certificate showing vaccination against feline enteritis. Presently, there are no required quarantine periods for cats entering the USA. However, a current health certificate, no more than ten days old, must be produced. In addition, vaccination against rabies and other major feline diseases is strongly recommended. Translations of health certificates (for example, those in Spanish or French) are not required by law, but their availability will help prevent delay caused by language difficulties.

IMPORTANT NOTICE

The comments made here are intended only as an approximate guide to the regulations that may be in force at any one time and in any particular country. The exact documentation required can only be established by contacting both the ministry or department of the exporter's country, which controls animal movements to and from that country, and that of the country to which the cat is to be exported. If the cat is to pass through one or more other countries en route to its final destination, then the regulations of those countries should also be obtained.

In the event that a large number of cats are to be exported (e.g., a relocating cattery owner), then the regulations may well differ from that of domestic pets, as they may be regarded as commercial exports, depending on the ultimate destination. Do allow yourself plenty of time to attend to documentation.

Someone let the Aby out of the bag (box)!! Before giving a cat as a gift, make sure the receiver will appreciate and properly care for it.

Bibliography

ACA; *Registration and Show Rules*, American Cat Association; Panorama City, California; 1988.

ACFA; *Show Rules*, American Cat Fanciers' Association; Point Lookout, Missouri; 1988.

Bass, S.; *This is the Maine Coon Cat*; T.F.H. Publications, Inc.; Neptune City, New Jersey; 1983.

Brearley, J.M.; *All About Himalayan Cats*; T.F.H. Publications, Inc.; Neptune City, New Jersey; 1976.

Burton, M., editor; *New Larousse Encyclopedia of Animal Life*, revised edition; Hamlyn; Feltham, Middlesex, United Kingdom; 1980.

Cain, A.J.; *Animal Species and their Evolution*; Hutchinson University Library; Hutchinson and Co.; London, United Kingdom; 1968.

CFA; *Show Rules, Cat Fanciers' Association, Inc.*; Ocean, New Jersey; 1988.

CFA; *Show Standards, Cat Fanciers' Association, Inc.*; Ocean, New Jersey; 1988.

CST; *Wild Cat*, Volume 1; The Cat Survival Trust; Welwyn, Hertfordshire, United Kingdom; 1977.

CST; *Wild Cat*, Volume 2; The Cat Survival Trust; Welwyn, Hertfordshire, United Kingdom; 1978.

CDPI; *Summary of Australian Plant and Animal Quarantine Requirements*; Commonwealth Department of Primary Industry; Canberra, ACT, Australia; 1987.

Crandell; *Management of Wild Animals in Captivity*; University of Chicago Press; Chicago, Illinois; 1964.

Edney, A.T.B., editor; *Dog and Cat Nutrition*; Pergamon Press; Oxford, United Kingdom; 1982.

Ewer, R.E.; *The Carnivores*; Weidenfeld and Nicolson; London, United Kingdom; 1973.

Faler, K.; *This is the Abyssinian Cat*; T.F.H. Publications, Inc.; Neptune City, New Jersey.

GCCF; *The Official Standard of Points*, Governing Council of the Cat Fancy; Bridgwater, Somerset, United Kingdom; 1983.

GCCF; *The Rules of the GCCF*, Governing Council of the Cat Fancy; Bridgwater, Somerset, United Kingdom; 1986.

GCC; *Ninth All-Breeds Championship Show Schedule*; Gwynedd Cat Club; Gwynedd, United Kingdom; 1987.

Grzimek, H.C.B., editor; *Animal Life Encyclopedia*, Volume 12, Mammals 3; Van Nostrand Reinhold; New York, New York; 1975.

Grzimek, H.C.B., editor; *Encyclopedia of Evolution*; Van Nostrand Reinhold; New York, New York; 1976.

Hackmann, A.; *Birmakatzen*; Rudolf Müller; Cologne, West Germany; 1982.

IUBS; *International Code of Zoological Nomenclature*; International Union of Biological Sciences; British Museum of Natural History; London, United Kingdom; 1985.

Kelsey-Wood, D.; "The Classification and Evolution of the Dog," *Dog Shows and Show Dogs*; K & R Books; Edlington, Lincolnshire, United Kingdom; 1980.

Lambert, D.; *The Cambridge Field Guide to Prehistoric Life*; Cambridge University Press; Cambridge, United Kingdom; 1985.

Lindley, J.; *The Handbook of the Calico Cat Registry International*; Morongo Valley, California; 1979.

Pinniger, R.S., editor; *Jone's Animal Nursing*, second edition; Pergamon Press; Oxford, United Kingdom; 1973.

Pond, G., and Dunhill, M.; *Cat Shows and Successful Showing*; Blandford Press; Poole, Dorset, United Kingdom; 1985.

Ramsdale, J.; *Persian Cats and Other Longhairs*; T.F.H. Publications, Inc.; Neptune City, New Jersey; 1976.

Reid, B.; *The Cat's Whiskers*; Ebury Press; London, United Kingdom; 1986.

Reagan, Ron; *Siamese Cats*; T.F.H. Publications, Inc.; Neptune City, New Jersey; 1988.

Robinson, R.; *Genetics for Cat Breeders*, second edition; Pergamon Press; Oxford, United Kingdom; 1977.

Robinson, R.; "Color Inheritance in Small Livestock," *Fur and Feather*; Bradford, West Yorkshire, United Kingdom; 1978.

Swantek, M.; *The Manx Cat*; T.F.H. Publications, Inc.; Neptune City, New Jersey; 1987.

Taylor, D.; *You and Your Cat*; Dorling Kindersley; London, United Kingdom; 1986.

TICA; *By-Laws: Registration Rules*, The International Cat Association; Harlingen, Texas; 1988.

Theis, Dagmar; *Cat Care*; T.F.H. Publications, Inc.; Neptune City, New Jersey; 1988.

Urcia, I.; *All About Rex Cats*; T.F.H. Publications, Inc.; Neptune City, New Jersey; 1982.

Urcia, I.; *This is the Russian Blue*; T.F.H. Publications, Inc.; 1983.

Willis, M.B.; "Principles of Genetics," *The German Shepherd Dog, Its History, Development, and Genetics*; K & R Books; Queniborough, Leicester, United Kingdom; 1977.

Wilson, M.D.; *Encyclopedia of American Cat Breeds*; T.F.H. Publications, Inc.; Neptune City, New Jersey; 1978.

A brown tabby and white household pet.

Index

Above: A blue male Abyssinian. **Below:** Shaded silver American Shorthairs, kitten and dam.

Above: Brown tabby and white household pet. Household pets are often called domestic shorthairs; purebred American Shorthairs were often called by this name in the past. **Below:** A tabby shorthair household pet.

A ruddy Abyssinian.